401 GREAT LETTERS

D1605515

401 GREAT LETTERS

NEW HANOVER COUNTY
PUBLIC LIBRARY
201 CHESTNUT STREET
WILMINGTON, N C 28401

KIM KOMANDO

Business One Irwin
Burr Ridge, Illinois
New York, New York

This symbol indicates that the paper in this book is made of recycled paper. Its fiber content exceeds the recommended minimum of 50% waste paper fibers as specified by the EPA.

© RICHARD D. IRWIN, INC., 1994

All rights reserved. No part of this publication may be reproduced, stored in a retrieval system, or transmitted, in any form or by any means, electronic, mechanical, photocopying, recording, or otherwise, without the prior written permission of the publisher.

This publication is designed to provide accurate and authoritative information in regard to the subject matter covered. It is sold with the understanding that neither the author nor the publisher is engaged in rendering legal, accounting, or other professional service. If legal advice or other expert assistance is required, the services of a competent professional person should be sought.

From a Declaration of Principles jointly adopted by a Committee of the American Bar Association and a Committee of Publishers.

Sponsoring editor: Cynthia A. Zigmund
Project editor: Gladys True
Production manager: Diane Palmer
Designer: Larry J. Cope
Compositor: BookMakers
Typeface: 10.5/12 Times Roman
Printer: Edwards Brothers, Inc.

Library of Congress Cataloging-in-Publication Data

Komando, Kim.
    401 great letters / Kim Komando.
        p.   cm.
    ISBN 1-55623-833-9   ISBN 1-55623-835-5 (disk with text)
        1. Commercial correspondence—Handbooks, manuals, etc.   I. Title.
    II. Title: Four hundred one great letters.   Title: Four hundred
    and one great letters.
    HF5726.K63   1994
    658.7'5—dc20   92–42422

Printed in the United States of America
1 2 3 4 5 6 7 8 9 0 EB 0 9 8 7 6 5 4 3

Living within these pages memories of my love reside. To him and his life's ending I dedicate this book. Moving forward now full of his eternal enthusiasm, I am thankful for my parents, Richard and Virginia. Their joy, love, and encouragement in my life are truly beyond description.

PREFACE

Boring. Impersonal. Easily forgotten.

Does that sound like you? Probably not. Odds are, you are intelligent. You are warm. You are memorable. You are friendly. For some reason, however, we camouflage the most cherished human characteristics in our business writings. Congratulations on taking the first step toward increasing your presence in business, with customers, around the office, and in personal affairs.

From the highest ranks of public and private companies to the equally important support staff, people have applauded this collection of instant letters as a proven way to save time and energy and generate astounding results. Any professional should have this book on his or her desk and computer. There are 115 business letters, 115 customer letters, 115 interoffice letters, and 56 personal letters totaling 401 Great Letters.

Today, composing a powerful, cost-effective letter takes five minutes or less with my book. All the writing is done; all you do is fill in the blanks. Drafting just one letter designed for maximum performance like these could take hours. To save even more time, we offer every letter on a disk that you can use with your current IBM-compatible word processing software or as a DOS and Windows stand-alone application software program.

Cuts Correspondence Costs Dramatically.   The power of the written word has a price. Time is money, and it's no secret that effective letter writing can be pure torture for many people. Finding the right words, presenting facts properly, and simply making sure the letter is read require creativity, time, and hard work. But you will never have to worry about any of those things again, thanks to this book.

I could claim that the value of this book is actually close to $5,000. The Dartnell Corporation's Institute of Business Research and the authors of *From Nine to Five* have conducted extensive research on the cost of a conventional, 185-word business letter. Mind you, these letters are the standard, impersonal "To whom it may concern" type taking ten minutes or less from start to finish.

In 1992, the analysts found that the cost of one business letter ranged anywhere from $11.91 to $18.03, depending on the dictation or typing method used. The days of wasting money by sending a letter destined to end up in someone's in basket or round file are long gone with *401 Great Letters*.

Change with the Times or You'll Fall Behind.   We have grown tired of being treated like robots. The prevalence of human relations and self-improvement programs and seminars proves it. We have learned that money is not everything. We have come to appreciate the individualism each of us possesses.

Adding to the impersonal pie is the onslaught of technology in this information age. Computers, electronic mail, facsimile machines, and voice mail speed communication, forcing us to act and react faster than ever before. In keeping up with the race, many fall short in their correspondence and send cryptic notes that are often misunderstood by the recipient.

There is no replacement for the impact of a well-written letter. And why do we spend so much energy and time composing letters? Let's face it; any time we write a letter we want something. The key is telling the person what you want with diplomacy. Abruptness was the old order. Sincerity works wonders.

The Personal Touch.   It's important to get the point here. So many letters are mailed every day that you must make your letter stand out on the recipient's desk. Your words are what I call a letter's *presence factor*—the power contained in three paragraphs or less. The overused "enclosed please find" puts you at the very bottom of the stack.

Moving to the top takes diplomacy, which works for letters of all kinds. The first time I experienced positive effects with this principle was in my early career as a computer sales representative for a FORTUNE 500 company. Faced with a list of prospects, I worked up my nerve, picked up the telephone, and tried to make appointments.

Like the calls from direct marketing companies that we receive at our homes, unsolicited business calls provoke the "Thanks, I'm not interested" response. During one call, I managed to squeeze in a few words before the fatal words were spoken. I then sent the prospect a thank you note that literally said, "This is my first job. I'm fresh out of college, and thanks for not hanging up on me."

He called to make an appointment with me, and when I walked into his office a few days later, I saw the letter I had sent him framed, hanging on the wall! More important, everyone in his company knew who I was, and I clearly had an advantage in closing the deal.

I wondered why my letter received attention, and from the conclusions I drew with feedback from business associates, customers, peers, and others came the start of this letter book. I can give you many examples of letters just like the ones in this book that have been published, photocopied and distributed throughout corporate offices, and remembered many years later, or have achieved unbelievable results. I have used letters like these in and out of the most formal FORTUNE 500 companies. When was the last time you received a telephone call from a customer service representative at a large company who phoned to say he or she liked your complaint letter? It's no big deal any longer in our home. People will go the extra mile on your behalf if you sound like a nice person. Share a part of yourself by being open, honest, and compassionate. Try it, and I am confident you will agree that the benefits are incredible.

Anatomy of a Great Letter.   Inside, you'll find letters for every occasion and letters you might not have thought of before but really should have. You never have to get lost in the shuffle again.

The premise of each letter is simple: get attention with reader appeal in the first sentence. Make the reader nod in agreement or provide an interesting fact. Move thorough the letter with a positive tone, even under the most negative conditions, and wrap it up on a final positive note. The result is a letter that will be read, understood, and acted upon.

Leading writing guides agree that every great letter has several key parts, which are presented in a fairly standard format. At the top of the page is usually your return address or letterhead, the date, the name of the addressee or recipient, the salutation, the body, your signature, and sometimes an indication of a copy or enclosure.

Your Address.   People routinely send business and customer-related correspondence on company letterhead. Interoffice memorandums do not need a return address; memos have a format all their own. Personal letters display your return address near the top of the page.

Date.   The date is placed between your return address and the recipient's address.

Recipient.   Under the date, the the name and address of the recipient appear. In this area of the letter, you will see any, or all, of the following information, depending on the type of letter you are writing:

[Mr./Mrs./Ms./Dr.] [FIRST AND LAST NAME]
[TITLE]
[COMPANY]
[ADDRESS]
[CITY], [STATE] [ZIP CODE]

Exceptions are interoffice letters, or memorandums, for which standard formats are used. Interoffice letters include places in the page heading space for the recipient's name, your name and title, date, copies, and subject matter.

Salutation.   Before the body of the letter, a polite greeting is inserted—Dear [Mr./Mrs./Ms./Dr.] [LAST NAME]. Depending on the formality of the letter, you will use either the recipient's first name or his or her entire proper greeting as in Mr./Mrs./Ms./Dr.

Body.   The text in which you describe the purpose of the letter falls between the salutation and the closing and contains powerful sentences and generic, fill-in-the blank fields. Fill-in-the-blank fields in the letter are called "items" and are numbered in sequence. Items and their associated numbers appear throughout the body in brackets [ ].

Signature.   With the exception of interoffice memorandums, the complimentary closing, your name, and when appropriate, your title appear on every letter.

Copies.   When a copy of a letter is sent to another person in addition to the recipient, his or her name is indicated below the signature line with the cc: notation. This is a very easy thing to add, so I have not included any cc: notations in this book.

By adhering to fundamental writing rules, *401 Great Letters* addresses the needs of most people. For example, you are more likely to address a friend by his or her first name than a politician, and the book takes this into consideration. Offices use a standard format shown in the interoffice memorandums. And, personal letters sometimes have a different look. You should have no trouble matching the letters in *401 Great Letters* with the situations and events in your own life.

Organization of 401 Great Letters.   To find the letter you want, start by determining the letter's overall purpose. To do this, ask yourself four questions: Is it directly related to my company? Does it concern a customer? Is it about something in my office? Is it a personal matter?

This book, *401 Great Letters*, is organized in four sections:

1. Business, for business-to-business correspondence.
2. Customer, for business-to-customer correspondence.
3. Interoffice, for internal company correspondence.
4. Personal, for personal correspondence.

Letters are first categorized by whether they deal with business, customer, interoffice, or personal matters. Next, under each category, the letters are sorted alphabetically by topic. And finally, the letters within each topic are arranged alphabetically. The table of contents contains a complete listing of letters by category, topic, and title.

Open to the appropriate section, and you're ready to command attention. At the beginning of each section are secrets and tricks of the trade. You might want to read through these before starting on your first letter.

The listing of letters is all-encompassing, covering topics you probably never thought of as ways to promote yourself and your company. Let's look at some real-life examples and find the right great letter to use in each.

Scenario One.   *You are in an awkward position when a worthy organization approaches your company for donations. When times were better, you contributed, because you believe in the good work the charity is doing.*

Company profits are declining and putting a strain on expenses. Even though your company would like to make a donation, it's just not possible at present.

This letter concerns your company, so it is located in the Business category. Charitable acts relate to Good Will, and under this heading, a Donations-No letter will handle the situation.

Scenario Two.   *You have a customer who has been sitting on the fence. The customer hasn't said, "Bring the contract" or "I'm sorry but we aren't interested." Any decision would be great; at least you would know whether to spend more time with them or move on to customers with greater potential.*

Because the letter is to a customer, go to the Customer letters. There is a deal pending, so you look at the list of customer letter subjects and find Deal Closers. You want the customer to get off the fence; choose the Make Decision letter.

Scenario Three.   *You've been doing a good job. While your salary is competitive, a little extra money would be welcome in your bank account. You never seem to have enough money to live the way you want to, and getting another, or second, job isn't very appealing. It's been some time since you had a raise, and you want to ask your manager if (or when) one is available.*

This is an internal company letter or an Interoffice memorandum that is asking—making a Request—for something—in this case, a Salary Increase.

Scenario Four   *You made a personal loan to someone to help him or her out of a bad situation. It seems he or she has forgotten about the repayment plan. While money is not the most important thing in life, a promise is a promise. You'd like the money back but are not quite sure how to ask.*

This is obviously a personal matter, which will be found in the Personal section. You aren't terribly happy about the situation and probably want to complain. Pick the Complaint topic and select the letter title, Someone Owes You Money.

Personalizing a Great Letter.   We are all unique, which is precisely why *401 Great Letters* uses fill-in-the-blank areas and promotes personalizing of all letters. Fill-in-the-blank areas are always indicated with the word ITEM in capital letters enclosed in brackets [ ]. This way they are easy to find.

Fill-in-the-blank items are numbered sequentially within the letter from top to bottom. For example, the first item requiring specific information appears as [ITEM 1], the second as [ITEM 2], and so on. The item numbers for each letter are listed at the bottom of the page along with descriptions of the information you must enter.

Fill-in-the-blank areas that refer to the recipient in the inside address and within the letter are enclosed in brackets too. For example, [Mr./Mrs./Ms./Dr.] [FIRST AND LAST NAME], [TITLE], [COMPANY], [ADDRESS], [CITY], [STATE], and [ZIP CODE] always refer to the recipient. [YOUR COMPANY NAME] is the name of your company.

Power Writing for the Rest of Your Life.   By now you are probably wondering how to make the letters more "you." The best part of this book is that it allows you to develop individual writing styles and discover hidden writing talents. You can mix and match paragraphs between letters and sections, even add a few sentences so it sounds like you. Soon, your own personality will emerge in your writing.

401 Great Letters will help you to save much of the time and energy you have wasted fretting over correspondence in the past. In addition, you will acquire writing skills to use for the rest of your life. I cannot guarantee that you'll get the answer you want every time in your correspondence. I can guarantee that the odds in your favor will increase significantly when you use the power of the written word contained within this book.

CONTENTS

SECTION 4   Personal Correspondence

SECTION 5   Letters for Your Computer

SECTION 1

Business-to-Business Correspondence

Put it in writing. Nowhere is this more true than in today's business world. Busy executives often spend more time writing letters to their customers—the companies with which they do business—than they spend on any other type of correspondence. Every letter sent under a company's letterhead represents an opportunity to boast about a company's management prowess and market strength.

Desk-to-Desk Advertising.   Companies spend thousands of dollars on advertising just to let other companies know they exist. Take a look at some current advertisements, and you will notice that many are not selling products anymore. Much of today's advertising describes the company's placement in its industry and its commitment to environmental concerns or the ideals under which it purports to operate.

A well-written letter contains many key goodwill statements and can have greater impact on its recipient than a $20,000 full-page magazine advertisement. The personal business letter spreads company doctrine for very little money and has a better chance of being noticed than even the best-targeted ad.

Speak the Language.   Business letters differ from other kinds of correspondence. One technique that is useful in business-to-business letters is using the same words the reader uses. You will notice, for example, that the claim letters in this section incorporate the ideas of loss protection and risk minimization—ideas the agent probably used when he or she presented the insurance company to you.

The letters in this section, which cover nearly every imaginable business need, include the buzz words that are peculiar to each addressee's industry. Speaking their language speaks well for your expertise in, and out of, your industry; it lets the reader know that you are an articulate, informed executive worthy of respect.

You Are the Company.   Go ahead, throw your weight around. Executives who make decisions for companies affect the professional and personal lives of employees and their families. Business letters represent not just the writer but his or her entire company.

Business growth, employee relations, legal matters, and ways to save money are a few of the areas you can explore. These and many other kinds of letters identify the person signing the page as self-confident, professional, and successful. Challenge yourself to be more effective in business-to-business correspondence. The results can be far-reaching.

[DATE]

[Mr./Mrs./Ms./Dr.] [FIRST AND LAST NAME]
[TITLE]
[COMPANY]
[ADDRESS]
[CITY], [STATE] [ZIP CODE]

Dear [Mr./Mrs./Ms./Dr.] [LAST NAME]:

By now, you've probably noticed that [YOUR COMPANY NAME] is a bottom-line-oriented company constantly checking and double-checking its facts and figures. Although [COMPANY] has done a fine job managing our books and advising us on tax matters, I question the calculations on the latest bill we received. The total amount due is not reasonable, and I'm sure a review will result in a favorable adjustment for [YOUR COMPANY NAME].

[YOUR COMPANY NAME] appreciates our affiliation with [COMPANY], but I cannot justify bills of this nature. You have always handled our statements very professionally, so I ask that you personally analyze this bill and the amount owed to [COMPANY]. Thank you in advance for your assistance. Even the masters are subject to error at times.

Respectfully yours,

[YOUR NAME]
[YOUR TITLE]

[DATE]

[Mr./Mrs./Ms./Dr.] [FIRST AND LAST NAME]
[TITLE]
[COMPANY]
[ADDRESS]
[CITY], [STATE] [ZIP CODE]

Dear [Mr./Mrs./Ms./Dr.] [LAST NAME]:

There is no doubt about it; mistakes happen. In today's computer age, information management is supposedly above reproach. [YOUR COMPANY NAME] understands that just one incorrect keystroke can add the wrong column of figures or erase an entire file of customer requests. It appears that this was the case on invoice number [ITEM 1] recently sent by [COMPANY].

Upon checking our records authorizing the purchase of [ITEM 2], we have discovered that [ITEM 3] contains an error. The correct [ITEM 3] should be [ITEM 4]. I am confident that [COMPANY]'s due diligence will result in the same correction arrived at by our staff.

Over the years, I have learned computers are merely machines and only as good as the humans and programs that control them. We are prone to error, and so are the machines. Thank you for your prompt attention in this matter and your help in making the necessary billing adjustments. It takes one more pressure off my day.

Sincerely yours,

[YOUR NAME]
[YOUR TITLE]

[ITEM 1] = Number generated by [COMPANY] on the invoice
[ITEM 2] = Describe and list by number [YOUR COMPANY NAME] purchases within [ITEM 1]
[ITEM 3] = Place where there is an error in [ITEM 1]
[ITEM 4] = Describe the correction needed

[DATE]

[Mr./Mrs./Ms./Dr.] [FIRST AND LAST NAME]
[TITLE]
[COMPANY]
[ADDRESS]
[CITY], [STATE] [ZIP CODE]

Dear [Mr./Mrs./Ms./Dr.] [LAST NAME]:

Fundamentally, business is a dynamic entity whose plans made in good faith are subject to laws of economic warfare. [YOUR COMPANY NAME]'s battlefield position and other extenuating circumstances require an immediate change in plans. We have been forced to reconsider our original intention to stay for the duration of the lease.

Much to my regret, I must realign the troops in a considerably smaller location. After extensive review, we have no alternative but to relocate effective [ITEM 1] days from today's date.

The entire [COMPANY] has been so professional in the past that I wanted to tell you just as soon as this unfortunate decision was made. In addition, we understand that our move affects the building's management. Please know our office is open to prospective tenants during normal business hours.

If you need to conduct tours over weekends, we will be happy to accommodate you; it is the least we can do in return for your professional consideration in this matter. [ITEM 2], thank you for all you have done for [YOUR COMPANY NAME].

Sincerely yours,

[YOUR NAME]
[YOUR TITLE]

[ITEM 1] = Number of days [YOUR COMPANY NAME] is moving from date letter sent
[ITEM 2] = First name of person receiving letter

[DATE]

[Mr./Mrs./Ms./Dr.] [FIRST AND LAST NAME]
[TITLE]
[COMPANY]
[ADDRESS]
[CITY], [STATE] [ZIP CODE]

Dear [Mr./Mrs./Ms./Dr.] [LAST NAME]:

By nature, most people throughout the world are quite alike. Investing in an education gives one a variety of options—particularly for the pursuit of specialized professions. I admire your dedication and appreciate the years you spent in school, both of which have enabled you to represent [YOUR COMPANY NAME].

I am, however, inclined to hold you in contempt of court. Frankly, when I looked at the bill for your services regarding [ITEM 1], I did a double-take. Perhaps we have simply had a misunderstanding over fees and expenses, or perhaps my records have somehow been confused with those of another client. Regardless, I ask you to review the bill for any possible adjustments and advise me of your position as soon as possible.

I thank you for your professional courtesy in this matter. Off the record, it's no secret that money is tight in our economy. Anything you can do to reduce the total is greatly appreciated.

Respectfully yours,

[YOUR NAME]
[YOUR TITLE]

[ITEM 1] = Describe work performed by [COMPANY]

[DATE]

[Mr./Mrs./Ms./Dr.] [FIRST AND LAST NAME]
[TITLE]
[COMPANY]
[ADDRESS]
[CITY], [STATE] [ZIP CODE]

Dear [Mr./Mrs./Ms./Dr.] [LAST NAME]:

Chasing the dollar in business hardly ever leads to success. We must take pride in our work, promote quality in our products, and foster trust in our customer relationships. It was for these reasons that [YOUR COMPANY NAME] originally purchased [ITEM 1] from [COMPANY].

Recently, however, [COMPANY] did not honor these values when repairing [ITEM 1] on [ITEM 2]. [YOUR COMPANY NAME] was wrongly charged $[ITEM 3] for the repair, as [ITEM 1] is still protected under the warranty.

I would like to think that this was simply an oversight by your service department. Pride, quality, and trust are very hard to reestablish once a relationship is severed. There will be no chance of this happening if [COMPANY] issues an immediate refund. Thank you for fulfilling your commitment to, among other things, our complete customer satisfaction.

Sincerely yours,

[YOUR NAME]
[YOUR TITLE]

[ITEM 1] = Name of product repaired
[ITEM 2] = Date [ITEM 1] was repaired
[ITEM 3] = Dollar amount of charge incurred on [ITEM 2] when [ITEM 1] was repaired

[DATE]

[Mr./Mrs./Ms./Dr.] [FIRST AND LAST NAME]
[TITLE]
[COMPANY]
[ADDRESS]
[CITY], [STATE] [ZIP CODE]

Dear [Mr./Mrs./Ms./Dr.] [LAST NAME]:

Business success does not require a Bachelor or Master's degree. Notwithstanding formal education's benefits, companies thrive with an enduring M.A.P. degree. That is, practicing the lessons of Management, Advertising, and Positioning in daily operations.

Taking the "A" from our diploma, I am exploring advertising and promotional efforts for [YOUR COMPANY NAME]. I cannot honestly say I have read every issue of your publication. From what I have seen, however, it appears that we may have a fit between your audience and our customers.

To make my decision, I require the hard facts normally contained in a publication's media kit. This can be sent to me at [ITEM 1]. Please be sure that the package includes your advertising rates, audience demographic profile, average life span per issue, one sample issue, publication frequency, and circulation data, including a complete breakdown of complimentary and paid subscriptions.

I look forward to receiving [COMPANY]'s literature and making a well-informed decision as another contribution to our company's core M.A.P. curriculum.

Sincerely yours,

[YOUR NAME]
[YOUR TITLE]

[ITEM 1] = [YOUR COMPANY NAME]'s address

[DATE]

[Mr./Mrs./Ms./Dr.] [FIRST AND LAST NAME]
[TITLE]
[COMPANY]
[ADDRESS]
[CITY], [STATE] [ZIP CODE]

Dear [Mr./Mrs./Ms./Dr.] [LAST NAME]:

Marketing without a shrewd advertising plan can be hazardous to a business's health. [YOUR COMPANY NAME] is interested in the services offered by [COMPANY] to help us spread our good word. Before proceeding any further, we would like a little information about your advertising background and success stories.

Please forward to my attention the following materials: company profile, client list, basic fee schedule, and professional references. These can be sent to [ITEM 1].

We do not require a formal advertising plan now; this can be determined later. However, if you have a general notion of how our account would be handled, by all means jot it down. I look forward to reviewing your firm's package. When I receive the material, I may telephone and set a meeting time because the health of our business is a vital asset.

Sincerely yours,

[YOUR NAME]
[YOUR TITLE]

————————————————◆————————————————

[ITEM 1] = [YOUR COMPANY NAME]'s address

BUSINESS \ Advertising
Agency Review Request

[DATE]

[Mr./Mrs./Ms./Dr.] **[FIRST AND LAST NAME]**
[TITLE]
[COMPANY]
[ADDRESS]
[CITY], [STATE] [ZIP CODE]

Dear [Mr./Mrs./Ms./Dr.] [LAST NAME]:

Often, when we compare business goals with actual performance, we identify areas of resource mismanagement. Since the agreement with your firm was entered into on [ITEM 1], [YOUR COMPANY NAME] has not noticed a dramatic increase in public awareness. We understand that this may, or may not, be totally advertising related.

Therefore, [YOUR COMPANY NAME] is reviewing our entire marketing and promotional efforts in search of weaknesses that may be inhibiting growth. I'm positive [COMPANY]'s participation is a piece of the business puzzle. Your firm has the opportunity to gather supporting materials on our entire advertising campaign.

Please telephone me at your earliest convenience to arrange a meeting. At that time, [YOUR COMPANY NAME] expects to examine what your firm has done to date, all projects in process, and all future campaign directions. Thank you for your prompt assistance. [COMPANY]'s facts will facilitate an accurate analysis of yesterday's expectations and today's results.

Sincerely yours,

[YOUR NAME]
[YOUR TITLE]

[ITEM 1] = Date agency agreement was signed between [YOUR COMPANY NAME] and [COMPANY]

RECITALS:

This is [YOUR COMPANY NAME]'s standard agreement to confirm a freelance work arrangement where we are referred to as "Customer" and [COMPANY] is the "Contractor."

FREELANCE WORK AGREEMENT

Customer hereby requests Contractor to prepare the following:

Description of Work: [ITEM 1]Date Due: [ITEM 2]

Customer agrees to pay Contractor $[ITEM 3] upon timely receipt and acceptance of the work. All work done under this Freelance Work Agreement is considered "work for hire," meaning that Contractor is not an employee of Customer, and Contractor is solely responsible for any and all taxes (state, federal, and local), worker's compensation insurance payments, disability payments, social security payments, unemployment insurance payments, other insurance payments, and any similar type of payment for Contractor or employee thereof. Contractor warrants the work is an original work that has not been previously created and is free of any unauthorized derivations from other sources. Customer retains the right to refer to Contractor in any advertising or promotional material.

Please acknowledge your acceptance of this Freelance Work Agreement by completing the areas below, and return one copy to my attention. Thank you in advance for your assistance.

[YOUR NAME]
[YOUR TITLE]

I, [ITEM 4] on behalf of [COMPANY], agree to perform the work indicated above under the terms and conditions of this Freelance Work Agreement.

Signature and Date	Social Security Number

[ITEM 1] = Describe and list by number work performed by [COMPANY]
[ITEM 2] = Date [ITEM 1] is due
[ITEM 3] = Cost of [ITEM 1]
[ITEM 4] = First and last name of [COMPANY]'s representative

BUSINESS \ Advertising
Hiring the Agency

[DATE]

[Mr./Mrs./Ms./Dr.] [FIRST AND LAST NAME]
[TITLE]
[COMPANY]
[ADDRESS]
[CITY], [STATE] [ZIP CODE]

Dear [Mr./Mrs./Ms./Dr.] [LAST NAME]:

Today, more than ever, transactions speak in the loudest voice. After careful review, [YOUR COMPANY NAME] has decided that your firm is best equipped to help us achieve our advertising goals. The campaign [COMPANY] presented was excellent, and our entire management team is excited by its profit potential.

Due to the nature of our business, [YOUR COMPANY NAME] requires final approval of all media placements before publication. Do call upon me for comments and suggestions during the idea-to-print process. Should [COMPANY] receive any sales inquiries during the term of our contract, please refer them to [ITEM 1].

Let's talk soon, as there are still contracts to sign and financial arrangements to solidify. I look forward to a long and rewarding relationship and extend a big "Congratulations!" for winning [YOUR COMPANY NAME]'s account.

Sincerely yours,

[YOUR NAME]
[YOUR TITLE]

[ITEM 1] = First and last name of [YOUR COMPANY NAME]'s contact for sales inquiries

[DATE]

[Mr./Mrs./Ms./Dr.] [FIRST AND LAST NAME]
[TITLE]
[COMPANY]
[ADDRESS]
[CITY], [STATE] [ZIP CODE]

Dear [Mr./Mrs./Ms./Dr.] [LAST NAME]:

It's unfortunate when any business relationship comes to an unanticipated ending. Yet, there are times when the reasons to separate outweigh any justification we may have to join forces. [YOUR COMPANY NAME] has given serious consideration to the question of whether our best interest continues to be served by retaining [COMPANY]'s advertising services.

After evaluating the costs versus the results, management has decided to terminate our relationship with your firm effective [ITEM 1]. This letter serves as formal notification that [YOUR COMPANY NAME] no longer requires your assistance. Please close out our account, cancel any pending media placements, and forward the final invoice to [ITEM 2]'s attention.

Thank you for your professional handling of this matter. Time brings about change, and the world is a very small place. Perhaps we will have a chance to work together in the future when circumstances are different.

Sincerely yours,

[YOUR NAME]
[YOUR TITLE]

[ITEM 1] = Date relationship with [COMPANY] ends
[ITEM 2] = First and last name of person in [YOUR COMPANY NAME] responsible for invoices

[DATE]

[Mr./Mrs./Ms./Dr.] [FIRST AND LAST NAME]
[TITLE]
[COMPANY]
[ADDRESS]
[CITY], [STATE] [ZIP CODE]

Dear [Mr./Mrs./Ms./Dr.] [LAST NAME]:

Effort combined with knowledge and tenacity is the springboard of accomplishment. One feat alone does not result in success; an ongoing pattern unfolds every time a customer is encountered. [COMPANY]'s response to our specifications demonstrated, more than any other response we received, a thorough understanding of [YOUR COMPANY NAME]'s needs.

Therefore, this letter serves as formal notification that [YOUR COMPANY NAME] awards the contract for [ITEM 1], identified by [YOUR COMPANY NAME]'s bid number [ITEM 2], to [COMPANY]. We should meet within the upcoming week to review an action plan that will take us from start to finish as outlined in the proposal. As [COMPANY]'s professionalism won our business, know that your adherence to commitments made by [COMPANY] during the bidding process is paramount.

The way in which this project is handled may result in additional business opportunities for [COMPANY]. With that said and understood, congratulations on positioning your company with [YOUR COMPANY NAME]. Obviously, you spent many hours in and out of our offices preparing the successful proposal. I look forward to getting started on "our" project.

Sincerely yours,

[YOUR NAME]
[YOUR TITLE]

[ITEM 1] = Describe what the bid was for
[ITEM 2] = Provide [YOUR COMPANY NAME]'s bid tracking number relating to [ITEM 1]

[DATE]

[Mr./Mrs./Ms./Dr.] [FIRST AND LAST NAME]
[TITLE]
[COMPANY]
[ADDRESS]
[CITY], [STATE] [ZIP CODE]

Dear [Mr./Mrs./Ms./Dr.] [LAST NAME]:

In any contest, there can be only one winner. [YOUR COMPANY NAME] challenges [COMPANY] to provide the most competitive bid and detailed proposal for [ITEM 1]. Budgetary funds are allocated for [ITEM 1], [YOUR COMPANY NAME] bid number [ITEM 2]; our anticipated procurement date is [ITEM 3].

[COMPANY]'s proposal should include specific details organized by chapter number in the following manner:

1. [COMPANY] Introduction and Background
2. [ITEM 1] Features and Warranty Information
3. [COMPANY] References
4. [ITEM 1] Pricing
5. [ITEM 1] Documentation and Literature

[YOUR COMPANY NAME] is holding a bidders' conference to address specific requirements and evaluation criteria on [ITEM 4] at [ITEM 5] beginning at [ITEM 6]. To ensure equality among the respondents, no questions pertaining to the bid will be answered before the conference. I look forward to seeing you there.

Sincerely yours,

[YOUR NAME]
[YOUR TITLE]

[ITEM 1] = Describe what the bid is for
[ITEM 2] = Provide [YOUR COMPANY NAME]'s bid tracking number relating to [ITEM 1]
[ITEM 3] = Date [ITEM 1] will be procured
[ITEM 4] = Date of bidders' conference
[ITEM 5] = Location of bidders' conference
[ITEM 6] = Time bidders' conference begins

BUSINESS \ Bids and Quotes
Finalists' Best Price Request

[DATE]

[Mr./Mrs./Ms./Dr.] [FIRST AND LAST NAME]
[TITLE]
[COMPANY]
[ADDRESS]
[CITY], [STATE] [ZIP CODE]

Dear [Mr./Mrs./Ms./Dr.] [LAST NAME]:

The results are in. Congratulations on [COMPANY]'s selection as a finalist for [YOUR COMPANY NAME]'s competitive bid number [ITEM 1] for [ITEM 2]. The proposal submitted clearly reflects [COMPANY]'s market and product awareness.

However, the decision committee requires your assistance once more before determining the winner. Respondent bids are quite similar. We are giving finalists the opportunity to submit their best and final pricing offers for [ITEM 2] under the bid's existing conditions, quantity, and terms.

While a pricing revision is not required to remain a finalist, a response either way must be in our office by the close of business on [ITEM 3]. Be advised that all finalists have received this letter, and obviously, it is in [COMPANY]'s best interest to revisit the pricing. On behalf of [YOUR COMPANY NAME], thank you for your continued professionalism. We look forward to receiving what could be the winning bid.

Sincerely yours,

[YOUR NAME]
[YOUR TITLE]

———————————◆———————————

[ITEM 1] = Provide [YOUR COMPANY NAME]'s bid tracking number relating to [ITEM 2]
[ITEM 2] = Describe what the bid is for
[ITEM 3] = Date response is due

[DATE]

[Mr./Mrs./Ms./Dr.] [FIRST AND LAST NAME]
[TITLE]
[COMPANY]
[ADDRESS]
[CITY], [STATE] [ZIP CODE]

Dear [Mr./Mrs./Ms./Dr.] [LAST NAME]:

Competition is beneficial to both buyers and sellers. During a bidding process, customer demands test vendor operations. The customer then chooses the one company best suited to be its partner for the next project.

It was evident that you and [COMPANY] expended much time and effort in completing [YOUR COMPANY NAME]'s bid for [ITEM 1]. I know well how costly and time-intensive a bid of this nature is to complete accurately and thoroughly. Please be advised, however, that the decision committee did not select [COMPANY] as the winner.

Although [COMPANY] was not awarded this bid, I hope to see your company name in future competitive situations. It may be possible for us to join forces under different conditions. [ITEM 2], thank you for your response. I assure you that our decision is not a reflection on your expertise or professionalism.

Sincerely yours,

[YOUR NAME]
[YOUR TITLE]

[ITEM 1] = Describe what the bid was for
[ITEM 2] = First name of person receiving letter

[DATE]

[Mr./Mrs./Ms./Dr.] [FIRST AND LAST NAME]
[TITLE]
[COMPANY]
[ADDRESS]
[CITY], [STATE] [ZIP CODE]

Dear [Mr./Mrs./Ms./Dr.] [LAST NAME]:

As additional information is gathered, decisions are subject to change. Many respondents to [YOUR COMPANY NAME]'s bid, number [ITEM 1], for [ITEM 2], have requested [ITEM 3]. The decision committee considered the issue and decided to [ITEM 4].

Therefore, please revise [COMPANY]'s bid response to incorporate the aforementioned. Any questions pertaining to this modification must be submitted in writing to promote fairness among the respondents.

Upon our receipt of a question, we will promptly provide the question and answer to all bid participants. Thank you for your assistance in ensuring that [YOUR COMPANY NAME] ethics are maintained during the bid process. It's important for both of us.

Sincerely yours,

[YOUR NAME]
[YOUR TITLE]

[ITEM 1] = Provide [YOUR COMPANY NAME]'s bid tracking number relating to [ITEM 2]
[ITEM 2] = Describe what the bid is for
[ITEM 3] = Describe and list by number bid respondent's request
[ITEM 4] = Describe and list by number the revision

[DATE]

[Mr./Mrs./Ms./Dr.] [FIRST AND LAST NAME]
[TITLE]
[COMPANY]
[ADDRESS]
[CITY], [STATE] [ZIP CODE]

Dear [Mr./Mrs./Ms./Dr.] [LAST NAME]:

There is never a good time for misfortune to occur. [YOUR COMPANY NAME] was recently reminded of this when one of our company vehicles was involved in an accident. After reviewing our [COMPANY] insurance policy, number [ITEM 1], this letter is sent in full compliance within the time limitations governing damage reimbursement.

The vehicle involved in the accident is car number [ITEM 2] on the policy, a [ITEM 3]. Reconstructing the accident in words alone is awkward. However, to the best of my knowledge, the driver, [ITEM 4], a [YOUR COMPANY NAME] employee, was [ITEM 5]. Then, [ITEM 6].

Damage estimates are attached for your reference. Please advise what effect, if any, this accident claim will have on our premiums and how we should proceed from here. Thank you for your assistance in securing reimbursement at the earliest date. I would like to move past this situation as quickly as possible.

Sincerely yours,

[YOUR NAME]
[YOUR TITLE]

[ITEM 1] = [YOUR COMPANY NAME]'s insurance policy number assigned by [COMPANY]
[ITEM 2] = Number of car described on [ITEM 1]
[ITEM 3] = Describe vehicle with year, make, model and serial number as relates to [ITEM 2]
[ITEM 4] = First and last name of driver involved in accident
[ITEM 5] = Describe and list by number what happened before accident
[ITEM 6] = Describe and list by number how accident occurred

BUSINESS \ Claim
Error in Claim

[DATE]

[Mr./Mrs./Ms./Dr.] [FIRST AND LAST NAME]
[TITLE]
[COMPANY]
[ADDRESS]
[CITY], [STATE] [ZIP CODE]
Reference Claim Number: [ITEM 1]

Dear [Mr./Mrs./Ms./Dr.] [LAST NAME]:

Life's best lessons are mastered during difficult and trying times. Following a calamity, only after the dust settles can a clearer picture appear. When [ITEM 2] on [ITEM 3], I tried hard throughout the initial tumultuous time to secure an accurate damage estimate.

Those efforts are now merely a good place to start. Upon careful review of the damages listing, some areas definitely require reassessment. I need your help correcting errors in our insurance claim covered under policy number [ITEM 4]. These are as follows: [ITEM 5].

I regret the extra effort required to meet our expectations as a [COMPANY] client. Please know I am here to make your job easier by answering any questions that simplify prompt reimbursement.

[ITEM 6], your professionalism then, and today, does not go unnoticed. Thank you for your assistance and understanding. Speaking for the entire team at [YOUR COMPANY NAME], I appreciate organizations that maintain high standards to sustain life-long relationships with customers.

Sincerely yours,

[YOUR NAME]
[YOUR TITLE]

[ITEM 1] = Claim number assigned to incident by [COMPANY]
[ITEM 2] = Describe the event that happened covered by insurance
[ITEM 3] = Date [ITEM 2] occurred
[ITEM 4] = [YOUR COMPANY NAME]'s insurance policy number assigned by [COMPANY]
[ITEM 5] = Describe and list by number the corrections
[ITEM 6] = First name of person receiving letter

[DATE]

[Mr./Mrs./Ms./Dr.] [FIRST AND LAST NAME]
[TITLE]
[COMPANY]
[ADDRESS]
[CITY], [STATE] [ZIP CODE]

Dear [Mr./Mrs./Ms./Dr.] [LAST NAME]:

Even outstanding safety measures do not permanently protect businesses from Murphy's Law, "What can go wrong will go wrong." [YOUR COMPANY NAME] is a perfect example. At approximately [ITEM 1] on [ITEM 2], our company suffered a devastating tragedy. We were victims of one of life's perils and nature's wonders, a fire.

In full compliance with our [COMPANY] policy, number [ITEM 3], this damage estimate is submitted within the specified time limitations. As you might imagine, I am still gathering information. Therefore, the following represents a partial listing of the losses for [ITEM 4] reimbursement: [ITEM 5].

I must depend on your professional advice and expertise now. Our operations cannot resume normal activity without immediate reimbursement. Insurance inherently protects investments and limits losses in unforeseen circumstances. While you may not have used those exact words, today I am glad I followed your recommendations for [YOUR COMPANY NAME]'s insurance coverage. Thank you for your assistance.

Sincerely yours,

[YOUR NAME]
[YOUR TITLE]

[ITEM 1] = Time fire occurred
[ITEM 2] = Date fire occurred
[ITEM 3] = [YOUR COMPANY NAME]'s insurance policy number assigned by [COMPANY]
[ITEM 4] = Per insurance policy, "actual current value" or "replacement value"
[ITEM 5] = Describe and list by number damages or losses

[DATE]

[Mr./Mrs./Ms./Dr.] [FIRST AND LAST NAME]
[TITLE]
[COMPANY]
[ADDRESS]
[CITY], [STATE] [ZIP CODE]

Reference Claim Number: [ITEM 1]

Dear [Mr./Mrs./Ms./Dr.] [LAST NAME]:

Insurance. You pay for it. You may never need it. But when you do need it, you are supposed to be glad you have it. Reflecting back on [ITEM 2] when [ITEM 3], I found comfort in believing that [COMPANY] would abide by its promises of investment protection and loss minimization.

I want to continue to maintain that insurance makes misfortune more bearable. However, our company's experience with [COMPANY] makes me wonder if that belief is realistic. Pardon such frankness, but the settlement claim for [ITEM 3] covered under policy number [ITEM 4] is aggravating, not easing, the pain of our misfortune.

There are apparently errors or omissions in the list of the damages that have caused an inadequate claim settlement. Glancing at the settlement description, the obvious errors include: [ITEM 5]. It is my hope that [COMPANY] will take a proactive position resulting in an increased reimbursement. Only then, will a chance exist that [YOUR COMPANY NAME] will consider its insurance premiums money well spent. Thank you in advance for helping to increase our customer satisfaction.

Sincerely yours,

[YOUR NAME]
[YOUR TITLE]

[ITEM 1] = Claim number assigned to incident by [COMPANY]
[ITEM 2] = Date [ITEM 3] occurred
[ITEM 3] = Event that happened covered by insurance
[ITEM 4] = [YOUR COMPANY NAME]'s insurance policy number assigned by [COMPANY]
[ITEM 5] = Describe and list by number errors

[DATE]

[Mr./Mrs./Ms./Dr.] [FIRST AND LAST NAME]
[TITLE]
[COMPANY]
[ADDRESS]
[CITY], [STATE] [ZIP CODE]

Dear [Mr./Mrs./Ms./Dr.] [LAST NAME]:

The days of unlocked doors and front porch communities are long gone. Crime continues to pervade our nation, as the overpopulated prisons attest. I have learned that it really does not matter how secure your environment is anymore.

When a criminal wants to steal, he or she finds a way. On [ITEM 1] at approximately [ITEM 2], [YOUR COMPANY NAME] was victimized by theft. A police report was filed, and the criminal [ITEM 3] been apprehended. A partial list of the property discovered missing is as follows: [ITEM 4].

Because our [COMPANY] insurance policy, number [ITEM 5], covers theft, I hope to recoup our losses as soon as possible. Let me know how I can help you get the job done. Thank you for your professional assistance leading to a speedy settlement. It's a terrible shame that the illicit acts of a few force the rest of us to imprison ourselves within our environments.

Sincerely yours,

[YOUR NAME]
[YOUR TITLE]

[ITEM 1] = Date theft occurred
[ITEM 2] = Time theft occurred
[ITEM 3] = As relates to arrest of thief, "has" or "has not"
[ITEM 4] = Describe and list by number missing items
[ITEM 5] = [YOUR COMPANY NAME]'s insurance policy number assigned by [COMPANY]

BUSINESS \ Complaint
Bad Goods

[DATE]

[Mr./Mrs./Ms./Dr.] [FIRST AND LAST NAME]
[TITLE]
[COMPANY]
[ADDRESS]
[CITY], [STATE] [ZIP CODE]

Dear [Mr./Mrs./Ms./Dr.] [LAST NAME]:

I want to say good-bye to our post-purchase blues. Being consumer-conscious, [YOUR COMPANY NAME] practices standard buying etiquette. Purchases are investigated and opinions gathered before our company authorizes spending.

Our experience with [ITEM 1] bought on [ITEM 2] for $[ITEM 3] does not match the product literature or testimonial claims. Specifically, [ITEM 1] falls dramatically short in the following manner: [ITEM 4].

It is my hope that a refund will be expedited to protect our opinion of [COMPANY]. I have never believed the adage, "you get what you pay for." Money is an immaterial issue. Any product should, at the very minimum, leave a buyer satisfied with his or her purchase and the company that sold it. I look forward to the immediate refund that quells the "farewell" rising from my gullet.

Sincerely yours,

[YOUR NAME]
[YOUR TITLE]

[ITEM 1] = Name of bad product
[ITEM 2] = Date **[ITEM 1]** was purchased
[ITEM 3] = Dollar amount of **[ITEM 1]**'s purchase price
[ITEM 4] = Describe and list by number problems with **[ITEM 1]**

[DATE]

[Mr./Mrs./Ms./Dr.] [FIRST AND LAST NAME]
[TITLE]
[COMPANY]
[ADDRESS]
[CITY], [STATE] [ZIP CODE]

Dear [Mr./Mrs./Ms./Dr.] [LAST NAME]:

Have you seen the advertisements or noticed a trend in titles on the New York *Times* nonfiction best-seller list? Actually, you don't even need to pick up a book or magazine to see that service has become a thread that runs through the fabric of business the world over.

Today, the word "service" is thrown around as if it were something brand new. Service, however, has had the power to make or break sellers for as long as there have been buyers. I would like to help [COMPANY] by relating an incident exposing lack of respect and abominable service.

On [ITEM 1], [YOUR COMPANY NAME] had the unpleasant experience of [ITEM 2]. Not being a company to create waves, we handled the issue tactfully by [ITEM 3].

The average person is commonly believed to have at least 200 acquaintances. Bad news spreads like wildfire. I hope this type of experience is one your company calls the exception rather than the rule.

Sincerely yours,

[YOUR NAME]
[YOUR TITLE]

[ITEM 1] = Date of bad service
[ITEM 2] = Describe the incident
[ITEM 3] = Describe [YOUR COMPANY NAME]'s reaction to [ITEM 2]

[DATE]

[Mr./Mrs./Ms./Dr.] [FIRST AND LAST NAME]
[TITLE]
[COMPANY]
[ADDRESS]
[CITY], [STATE] [ZIP CODE]

Dear [Mr./Mrs./Ms./Dr.] [LAST NAME]:

We like to surround ourselves with knowledgeable and reputable winners. Assisting the next generation is equally important too. It's unfortunate that not all students recognize mentors in their professional lives.

One's immediate manager is not the sole source of practical education; a customer can teach too. My patience has worn increasingly thin with [ITEM 1]. I have neither the desire nor the authority to assume a disciplinary role. Trust me when I say that it is to [COMPANY]'s advantage that a new sales representative is assigned to handle [YOUR COMPANY NAME]'s business.

Rehashing the past is not always a productive venture. I'll just tell you [ITEM 1] needs remedial training in professional business practices. This is [COMPANY]'s task, not mine. I look forward to helping another representative develop his or her career. Hopefully, he or she will understand that learning is a life-long process and customer satisfaction is the highest priority.

Sincerely yours,

[YOUR NAME]
[YOUR TITLE]

[ITEM 1] = First and last name of [COMPANY]'s sales representative [YOUR COMPANY NAME] wants to replace

[DATE]

[Mr./Mrs./Ms./Dr.] [FIRST AND LAST NAME]
[TITLE]
[COMPANY]
[ADDRESS]
[CITY], [STATE] [ZIP CODE]

Dear [Mr./Mrs./Ms./Dr.] [LAST NAME]:

When a person inadvertently ingests a poisonous substance, we are taught to act quickly. The poison must be removed before damage is done. Accordingly, responses to our inquiries concerning unconventional business practices demand immediate attention.

I have contacted [COMPANY] on several occasions regarding [ITEM 1]. As a professional, I know this is not an insurmountable dilemma once the proper resources are dedicated. The key is making our concern a [COMPANY] priority by giving it attention.

[YOUR COMPANY NAME]'s stance has not changed. We still insist that [ITEM 2] be [ITEM 3] as soon as possible. Let's not waste any more valuable time; your unprofessionalism is destroying any possibility of future business with [YOUR COMPANY NAME]. I hope to hear from [COMPANY] within the next week with confirmation that the issue has been resolved to our mutual satisfaction. You know what it feels like when you're ignored.

Sincerely yours,

[YOUR NAME]
[YOUR TITLE]

[ITEM 1] = Describe the outstanding issue
[ITEM 2] = Subject of [ITEM 1]
[ITEM 3] = Describe and list by number actions [COMPANY] must take to resolve [ITEM 1]

BUSINESS \ Complaint
Price Increase

[DATE]

[Mr./Mrs./Ms./Dr.] [FIRST AND LAST NAME]
[TITLE]
[COMPANY]
[ADDRESS]
[CITY], [STATE] [ZIP CODE]

Dear [Mr./Mrs./Ms./Dr.] [LAST NAME]:

Anger results from disappointment. We believe that if the roles were reversed, the actions taken would not have been our own. Pardon my anger over receiving notification that [COMPANY] has increased the price dramatically for [ITEM 1].

I find it inconceivable, however, that [COMPANY]'s management could have approved such a ludicrous move. You are forcing many established customers, like [YOUR COMPANY NAME], to look elsewhere. [COMPANY] is not the only company selling [ITEM 1]. My professional career has formed around solid relationships and ours appears to be ending.

This is precisely why I have chosen to vent my disappointment through this letter. Up to now, I chose [COMPANY]. Your professional practices were quite respectable and consistent with our own. As this is no longer the case, know that we are evaluating other sources for our needs.

To stop other vendor proposals from entering my office, [COMPANY] must fulfill its customer satisfaction obligations and live up to our company's expectations. If this is possible, please telephone at your earliest convenience. I hope to hear from you shortly. Your price increase is a dangerous and losing proposition, but together we can change its direction.

Sincerely yours,

[YOUR NAME]
[YOUR TITLE]

[ITEM 1] = Describe product or service

[DATE]

[Mr./Mrs./Ms./Dr.] [FIRST AND LAST NAME]
[TITLE]
[COMPANY]
[ADDRESS]
[CITY], [STATE] [ZIP CODE]

Dear [Mr./Mrs./Ms./Dr.] [LAST NAME]:

Proper tools make our businesses run smoothly. In the perfect business world, every company would have the right equipment for every job it might have to undertake. However, this would eliminate the need for companies like [COMPANY] and, as your apparent success demonstrates, is not realistic.

[YOUR COMPANY NAME] runs a tight ship. When our goal attainment is dependent on another company's actions, our policy is to confirm those arrangements.

I trust the [ITEM 1] will be delivered to [ITEM 2] on [ITEM 3] around [ITEM 4] as we have agreed. Please take a moment today to verify the above details and advise me that everything is in order. Thank you for your continuing assistance and commitment to professional service. [COMPANY] is one of the tools of our trade.

Sincerely,

[YOUR NAME]
[YOUR TITLE]

[ITEM 1] = Describe and list by number equipment rented
[ITEM 2] = Address to which [ITEM 1] will be delivered
[ITEM 3] = Date [ITEM 1] will be delivered
[ITEM 4] = Time [ITEM 1] will be delivered

[DATE]

[Mr./Mrs./Ms./Dr.] [FIRST AND LAST NAME]
[TITLE]
[COMPANY]
[ADDRESS]
[CITY], [STATE] [ZIP CODE]

Dear [Mr./Mrs./Ms./Dr.] [LAST NAME]:

Can we ever be too efficient in business? [YOUR COMPANY NAME] doesn't think so. A little checking now eliminates errors later.

We usually receive an acknowledgment of some type when reservations are made for an event such as [ITEM 1]. Since we have not, I take this opportunity to confirm our reservation for [ITEM 1] on [ITEM 2] beginning at [ITEM 3].

The reservation is in the name(s) of [ITEM 4]. Unless we hear otherwise, we'll assume all systems are go and we are free to allow our anticipation to grow as the date nears. See you there!

Sincerely yours,

[YOUR NAME]
[YOUR TITLE]

[ITEM 1] = Name of event
[ITEM 2] = Date of event
[ITEM 3] = Time [ITEM 1] starts
[ITEM 4] = First and last name(s) of persons holding the reservation

[DATE]

[Mr./Mrs./Ms./Dr.] [FIRST AND LAST NAME]
[TITLE]
[COMPANY]
[ADDRESS]
[CITY], [STATE] [ZIP CODE]

Dear [Mr./Mrs./Ms./Dr.] [LAST NAME]:

Lack of consensus invariably leads to dissatisfaction. While our discussions are fresh, it is imperative that we have a mutual understanding of our potential business affiliation. Consequently, this letter serves as formal notification of our intent to [ITEM 1].

The terms and conditions of this offer are founded within the feedback obtained in our negotiations and additional outside research performed by [YOUR COMPANY NAME]. These are as follows: [ITEM 2].

This letter of intent expires, thus becoming null and void, [ITEM 3] days from today's date unless extended and agreed to by our respective organizations. We request that all information pertaining to the aforementioned be held in the strictest confidence until this letter expires or a final agreement is consummated. I await your positive response to this offer, which will foster a beneficial relationship between our respective companies.

Sincerely yours,

[YOUR NAME]
[YOUR TITLE]

[ITEM 1] = Purpose of letter of intent
[ITEM 2] = Describe and list by number all terms and conditions related to [ITEM 1]
[ITEM 3] = Number of days from the date the letter was sent the offer is good

BUSINESS \ Confirmation
Phone Conversation

[DATE]

[Mr./Mrs./Ms./Dr.] [FIRST AND LAST NAME]
[TITLE]
[COMPANY]
[ADDRESS]
[CITY], [STATE] [ZIP CODE]

Dear [Mr./Mrs./Ms./Dr.] [LAST NAME]:

By most estimates, there are between 3,000 and 4,000 languages in the world. Mandarin has the largest number of speakers; English the second. Although we speak the same language in more ways than one, miscommunication can sour any undertaking.

To confirm that our business dialects are complementary, a quick synopsis of our telephone conversation on [ITEM 1] is in order. It is my understanding that [YOUR COMPANY NAME] is to [ITEM 2]. [COMPANY] is planning to [ITEM 3].

If I am interpreting any area incorrectly, please advise me at your earliest convenience. Thank you for your professionalism now and in the future. While some languages have millions of speakers and others only 25, I am pleased ours is shared.

Sincerely yours,

[YOUR NAME]
[YOUR TITLE]

[ITEM 1] = Date telephone conversation took place
[ITEM 2] = Describe and list by number future actions by **[YOUR COMPANY NAME]**
[ITEM 3] = Describe and list by number future actions by **[COMPANY]**

[DATE]

[Mr./Mrs./Ms./Dr.] [FIRST AND LAST NAME]
[TITLE]
[COMPANY]
[ADDRESS]
[CITY], [STATE] [ZIP CODE]

Dear [Mr./Mrs./Ms./Dr.] [LAST NAME]:

Every day, millions of reservations are processed for everything from champagne balloon rides at sunrise to safaris crossing the African veldt. While I wish our reservations for [ITEM 1] were for one of the above adventures, the conventional importance of details must be addressed.

Therefore, I am confirming our reservation for [ITEM 1] on [ITEM 2]. [COMPANY] will be [ITEM 3]. Please take a moment to verify the above and advise me of any potential problem areas. Thank you for your assistance; who knows, maybe we'll experience eccentricity more than once in our lives. I hear African safaris are a natural wonder.

Sincerely yours,

[YOUR NAME]
[YOUR TITLE]

[ITEM 1] = Describe what reservation is for
[ITEM 2] = Date of reservation
[ITEM 3] = Describe and list by number actions need by [COMPANY] concerning [ITEM 1]

**BUSINESS \ Credit
Application for**

[DATE]

[Mr./Mrs./Ms./Dr.] [FIRST AND LAST NAME]
[TITLE]
[COMPANY]
[ADDRESS]
[CITY], [STATE] [ZIP CODE]

Dear [Mr./Mrs./Ms./Dr.] [LAST NAME]:

Believe it or not, success can be trendsetting and conservative simultaneously. Fortitude and wisdom achieve balance between innovation and risk protection. [YOUR COMPANY NAME] continues to master business's scales of justice by developing a healthy market and being, much to our liking, a little set in our ways.

We tip the scales more in the checks and balances tradition. Many other businesses our size probably would have extended themselves with credit already. In fact, I can't tell you how many creditors and suppliers have asked us if we wanted credit.

Today, credit with frequent suppliers like [COMPANY] is the next logical step in furthering growth and streamlining operations. We would like any purchases over a [ITEM 1]-day period totaled and invoiced. The benefits of reduced paperwork and processing hours for our respective organizations are obvious.

Please send a credit application and any other necessary paperwork to [ITEM 2]. [YOUR COMPANY NAME] is ready for credit now that the market rage we created has left us standing alone on enterprise's center stage.

Sincerely yours,

[YOUR NAME]
[YOUR TITLE]

[ITEM 1] = Time between invoices, i.e., 30, 60, or 90 days
[ITEM 2] = First and last name of the person at [YOUR COMPANY NAME] responsible for completing credit
applications

[DATE]

[Mr./Mrs./Ms./Dr.] [FIRST AND LAST NAME]
[TITLE]
[COMPANY]
[ADDRESS]
[CITY], [STATE] [ZIP CODE]

Dear [Mr./Mrs./Ms./Dr.] [LAST NAME]:

When great ideas have outlived their usefulness, it's time for a change. [YOUR COMPANY NAME]'s shift in direction has resulted in more than a few displacements as strategies have matured. Credit with [COMPANY] is one thing we no longer require for our long-term goal attainment.

Circumstances being what they are, I write on behalf of [YOUR COMPANY NAME] to cancel our [COMPANY] credit account, number [ITEM 1]. This is effective on [ITEM 2].

Please calculate the final balance as of the above date. To prevent any potential miscommunication, advise me of the total amount due in writing on [COMPANY] letterhead by [ITEM 3]. I appreciate your prompt attention and extend thanks for your participation in our growth.

Sincerely yours,

[YOUR NAME]
[YOUR TITLE]

[ITEM 1] = [YOUR COMPANY NAME]'s credit account number assigned by [COMPANY]
[ITEM 2] = Date the credit will be canceled
[ITEM 3] = Date the [COMPANY] should advise [YOUR COMPANY NAME] how much you owe

[DATE]

[Mr./Mrs./Ms./Dr.] [FIRST AND LAST NAME]
[TITLE]
[COMPANY]
[ADDRESS]
[CITY], [STATE] [ZIP CODE]

Dear [Mr./Mrs./Ms./Dr.] [LAST NAME]:

Good habits are essential to personal and professional security. By controlling our lives, we actually become freer to enjoy additional experiences. The availability and extension of credit from one company to another is a perfect example.

[YOUR COMPANY NAME] does its homework and confirms that the people involved with us take their credit seriously. We need [COMPANY]'s help. We are requesting a complete credit profile and report on [ITEM 1], located at [ITEM 2], for the years [ITEM 3]. The release from [ITEM 1] authorizing and granting permission to [YOUR COMPANY NAME] to investigate their credit history is [ITEM 4]. Please process payment for the credit report using [ITEM 5].

Business cannot afford to extend credit frivolously or to those who have not developed good track records. Thank you for your help in picking the winners.

Sincerely yours,

[YOUR NAME]
[YOUR TITLE]

[ITEM 1] = Customer [YOUR COMPANY NAME] needs the credit report on
[ITEM 2] = Address of [ITEM 1]
[ITEM 3] = Years [YOUR COMPANY NAME] wants information on
[ITEM 4] = Most credit bureaus require authorization from the customer, i.e., "enclosed" or "granted on our
         credit application"
[ITEM 5] = Method [YOUR COMPANY NAME] is paying for report, i.e., "enclosed check" or "our credit
         bureau account"

[DATE]

[Mr./Mrs./Ms./Dr.] [FIRST AND LAST NAME]
[TITLE]
[COMPANY]
[ADDRESS]
[CITY], [STATE] [ZIP CODE]

Dear [Mr./Mrs./Ms./Dr.] [LAST NAME]:

I always like to know where I stand. Having a complete understanding of where one is enables proactive decision making. Change for the sake of change is not as beneficial as change that is planned. In preparation for making financial moves promoting our imminent growth, [YOUR COMPANY NAME] needs your help.

We are requesting a complete report of our credit history with [COMPANY] over the past [ITEM 1], including the following: available line of credit; average, highest, and lowest balances; length of time the account has been active; number of times, if any, a late payment has been made; and outstanding amount due on the account. The above pertains to account number [ITEM 2].

As [YOUR COMPANY NAME] continues to take advantage of tremendous opportunities, your information facilitates business planning. My target date for receiving the report is [ITEM 3]. I realize that this may be short notice, and I want you to know that your assistance is appreciated. I look forward to [COMPANY]'s continued participation in our company's growth.

Sincerely yours,

[YOUR NAME]
[YOUR TITLE]

[ITEM 1] = Period credit inquiry report should cover
[ITEM 2] = [YOUR COMPANY NAME]'s credit account number assigned by [COMPANY]
[ITEM 3] = Date the [COMPANY] should provide credit inquiry report

BUSINESS \ Credit
Referral Request

[DATE]

[Mr./Mrs./Ms./Dr.] [FIRST AND LAST NAME]
[TITLE]
[COMPANY]
[ADDRESS]
[CITY], [STATE] [ZIP CODE]

Dear [Mr./Mrs./Ms./Dr.] [LAST NAME]:

Whether beginning a business or embarking on adulthood, minimizing risks increases the potential for achievement. The groundwork established pushes us to the next plateau. Suddenly, we realize that risk is necessary, and we must decide how much risk we are willing to take.

[YOUR COMPANY NAME] investigates the risk factor associated with every client who requests credit. The more information we can obtain about a client's past dealings, the better equipped we are to make decisions about his credit worthiness.

We were given [COMPANY]'s name as a reference by [ITEM 1]. Your information is crucial to our decision. In accordance with applicable laws, the areas about which we seek information are as follows: available line of credit; average, highest, and lowest balances; length of time the account has been active; number of times, if any, a late payment has been made; and outstanding amount due on the account. The above pertains to account number [ITEM 2].

You can forward this information to [ITEM 3]. Thank you for your assistance. From one business veteran to another, I appreciate your professional courtesy and prompt reply. We both know risk minimization assists profit maximization.

Sincerely yours,

[YOUR NAME]
[YOUR TITLE]

[ITEM 1] = Customer [YOUR COMPANY NAME] wants information on
[ITEM 2] = Customer's account number with [COMPANY]
[ITEM 3] = First and last name of person at [YOUR COMPANY NAME] who should receive information, or
          if yourself, "me"

[DATE]

[Mr./Mrs./Ms./Dr.] [FIRST AND LAST NAME]
[TITLE]
[COMPANY]
[ADDRESS]
[CITY], [STATE] [ZIP CODE]

Dear [Mr./Mrs./Ms./Dr.] [LAST NAME]:

Success often begets success. In our years of business, [YOUR COMPANY NAME] has prospered by adhering to the Golden Rule. Every kind gesture is returned eventually; in other words, what goes around comes around.

The credit reference for [ITEM 1] submitted by your company is my responsibility. As a professional, clearly you realize that the Consumer Protection Act and other statutes, legally limit the information about a business or individual's credit and payment history that can be disclosed.

Therefore, in accordance with the law, we provide the following credit facts for [ITEM 1], located at [ITEM 2], for the past [ITEM 3]: [ITEM 4]. Having this knowledge about our experience with [ITEM 1] should assist in [COMPANY]'s decision and success. If there are any questions, please do hesitate to contact me. It is my pleasure to help another company achieve its profit potential.

Sincerely yours,

[YOUR NAME]
[YOUR TITLE]

[ITEM 1] = Customer [COMPANY] needs the credit information on
[ITEM 2] = Address of [ITEM 1]
[ITEM 3] = Years [ITEM 1] information pertains to
[ITEM 4] = Credit information for [ITEM 1]

[DATE]

[Mr./Mrs./Ms./Dr.] [FIRST AND LAST NAME]
[TITLE]
[COMPANY]
[ADDRESS]
[CITY], [STATE] [ZIP CODE]

Dear [Mr./Mrs./Ms./Dr.] [LAST NAME]:

One way to build a successful company is to have assets in many areas. Financial statements and capital equipment are important, but a professional team builds security and increases profitability. We are increasing our wealth with the addition of hand-picked talent.

Because [COMPANY] targets a qualified audience, please place the following advertisement in your employment classified section under [ITEM 1]. We would like the advertisement to run [ITEM 2].

JOIN OUR WINNING TEAM

Our business is growing, and we are seeking quality people with a strong professional work ethic to share in our enthusiasm. Qualified, experienced [ITEM 3] should apply by [ITEM 4].

Upon receipt of this letter, please telephone with the estimated cost, and we'll arrange payment. Thank you for your assistance in keeping our assets strong.

Sincerely yours,

[YOUR NAME]
[YOUR TITLE]

[ITEM 1] = Industry or profession category under which advertisement should be placed
[ITEM 2] = Dates the advertisement should be put in publication
[ITEM 3] = Name of position open for applications
[ITEM 4] = Describe the actions taken by reader to apply for job

[DATE]

[Mr./Mrs./Ms./Dr.] [FIRST AND LAST NAME]
[ADDRESS]
[CITY], [STATE] [ZIP CODE]

Dear [Mr./Mrs./Ms./Dr.] [LAST NAME]:

Ability alone does not lead to achievement. Enthusiasm, knowledge, perseverance, and unity promote success. Because you possess these characteristics, [YOUR COMPANY NAME] is pleased to extend an offer to join our talented staff as a [ITEM 1] beginning on [ITEM 2].

In this position, you will be responsible for [ITEM 3]. Clearly, this is an incredible opportunity to utilize and develop your professional skills. The compensation of $[ITEM 4] per [ITEM 5] is quite competitive in today's market.

In addition, you will be eligible for bonuses and salary increases. [YOUR COMPANY NAME] rewards individual and team achievement based on the results of performance appraisals conducted every [ITEM 6]. I look forward to your acceptance of this offer and to welcoming you into [YOUR COMPANY NAME]'s team of professionals.

Sincerely yours,

[YOUR NAME]
[YOUR TITLE]

[ITEM 1] = Title of position offered to person receiving letter
[ITEM 2] = Start date of employment
[ITEM 3] = Describe and list by number responsibilities of [ITEM 1]
[ITEM 4] = Dollar amount paid per [ITEM 5]
[ITEM 5] = Length of time, i.e., "hour," "month," "week," or "year"
[ITEM 6] = Interval at which performance appraisals are conducted.

BUSINESS \ Employee
Jury Duty Excuse

[DATE]

[Mr./Mrs./Ms./Dr.] [FIRST AND LAST NAME]
[TITLE]
[COMPANY]
[ADDRESS]
[CITY], [STATE] [ZIP CODE]

Dear [Mr./Mrs./Ms./Dr.] [LAST NAME]:

It is truly an honor to be an American and live in this great nation. Respecting equality, freedom, and justice is every society member's responsibility. Through jury duty, the judicial system promotes appreciation of these ideals.

Far too many voices cry that laws and legislation are administered without regard for public opinion. Jury duty is a small price to pay for the benefits of United States citizenship. However, we regret that, due to circumstances beyond [YOUR COMPANY NAME]'s control, [ITEM 1] will be unable to report for jury duty on the date stated in [ITEM 2] summons.

Please know I have taken a personal interest in changing the situation that prevents [ITEM 1] from fulfilling [ITEM 2] responsibility. Under different circumstances, there would be no question of [ITEM 1]'s participation. Thank you for your understanding in the matter. As a law abiding company, we do wish things had been different.

Sincerely yours,

[YOUR NAME]
[YOUR TITLE]

[ITEM 1] = First and last name of employee
[ITEM 2] = Pronoun referring to [ITEM 1]'s gender, i.e., "his" or "her"

[DATE]

[Mr./Mrs./Ms./Dr.] [FIRST AND LAST NAME]
[ADDRESS]
[CITY], [STATE] [ZIP CODE]

Dear [Mr./Mrs./Ms./Dr.] [LAST NAME]:

    Protocols define accepted practices. Incorporating the standard phrase "References provided upon request" in a résumé is a common practice. Although we have spent only a brief time together, you probably have noticed [YOUR COMPANY NAME]'s rigorous attention to detail. Our success demands maintenance of high standards.

    Your credentials and presentation impressed me, so I would now like to take the next step in the hiring process, which calls for requesting references from three business associates.

    Please forward by [ITEM 1] a list to my attention that contains the following information for each reference: complete mail and telephone contact information, beginning date of affiliation with you, and a brief paragraph describing your relationship.

    I, or a member of my staff, will contact some or all of your references before our next meeting. Thank you for fulfilling your résumé's written commitment. I look forward to confirming my belief in your future with [YOUR COMPANY NAME].

Sincerely yours,

[YOUR NAME]
[YOUR TITLE]

[ITEM 1] = Date [YOUR COMPANY NAME] wants references by

BUSINESS \ Employee
Request for Résumé

[DATE]

[Mr./Mrs./Ms./Dr.] [FIRST AND LAST NAME]
[TITLE]
[COMPANY]
[ADDRESS]
[CITY], [STATE] [ZIP CODE]

Dear [Mr./Mrs./Ms./Dr.] [LAST NAME]:

From time to time, you hear of a person who possesses a certain successful air—a person who is admired and stands above the crowd in his or her chosen profession. [YOUR COMPANY NAME] looks for such presence and knowledge in our managers and employees.

I write with the hope that you are in a position to explore career alternatives. From what I know, we could be the company that precisely matches your short- and long-term goals. I am interested in receiving your professional profile or résumé if you are interested in a potential career move to [YOUR COMPANY NAME] as our newest [ITEM 1].

Timing is very important in life and I understand my initiative may not come at a convenient time. Nevertheless, I would appreciate a reply. Thank you for advising me of your thoughts in the matter. It is hard to find good people like you.

Sincerely yours,

[YOUR NAME]
[YOUR TITLE]

[ITEM 1] = Title of position available

[DATE]

[Mr./Mrs./Ms./Dr.] [FIRST AND LAST NAME]
[TITLE]
[COMPANY]
[ADDRESS]
[CITY], [STATE] [ZIP CODE]

Dear [Mr./Mrs./Ms./Dr.] [LAST NAME]:

First impressions are not always reliable. While trusting your conscience has merit, hiring decisions require certainty. We want not only the most experienced, knowledgeable, and team-oriented people, but people who will fit in with our corporate culture.

A former employee of [COMPANY], [ITEM 1], recently applied for a [ITEM 2] position with [YOUR COMPANY NAME] and gave your name as a reference.

In accordance with the law, please provide [ITEM 3] dates of employment and salary history. Thank you in advance for your assistance in our hiring process. As I'm sure you know, we need all the help we can get with the challenging process of hiring new employees.

Sincerely yours,

[YOUR NAME]
[YOUR TITLE]

[ITEM 1] = First and last name of employee
[ITEM 2] = Position [ITEM 1] is applying for at [YOUR COMPANY NAME]
[ITEM 3] = Pronoun referring to [ITEM 1]'s gender, i.e., "his" or "her"

[DATE]

To whom it may concern:

Skillful pilots gain a reputation maneuvering machines through both tranquil weather conditions and raging thunderstorms. Each situation requires a different approach, but a successful landing is always the ultimate goal. Employees like [ITEM 1] enable organizations to manage traffic patterns with professional skill.

It always gives me great pleasure to copilot, direct and manage a successful person's moves. Recently, I had such an experience when [ITEM 1] made important contributions to [YOUR COMPANY NAME] from [ITEM 2] through [ITEM 3]. [ITEM 4] achievements included [ITEM 5].

I can recommend [ITEM 4] knowledge, skills, and talents heartily. Beyond being achievement-oriented and enthusiastic, [ITEM 4] has the ability to get the job done. Any company that hires [ITEM 1] will defy gravity and successfully land time after time, no matter what the weather.

Sincerely yours,

[YOUR NAME]
[YOUR TITLE]

[ITEM 1] = First and last name of employee
[ITEM 2] = Starting date of [ITEM 1]'s employment with [YOUR COMPANY NAME]
[ITEM 3] = Ending date of [ITEM 1]'s employment with [YOUR COMPANY NAME]
[ITEM 4] = Pronoun referring to [ITEM 1]'s gender, i.e., "his" or "her," "he" or "she"
[ITEM 5] = Describe and list by number [ITEM 1]'s successes

[DATE]

[Mr./Mrs./Ms./Dr.] [FIRST AND LAST NAME]
[TITLE]
[COMPANY]
[ADDRESS]
[CITY], [STATE] [ZIP CODE]

Dear [Mr./Mrs./Ms./Dr.] [LAST NAME]:

In a world filled with talent that covers a myriad of business opportunities, acknowledgment of efforts is momentous. Even now as I write, I am flustered by the thrill of being looked upon with such high esteem. It is with the utmost honor and pleasure that [YOUR COMPANY NAME] gratefully accepts the [ITEM 1] award for [ITEM 2].

Undoubtedly, great things are possible when there is unity in action and spirit. Knowing [YOUR COMPANY NAME] may have created a better future with our small contribution makes our lives more worthwhile. With my sincerest appreciation and on behalf of [YOUR COMPANY NAME], thank you for recognizing our efforts and bestowing such an accolade. It means a great deal to us professionally and personally.

Sincerely yours,

[YOUR NAME]
[YOUR TITLE]

[ITEM 1] = Name of award
[ITEM 2] = Describe the reason [YOUR COMPANY NAME] received award

BUSINESS \ Goodwill
Congratulations to Peer

[DATE]

[Mr./Mrs./Ms./Dr.] [FIRST AND LAST NAME]
[TITLE]
[COMPANY]
[ADDRESS]
[CITY], [STATE] [ZIP CODE]

Dear [Mr./Mrs./Ms./Dr.] [LAST NAME]:

Wolfgang Amadeus Mozart wrote the opera "Don Giovanni" at one sitting, and it was played without any rehearsal the following day. Where innate talents exist, they must be challenged and developed. Your achievement in [ITEM 1] obviously required similar proficiency.

No one can give a person a need for success—a desire to do his very best every moment of every day. I believe your inherent desire for accomplishment is the spark that lights the fire from which [COMPANY] derives the warmth that sustains it. I extend my heartiest congratulations and wishes for continued success in, and out of, business's symphony halls.

Sincerely yours,

[YOUR NAME]
[YOUR TITLE]

[ITEM 1] = Describe the achievement performed by peer

[DATE]

**[Mr./Mrs./Ms./Dr.] [FIRST AND LAST NAME]
[TITLE]
[COMPANY]
[ADDRESS]
[CITY], [STATE] [ZIP CODE]**

Dear [Mr./Mrs./Ms./Dr.] [LAST NAME]:

With admiration and respect, I read [COMPANY]'s literature describing your efforts to better humanity. I write with much regret to say that our previous generosity is just not possible this year. In these economically troubled times, added budgetary strains have demanded cutbacks across the board.

Although donations are included in this category, please know this will not be forever. I have taken a keen interest in making sure that donations to [COMPANY] have the highest priority when the numbers are better.

Please keep me advised of your activities. I assure you that when times are better again our support will extend beyond words of encouragement. [ITEM 1], thank you for understanding. I have often thought of leaving this rat race to enter a world where goodwill is appreciated and revered. I envy your ability to live my dream.

Sincerely yours,

**[YOUR NAME]
[YOUR TITLE]**

[ITEM 1] = First name of person receiving letter

BUSINESS \ Goodwill
Donations—Yes

[DATE]

[Mr./Mrs./Ms./Dr.] [FIRST AND LAST NAME]
[TITLE]
[COMPANY]
[ADDRESS]
[CITY], [STATE] [ZIP CODE]

Dear [Mr./Mrs./Ms./Dr.] [LAST NAME]:

    Andrew Carnegie, one of the wealthiest men in United States history, never failed to remember the less fortunate. He devoted himself to philanthropy and donated more than $350 million to various causes in his lifetime. Mr. Carnegie gave back to society what he and his family were blessed in receiving.

    Similarly, [YOUR COMPANY NAME] strongly believes in supporting good causes. I am impressed that [COMPANY] has taken the initiative in aiding [ITEM 1]. Please accept our company's donation in the amount of $[ITEM 2] to help in your humanitarian efforts. While there is still much work to be done, your entire organization should be proud that because of their generosity, [ITEM 1] has a new lease on life.

Sincerely yours,

[YOUR NAME]
[YOUR TITLE]

[ITEM 1] = Subject of [ITEM 1]'s cause and efforts
[ITEM 2] = Dollar amount of [YOUR COMPANY NAME]'s donation

[DATE]

[Mr./Mrs./Ms./Dr.] [FIRST AND LAST NAME]
[TITLE]
[COMPANY]
[ADDRESS]
[CITY], [STATE] [ZIP CODE]

Dear [Mr./Mrs./Ms./Dr.] [LAST NAME]:

Distinguishing one business from another through the advertising hype that pervades our world is a tiring adventure. Many companies claim superiority because of low prices or unparalleled service. Withstanding the test of promotion is the axiom, "People want to do business with people, not companies."

Whenever someone does an outstanding job, it's imperative to recognize his or her extra effort. I had the pleasure recently of meeting a [COMPANY] employee, [ITEM 1], to [ITEM 2]. [ITEM 3] diligence and professionalism have reassured [YOUR COMPANY NAME] that there are other companies like us that fulfill their promises.

Human nature normally responds only when things go wrong. For this reason, I write to give your company, and especially [ITEM 1], a big pat on the back. I hope this dedication typifies your company. People like [ITEM 1] are [COMPANY]'s best advertisement.

Sincerely yours,

[YOUR NAME]
[YOUR TITLE]

[ITEM 1] = First and last name of person you are complimenting
[ITEM 2] = Task you worked with [ITEM 1] to complete
[ITEM 3] = Pronoun referring to [ITEM 1]'s gender, i.e., "his" or "her"

BUSINESS \ Goodwill
Support of Position

[DATE]

[Mr./Mrs./Ms./Dr.] [FIRST AND LAST NAME]
[TITLE]
[COMPANY]
[ADDRESS]
[CITY], [STATE] [ZIP CODE]

Dear [Mr./Mrs./Ms./Dr.] [LAST NAME]:

    Fire must be controlled; otherwise everything in its path is destroyed. Powerful issues like [ITEM 1] are subject to elements that alone cannot create combustion. However, once the properties are combined, restraint is the only means of keeping order.

    [YOUR COMPANY NAME] supports [COMPANY]'s efforts in promoting public awareness of the danger inherent in [ITEM 1]. Personally and professionally, I believe [ITEM 2] is vital for the future of our industry, nation, and succeeding generations. I am certain that [COMPANY]'s efforts are endorsed just as strongly by others who simply don't have the time to write a note such as this.

    If there is anything either [YOUR COMPANY NAME] or I can do in support of the cause, please notify me. Best wishes in the fight, and remember, there are many more people ready to take action. Enough water could eliminate [ITEM 1]'s fire and leave only ashes behind.

Sincerely yours,

[YOUR NAME]
[YOUR TITLE]

--------------------------◆--------------------------

[ITEM 1] = Describe the issue in one or two words
[ITEM 2] = Describe what [COMPANY] is trying to accomplish

[DATE]

[Mr./Mrs./Ms./Dr.] [FIRST AND LAST NAME]
[TITLE]
[COMPANY]
[ADDRESS]
[CITY], [STATE] [ZIP CODE]

Dear [Mr./Mrs./Ms./Dr.] [LAST NAME]:

It's good to have strong partners. In personal and professional relationships, I strive for a sharing of beliefs, goals, interests, and values. Joining forces with like-minded people can have a decidedly positive effect on our lives.

Believing we may have complementary aspirations, I am interested in [COMPANY]. Please send an introductory membership package to my attention at [ITEM 1]. Specifically, I would like to review the dues, meeting schedule, typical member profile, and any educational seminars sponsored by the group.

Thank you for your reply to my inquiry about what may prove a mutually beneficial relationship. Networking with other professionals has proven repeatedly to be both a learning and a rewarding experience.

Sincerely yours,

[YOUR NAME]
[YOUR TITLE]

[ITEM 1] = [YOUR COMPANY NAME] address

[DATE]

[Mr./Mrs./Ms./Dr.] [FIRST AND LAST NAME]
[TITLE]
[COMPANY]
[ADDRESS]
[CITY], [STATE] [ZIP CODE]

Dear [Mr./Mrs./Ms./Dr.] [LAST NAME]:

To say we are better than other people is limiting. We all have talents in diverse areas. The key to success is recognizing the areas in which we lack talent and finding it elsewhere.

A metamorphosis that will require additional resources is underway at [YOUR COMPANY NAME]. Our management believes that [COMPANY] may be the vehicle taking us from where we are to where we plan to be. Please forward the following materials pertaining to your firm: company profile, client list, basic fee schedule, and professional references. This information can be sent to [ITEM 1].

Give me a week or so to review the package before following up on our interest in [COMPANY]. Focusing on specialization has contributed greatly to our success. I look forward to learning if our professional goals and practices are complementary.

Sincerely yours,

[YOUR NAME]
[YOUR TITLE]

[ITEM 1] = [YOUR COMPANY NAME] address

[DATE]

[Mr./Mrs./Ms./Dr.] [FIRST AND LAST NAME]
[TITLE]
[COMPANY]
[ADDRESS]
[CITY], [STATE] [ZIP CODE]

Dear [Mr./Mrs./Ms./Dr.] [LAST NAME]:

Is there such a thing as a formula for success? The myriad business and consumer variables that envelope every industry has always kept me from believing so—that is, until I visited a [COMPANY] location in [ITEM 1]. The operation was efficient and, at first glance, appears to be a profitable enterprise.

[YOUR COMPANY NAME] is interested in learning more about [COMPANY] with a particular curiosity about growth opportunities in [ITEM 2]. Please forward the following materials: [COMPANY] background, break-even analysis, estimated franchise earnings, franchisee fees, financing alternatives, approved government assistance programs, and a successful franchise's demographic profile. In addition, we are interested in obtaining [COMPANY]'s "Uniform Franchise Offering Circular." All the above can be sent to [ITEM 3].

I look forward to reviewing the information and discovering [COMPANY]'s formula for franchise success. Thank you in advance for your reply. [YOUR COMPANY NAME] would like to share in your breakthrough.

Sincerely yours,

[YOUR NAME]
[YOUR TITLE]

———————————————◆———————————————

[ITEM 1] = City in which you visited a [COMPANY] location
[ITEM 2] = City [YOUR COMPANY NAME] is interested in placing a [COMPANY] location
[ITEM 3] = [YOUR COMPANY NAME] address

[DATE]

[Mr./Mrs./Ms./Dr.] [FIRST AND LAST NAME]
[TITLE]
[COMPANY]
[ADDRESS]
[CITY], [STATE] [ZIP CODE]

Dear [Mr./Mrs./Ms./Dr.] [LAST NAME]:

Picture running a company in today's fast-moving environment with early 20th century tools. There were no copy machines, no overnight package deliveries, no ways to access information instantaneously, and telephone service was shaky at best. These devices and services, along with many others, have developed over time into business advantages and necessities.

To remain competitive, [YOUR COMPANY NAME] has determined a probable need to lease or purchase a [ITEM 1]. Therefore, I am requesting information on cost-effective ways to meet our current and future business requirements.

Please have a [COMPANY] sales representative contact me and arrange a time to evaluate our present requirements. The best time to call is around [ITEM 2]. I look forward to hearing from [COMPANY] in the near future.

One can only surmise what office equipment will be like 100 years from now. What will a citizen of the late 21st century think of today's high-tech tools? Undoubtedly, great change is an accurate prediction.

Sincerely yours,

[YOUR NAME]
[YOUR TITLE]

[ITEM 1] = Describe and list by number office equipment [YOUR COMPANY NAME] needs
[ITEM 2] = Time of day you would like to receive [COMPANY]'s telephone call

[DATE]

[Mr./Mrs./Ms./Dr.] [FIRST AND LAST NAME]
[TITLE]
[COMPANY]
[ADDRESS]
[CITY], [STATE] [ZIP CODE]

Dear [Mr./Mrs./Ms./Dr.] [LAST NAME]:

As it parallels the economic product life cycle model, a business moves through many stages of development. Controlling progress is essential to the success of any company. If progress is not kept under control, the business may suffer decline or, even worse, demise.

Although [YOUR COMPANY NAME] is prospering, budgetary constraints do not guarantee another employee long-term stability. Caught in the precarious position of needing assistance, we seek a temporary worker to join our team of professionals as a [ITEM 1].

This person should be available [ITEM 2] hours per week starting on [ITEM 3]. The following skills are necessary: [ITEM 4]. I anticipate that this person will be with our company for [ITEM 5].

Please forward any [COMPANY] contracts, forms, and professional referrals to my attention. While I am positive that [COMPANY] performs extensive screening, [YOUR COMPANY NAME] requests three candidate interviews before choosing our new "employee." Thank you for the assistance that will enable us to continue growing strong.

Sincerely yours,

[YOUR NAME]
[YOUR TITLE]

-----------------------------◆-----------------------------

[ITEM 1] = Name of position open by [COMPANY]
[ITEM 2] = Number of hours worked per week in [ITEM 1]
[ITEM 3] = Date the person for [ITEM 1] should begin work
[ITEM 4] = Describe and list by number skills needed to perform [ITEM 1]
[ITEM 5] = Length of time [YOUR COMPANY NAME] needs [ITEM 1]

[DATE]

[Mr./Mrs./Ms./Dr.] [FIRST AND LAST NAME]
[TITLE]
[COMPANY]
[ADDRESS]
[CITY], [STATE] [ZIP CODE]

Dear [Mr./Mrs./Ms./Dr.] [LAST NAME]:

The plot of our story is not new: great enterprise shocks marketplace but needs additional funding. Delving beneath the headline, it becomes evident the majority of venture capital criteria have already been satisfied. Your success with other companies in our situation makes this obvious once our whole story is told.

Briefly, [YOUR COMPANY NAME] is on the leading edge of the growing [ITEM 1] industry. An influx of money will determine not if we will grow but, rather, how fast. The funding will be dedicated to [ITEM 2]. After extensive market analysis, additional revenues are within reach.

In order for us to meet our stated objectives, we require an estimated $[ITEM 3] in the form of either straight financing or joint venture arrangements. However, our company policy requires that a nondisclosure form be signed by an authorized [COMPANY] principal prior to any in-depth discussions. If you are interested in learning more about [YOUR COMPANY NAME], please telephone to arrange delivery of the nondisclosure form. Once you have had an opportunity to review our plans, I am sure you will agree that we have the makings of another American Dream.

Sincerely yours,

[YOUR NAME]
[YOUR TITLE]

[ITEM 1] = Industry [YOUR COMPANY NAME] is in
[ITEM 2] = Describe in an overview why the money is needed
[ITEM 3] = Dollar amount required by [YOUR COMPANY NAME]

[DATE]
[Mr./Mrs./Ms./Dr.] [FIRST AND LAST NAME]
[TITLE]
[COMPANY]
[ADDRESS]
[CITY], [STATE] [ZIP CODE]

Dear [Mr./Mrs./Ms./Dr.] [LAST NAME]:

    This letter serves as official notice that we have assigned all duties, obligations, performance requirements, and rights of our [ITEM 1] Agreement, dated and executed on [ITEM 2], with [COMPANY] to [ITEM 3] as of [ITEM 4]. Therefore, [ITEM 3] has assumed fully our position in the agreement here and as above described.

    I have enclosed a duplicate copy of this Contract Assignment notice for your signature to acknowledge receipt of this letter. Please return one signed original to my attention. If there are any questions, please do not hesitate to contact me. Thank you in advance for your prompt attention.

Sincerely yours,

[YOUR NAME]
[YOUR TITLE]

Agreed and Consented by:

[COMPANY]

_____
Signature

_____
Printed Name and Title

_____
Date

———————————————◆◆———————————————

[ITEM 1] = Name of the agreement
[ITEM 2] = Date [YOUR COMPANY NAME] and [COMPANY] signed [ITEM 1]
[ITEM 3] = Name of company to which [YOUR COMPANY NAME] is assigning [ITEM 1]
[ITEM 4] = Date the contract is assigned

NONDISCLOSURE AGREEMENT

Representatives of [YOUR COMPANY NAME], hereinafter referred to as "[YOUR COMPANY NAME]," and representatives of [COMPANY], hereinafter referred to as "Organization," are discussing and meeting for the purpose of [YOUR COMPANY NAME] sharing confidential and/or proprietary information relating to [ITEM 1]. Any and all discussions, presentations, and meetings may include information regarding company and/or product specifications, availability, pricing, marketing, and business data, all of which are considered proprietary information of [YOUR COMPANY NAME]. Organization agrees that all information it receives from [YOUR COMPANY NAME] at any time concerning [ITEM 1] or related plans will be treated in a confidential manner, will not be used except as authorized, and will not be disclosed to any third party. Organization will be released from the above obligations when the information and/or products are announced by [YOUR COMPANY NAME]. Confidential disclosure of information relating to unreleased company and/or product specifications does not imply an undertaking that any future activities will necessarily conform to specifications, prices, or availability dates disclosed under this Agreement.

[YOUR COMPANY NAME]   Organization

_____   _____
Authorized Representative's   Authorized Representative's
Printed Name and Title   Printed Name and Title

_____   _____
Signature   Signature

_____   _____
Date   Date

[ITEM 1] = Describe and list by number the subject requiring nondisclosure

[DATE]

[Mr./Mrs./Ms./Dr.] [FIRST AND LAST NAME]
[TITLE]
[COMPANY]
[ADDRESS]
[CITY], [STATE] [ZIP CODE]

Dear [Mr./Mrs./Ms./Dr.] [LAST NAME]:

An equitable deal goes beyond the immediate benefits to the two parties signing a contract. The business world is small, and we cross paths with our associates again and again. [YOUR COMPANY NAME]'s goal in a negotiation is to ensure that when, and if, that happens our ethics will be remembered favorably.

In a clearly win-win proposition, we hereby submit an offer to purchase from [COMPANY] the following: [ITEM 1]. It is understood the payment for said purchase will be made in the form of [ITEM 2] totaling $[ITEM 3], which includes all past, present, and future interests in, ownership of, and titles to [ITEM 1].

We reserve the right to review particular [ITEM 1] documentation and financial data prior to completing the purchase. [YOUR COMPANY NAME] stands by its commitment to making the present our future. I look forward to receiving [COMPANY]'s positive response to our offer.

Sincerely yours,

[YOUR NAME]
[YOUR TITLE]

[ITEM 1] = Describe and list by number of what [YOUR COMPANY NAME] wants to purchase from [COMPANY]
[ITEM 2] = Describe the manner in which [YOUR COMPANY NAME] is going to pay [COMPANY] for [ITEM 1]
[ITEM 3] = Dollar amount [YOUR COMPANY NAME] is going to pay [COMPANY] for [ITEM 1]

BUSINESS \ Legal
Rejection of Goods

[DATE]

[Mr./Mrs./Ms./Dr.] [FIRST AND LAST NAME]
[TITLE]
[COMPANY]
[ADDRESS]
[CITY], [STATE] [ZIP CODE]

Dear [Mr./Mrs./Ms./Dr.] [LAST NAME]:

Many companies fear the judicial system's increasing interference in commercial enterprise. Yet, there is no reason for apprehension when business practices are fair and in compliance with existing agreements. Much to our dismay, [YOUR COMPANY NAME] has been forced to question [COMPANY]'s adherence to oral and written commitments.

[YOUR COMPANY NAME]'s recent order of [ITEM 1] does not conform to the representations made by [COMPANY]. As clearly stated within [COMPANY]'s [ITEM 2], [ITEM 1] was to be [ITEM 3]. The contradictions are obvious to anyone who so much as glances at [ITEM 1] and [ITEM 2].

Therefore, we have no choice but to reject, and return, [ITEM 1] for a full refund in the amount of $[ITEM 4]. I suggest that [COMPANY] investigate the displeasure caused by this unfortunate situation. It may yield results that will benefit future customer relationships.

Sincerely yours,

[YOUR NAME]
[YOUR TITLE]

———————————◆———————————

[ITEM 1] = Description of product rejected
[ITEM 2] = Document containing [ITEM 1]'s product information
[ITEM 3] = Description of [ITEM 1] as presented in [ITEM 2]
[ITEM 4] = Dollar amount paid for [ITEM 1]

[DATE]

[Mr./Mrs./Ms./Dr.] [FIRST AND LAST NAME]
[TITLE]
[COMPANY]
[ADDRESS]
[CITY], [STATE] [ZIP CODE]

Dear [Mr./Mrs./Ms./Dr.] [LAST NAME]:

The letter serves as official notice that the [ITEM 1] agreement, dated [ITEM 2], by and between [YOUR COMPANY NAME] and [COMPANY], shall be hereby considered terminated effective on [ITEM 3]. Therefore, as of [ITEM 3] we are no longer bound or obligated to fulfill any terms and conditions contained within [ITEM 1] here and as above described.

I have enclosed a duplicate copy of this Termination of Contract notice for your signature to acknowledge receipt of this letter. Please return one signed original to my attention. If there are any questions, please do hesitate to contact me. Thank you in advance for your prompt attention.

Sincerely yours,

[YOUR NAME]
[YOUR TITLE

Agreed and Consented by:

[COMPANY]

_____
Signature

_____
Printed Name and Title

_____
Date

◆—————◆

[ITEM 1] = Name of the agreement
[ITEM 2] = Date [YOUR COMPANY NAME] and [COMPANY] signed [ITEM 1]
[ITEM 3] = Date the contract is terminated

RECITALS:

This is [YOUR COMPANY NAME]'s standard agreement to confirm a Work for Hire arrangement in which we are referred to as "Customer" and [COMPANY] is the "Contractor."

WORK FOR HIRE AGREEMENT

Contractor shall be paid the sum of $[ITEM 1] by Customer for the services described herein. The sum shall be paid upon the timely completion of all of the duties described herein on, or before, [ITEM 2]. Contractor agrees to use best efforts to provide [ITEM 3] according to the specifications presented by Customer. Contractor shall, at all times, use his or her own tools and employees to complete the terms of this Agreement. Contractor shall not be supervised by Customer but shall proceed to accomplish the task hereunder in whatsoever manner is deemed appropriate within the scope of this Agreement. Customer is aware that Contractor may have other customers and jobs simultaneous with this job. This Agreement does not constitute an employment Agreement, and Contractor shall be considered only as an independent contractor and not as an employee, agent, partner, or joint venturer of Customer. Contractor shall be solely responsible for any and all safety measures and taxes (state, federal, and local); worker's compensation insurance payments; disability payments; social security payments; unemployment insurance payments; other insurance payments; and any similar type of payment for Contractor or any employee thereof, and shall hold Customer harmless from any and all accidents and payments.

Please acknowledge your acceptance of this Work for Hire Agreement by completing the areas below and returning one copy to my attention. Thank you in advance for your assistance.

_____

[YOUR NAME]
[YOUR TITLE]

I, [ITEM 4], on behalf of [COMPANY], am authorized to agree to perform the work indicated above under the terms and conditions of this Work for Hire Agreement.

_____   _____
Signature   Social Security Number

_____

[ITEM 1] = Cost of [ITEM 3]
[ITEM 2] = Date [ITEM 3] is due
[ITEM 3] = Describe and list by number of all work performed by [COMPANY]
[ITEM 4] = First and last name of person from [COMPANY] signing the Work for Hire Agreement

[DATE]

[Mr./Mrs./Ms./Dr.] [FIRST AND LAST NAME]
[TITLE]
[COMPANY]
[ADDRESS]
[CITY], [STATE] [ZIP CODE]

Dear [Mr./Mrs./Ms./Dr.] [LAST NAME]:

Long before paper currency was invented in China around the 11th century, trade was the primary means of obtaining goods and services. Today, hundreds of years later, bartering is still an efficient and effective way of conducting business. Simply stated, you have something I need and I have something you desire.

Considering our respective business interests, I foresee an even exchange. To better our operations, [YOUR COMPANY NAME] has investigated various offerings for [ITEM 1] by companies like [COMPANY]. Your company is one of the leaders. Rather than paying cash for [ITEM 2], I propose a trade for [YOUR COMPANY NAME]'s [ITEM 3].

Looking at the hard costs involved, value is well-covered without any currency exchange. [ITEM 4], think about it and if this is not acceptable, perhaps you can suggest another way to achieve the same goal. The key is to strike a fair and equitable trade for the mutual benefit of the parties involved. I look forward to hearing from you in the near future.

Sincerely yours,

[YOUR NAME]
[YOUR TITLE]

[ITEM 1] = Name of product or service [YOUR COMPANY NAME] needs
[ITEM 2] = Specific name of product or service offered by [COMPANY]
[ITEM 3] = Specific name of product or service offered by [YOUR COMPANY NAME]
[ITEM 4] = First name of person receiving letter

[DATE]

[Mr./Mrs./Ms./Dr.] [FIRST AND LAST NAME]
[TITLE]
[COMPANY]
[ADDRESS]
[CITY], [STATE] [ZIP CODE]

Dear [Mr./Mrs./Ms./Dr.] [LAST NAME]:

    Complementary business ventures are often advantageous to both parties. Sharing achievements and resources enables mutual gain and profit. Because of [COMPANY]'s prominence, I am contacting you in the hope that my proposal will be given the highest professional consideration.

    [YOUR COMPANY NAME] is at a critical point in its development. In formulating a strategic plan to expand our existing customer base, we have decided to pursue markets possessing demographic profiles much like that of [COMPANY]. Hence, we are interested in renting your customer list to further our marketing efforts.

    [YOUR COMPANY NAME] will use the names to [ITEM 1]. We are prepared to pay the normal charges, provided the customer list has been updated recently and reflects accurate information. If you are interested, please send pricing and customer profile information. Thank you in advance for your response. Clearly, sharing resources can improve our future while compensating you for efforts already put forth.

Sincerely yours,

[YOUR NAME]
[YOUR TITLE]

[ITEM 1] = Describe the action [YOUR COMPANY NAME] will take with [COMPANY]'s customer names

[DATE]

[Mr./Mrs./Ms./Dr.] [FIRST AND LAST NAME]
[TITLE]
[COMPANY]
[ADDRESS]
[CITY], [STATE] [ZIP CODE]

Dear [Mr./Mrs./Ms./Dr.] [LAST NAME]:

Studying the past often reveals truths for today. The classic 17th century text on Japanese warfare by Miyamoto Musashi, *A Book of Five Rings,* contains valuable insight for both samurai warriors and business professionals. The pages of winning moves have taught me many lessons over the years.

While open to interpretation, one of the things I have learned is that achievers need to "see distant things as if they were close." I congratulate you on successfully creating in [COMPANY] a dominant force in the [ITEM 1] industry. It took a great deal of hard work and vision to achieve such stature.

Because of this, [YOUR COMPANY NAME] is interested in learning more about [COMPANY] with a specific goal. Our staff has identified your company from a distance as one that we might be interested in acquiring. If this looks like a winning move for you and [COMPANY], please assume a proactive stance by telephoning me at your convenience. I look forward to future discussions with you and your associates.

Sincerely yours,

[YOUR NAME]
[YOUR TITLE]

[ITEM 1] = Describe [COMPANY]'s main business emphasis

[DATE]

[Mr./Mrs./Ms./Dr.] [FIRST AND LAST NAME]
[TITLE]
[COMPANY]
[ADDRESS]
[CITY], [STATE] [ZIP CODE]

Dear [Mr./Mrs./Ms./Dr.] [LAST NAME]:

Many professionals wrongly believe marketing tactics are the same as marketing strategies. Although interrelated, the two are distinct. Tactics are the techniques used by corporate armies to secure the strategy's goals.

[YOUR COMPANY NAME] implemented this distinction throughout the ranks long ago. One of our tactics is to join forces with allies to win customer support. [COMPANY]'s name was brought to my attention by our staff as the leader in the [ITEM 1] industry.

Clearly, we are not competitors, as our primary focus is [ITEM 2]. A collaboration through lead sharing would enhance both of our businesses. The many ways to achieve this goal warrant a meeting on the subject. If you are interested in pursuing this tactic, please telephone me to explore the implementation of a lead-sharing program. I look forward to exploring with you a mutually beneficial relationship.

Sincerely yours,

[YOUR NAME]
[YOUR TITLE]

[ITEM 1] = Describe [COMPANY]'s main business emphasis
[ITEM 2] = Describe [YOUR COMPANY NAME]'s main business emphasis

[DATE]

[Mr./Mrs./Ms./Dr.] [FIRST AND LAST NAME]
[TITLE]
[COMPANY]
[ADDRESS]
[CITY], [STATE] [ZIP CODE]

Dear [Mr./Mrs./Ms./Dr.] [LAST NAME]:

Abner Doubleday is given credit for inventing baseball, but Egyptians as far back as 3022 B.C. played the game. Those first games using a melon and shepherd's staff laid the foundation for today's big leagues. The point is that before anything can happen, someone must throw the first pitch.

Opportunities become successes when action is taken. Recently, I sent you a letter expressing interest in [YOUR COMPANY NAME]'s potential collaboration with [COMPANY]. I saw the beginning of a mutually beneficial relationship to [ITEM 1]. To date, I have not had a reply and am curious as to whether my correspondence dated [ITEM 2] was received.

Together, we could create the newest American legend, much like Mom, apple pie, and baseball. We have stepped up to the plate and are ready to play ball. Thank you in advance for your professional courtesy. I am waiting for [COMPANY] to enter the field by telephoning and expressing interest in discussing the matter.

Sincerely yours,

[YOUR NAME]
[YOUR TITLE]

[ITEM 1] = Describe business opportunity presented in letter
[ITEM 2] = Date of letter opportunity was first presented to [COMPANY]

BUSINESS \ Payment
Enclosed

[DATE]

[Mr./Mrs./Ms./Dr.] [FIRST AND LAST NAME]
[TITLE]
[COMPANY]
[ADDRESS]
[CITY], [STATE] [ZIP CODE]

Dear [Mr./Mrs./Ms./Dr.] [LAST NAME]:

Accounts receivable controls and maintenance are necessary for efficient business operations. [YOUR COMPANY NAME] appreciates prompt payment from our customers and assumes that [COMPANY] does too. In fulfilling our commitment, enclosed is $[ITEM 1], check number [ITEM 2], for invoice number [ITEM 3].

Our records show that this payment brings our balance to $[ITEM 4]. Should our calculations be in error, please contact me immediately. Thank you for your assistance in posting this payment to our account.

Sincerely yours,

[YOUR NAME]
[YOUR TITLE]

[ITEM 1] = Dollar amount of payment made with the enclosed check
[ITEM 2] = Number on [YOUR COMPANY NAME] check
[ITEM 3] = Invoice number issued by [COMPANY] for payment
[ITEM 4] = Balance on [YOUR COMPANY NAME] account with [COMPANY]

[DATE]

[Mr./Mrs./Ms./Dr.] [FIRST AND LAST NAME]
[TITLE]
[COMPANY]
[ADDRESS]
[CITY], [STATE] [ZIP CODE]

Dear [Mr./Mrs./Ms./Dr.] [LAST NAME]:

Poor business practices are remembered longer than respectable habits. I recently was informed by my staff that a potential mark may have been placed on [YOUR COMPANY NAME]'s character. While our account remittance policies are normally followed diligently, the paperwork authorizing payment to [COMPANY] was subject to pure negligence, and my staff has been reprimanded.

I have enclosed $[ITEM 1], check number [ITEM 2], for invoice number [ITEM 3]. Our balance after posting this payment is [ITEM 4].

[YOUR COMPANY NAME] is very much like [COMPANY] in many ways. We both appreciate prompt payment, if for no other reason than to keep the books under control. I extend my apology with sincere regret and thank you for your patience. Let's return to business as usual and put this embarrassing blunder behind us.

Sincerely yours,

[YOUR NAME]
[YOUR TITLE]

[ITEM 1] = Dollar amount of payment made with the enclosed check
[ITEM 2] = Number on [YOUR COMPANY NAME] check
[ITEM 3] = Invoice number issued by [COMPANY] for payment
[ITEM 4] = Balance on [YOUR COMPANY NAME] account with [COMPANY]

BUSINESS \ Payment
Made When Order Completed

[DATE]

[Mr./Mrs./Ms./Dr.] [FIRST AND LAST NAME]
[TITLE]
[COMPANY]
[ADDRESS]
[CITY], [STATE] [ZIP CODE]

Dear [Mr./Mrs./Ms./Dr.] [LAST NAME]:

Except for *Robert's Rules of Order* governing corporate boardroom etiquette, few books exist on business manners. Acceptable professional conduct is primarily a combination of common sense and past experience. Unfortunately, [COMPANY]'s request for payment on invoice number [ITEM 1] falls outside conventional [YOUR COMPANY NAME] standards.

We do not expect our customers to remit payment on incomplete orders. Nor do we release funds until our vendors fulfill their obligations. When [YOUR COMPANY NAME]'s order for [ITEM 2] is complete and passes quality assurance standards, payment will be processed promptly. As of this date, [ITEM 3] has not arrived.

Maintaining the highest customer satisfaction level is important to [YOUR COMPANY NAME]. The many books that exist on this subject have the common theme of putting customer priorities first. Thank you for your professional courtesy in the matter. Our goal now is to receive a complete order. Then, we can help you achieve your goal of obtaining payment.

Sincerely yours,

[YOUR NAME]
[YOUR TITLE]

[ITEM 1] = Invoice number from [COMPANY]
[ITEM 2] = Describe the order referenced by [ITEM 1]
[ITEM 3] = Describe and list by number what is missing from [ITEM 2]

[DATE]

[Mr./Mrs./Ms./Dr.] [FIRST AND LAST NAME]
[TITLE]
[COMPANY]
[ADDRESS]
[CITY], [STATE] [ZIP CODE]

Dear [Mr./Mrs./Ms./Dr.] [LAST NAME]:

Reaction normally requires more time and money than an initial proactive stance. However, receipt of new information sometimes forces drastic measures to correct unforeseen problems. At [YOUR COMPANY NAME]'s effort and expense, we have taken actions regarding our recent payment to [COMPANY].

On [ITEM 1], we ordered [ITEM 2] from [COMPANY] for $[ITEM 3]. Payment was processed, but after mailing the check, I received some disheartening news. Because [ITEM 2] is [ITEM 4], payment has been stopped on check number [ITEM 5].

Based on the above information, I am positive that [COMPANY] understands the reactionary position assumed by [YOUR COMPANY NAME]. Thank you in advance for your professional reply. Our company's intention is to resolve this issue. I wait for your suggestions on renewing our confidence as a [COMPANY] customer.

Sincerely yours,

[YOUR NAME]
[YOUR TITLE]

[ITEM 1] = Date [ITEM 2] was ordered
[ITEM 2] = Describe the product or service purchased from [COMPANY]
[ITEM 3] = Dollar amount of [ITEM 2]
[ITEM 4] = Describe and list by number problems with [ITEM 2]
[ITEM 5] = Number of [YOUR COMPANY NAME] check

[DATE]

[Mr./Mrs./Ms./Dr.] [FIRST AND LAST NAME]
[TITLE]
[COMPANY]
[ADDRESS]
[CITY], [STATE] [ZIP CODE]

Dear [Mr./Mrs./Ms./Dr.] [LAST NAME]:

Customer dissatisfaction is like a microscope that magnifies a company's inner workings. We learn the most about a company when it is presented with a problem. The manner in which problems are handled allows customers to decide whether a company is worthy of their business.

On [ITEM 1], [YOUR COMPANY NAME] agreed with [COMPANY] to [ITEM 2]. Instead, we ended up with [ITEM 3]. [COMPANY] was quick to ask for payment without any regard for our satisfaction or lack thereof. I will not authorize payment until [COMPANY] does the following: [ITEM 4].

There are no alternatives; there are no compromises. This is not a negotiation. [YOUR COMPANY NAME]'s success has been built on customer satisfaction levels that promote repeat business. Our recent experience with your company has left us disgusted and puzzled. I expect you to recognize the urgency of the matter and reply within the next five business days. I don't really like what I have seen so far.

Sincerely yours,

[YOUR NAME]
[YOUR TITLE]

[ITEM 1] = Date [ITEM 2] occurred
[ITEM 2] = Describe the reason [YOUR COMPANY NAME] called upon [COMPANY] on [ITEM 1]
[ITEM 3] = What the result of [ITEM 2] was
[ITEM 4] = Describe and list by number actions [YOUR COMPANY NAME] wants [COMPANY] to take

[DATE]

[Mr./Mrs./Ms./Dr.] [FIRST AND LAST NAME]
[TITLE]
[COMPANY]
[ADDRESS]
[CITY], [STATE] [ZIP CODE]

Dear [Mr./Mrs./Ms./Dr.] [LAST NAME]:

Journalists have a legal and moral responsibility to report accurately. Casebooks are full of decisions dealing with the consequences of gee-whiz headlines and sensational stories. I am confident that [COMPANY] is aware of the potential ramifications of incompetent reporting.

A person in your position clearly understands routine article research guidelines. I question whether the author, [ITEM 1], of the article about [YOUR COMPANY NAME] that appeared in your [ITEM 2] issue knows the definition of professional ethics.

Specifically, "[ITEM 3]," is poor journalism. The coverage could have been made accurate by including [ITEM 4].

If there were any questions, these should have been brought to our attention before the piece was submitted for editorial review or publication. [ITEM 1]'s inaccurate reporting has hurt [COMPANY]'s reputation more than [YOUR COMPANY NAME]'s. Our clients, many of whom are your readers, know how to distinguish fact from fiction.

Sincerely yours,

[YOUR NAME]
[YOUR TITLE]

[ITEM 1] = First and last name of author
[ITEM 2] = Date of publication
[ITEM 3] = Select what you consider the worst sentence from article
[ITEM 4] = Describe and list by number things that should have been in article

[DATE]

[Mr./Mrs./Ms./Dr.] [FIRST AND LAST NAME]
[TITLE]
[COMPANY]
[ADDRESS]
[CITY], [STATE] [ZIP CODE]

Dear [Mr./Mrs./Ms./Dr.] [LAST NAME]:

Seeing your name in print along with the names of great leaders is an experience that defies complete description. There is the initial thrill, then disbelief, and finally an acknowledgment that perhaps you really are worthy of such an honor. I experienced a wide range of professional reinforcement reading the [ITEM 1] issue of [COMPANY].

Of all the articles every written about [YOUR COMPANY NAME], yours was one of the best. It conveyed the enthusiasm that suffuses our entire team. Writing is an art, and you have talents that should not be ignored or underestimated.

Yet, there is another feeling that came over me while reading the article. I had a successful business mentor once tell me quite bluntly, "Never believe your own press clippings." Now, many years after his death, these words come back to me as I realize how much further we have to go. [ITEM 2], on behalf of [YOUR COMPANY NAME], thank you for a job well done.

Sincerely yours,

[YOUR NAME]
[YOUR TITLE]

[ITEM 1] = Date of publication
[ITEM 2] = First name of person receiving letter

[DATE]

[Mr./Mrs./Ms./Dr.] [FIRST AND LAST NAME]
[TITLE]
[COMPANY]
[ADDRESS]
[CITY], [STATE] [ZIP CODE]

Dear [Mr./Mrs./Ms./Dr.] [LAST NAME]:

The timing of events is very important in life. We seem either to need more time or to lose patience waiting for the "right" time. I realize that your deadline for the story on [YOUR COMPANY NAME] is approaching, and I appreciate the confidence and interest in our company that your request for an interview demonstrates.

Our company takes pleasure in assisting others in their professional quests. However, the timing is very inappropriate and forces me to decline your request.

I do not wish to dampen your enthusiasm, so keep [YOUR COMPANY NAME] in mind for a future story. Best wishes for success in your endeavor. I hope to hear from you in the future when the timing may be better.

Sincerely yours,

[YOUR NAME]
[YOUR TITLE]

[DATE]

[Mr./Mrs./Ms./Dr.] [FIRST AND LAST NAME]
[TITLE]
[COMPANY]
[ADDRESS]
[CITY], [STATE] [ZIP CODE]

Dear [Mr./Mrs./Ms./Dr.] [LAST NAME]:

Censorship was predictable in the old Soviet Union when the government controlled the official newspaper, *Pravda*. Rarely were both sides of a story revealed. Since 1776 when our great nation was founded, however, Americans have not tolerated censorship.

I must tell you that while reading the article about our company, [YOUR COMPANY NAME], printed in the [ITEM 1] issue of [COMPANY], I expected soldiers to come stomping through the door at any moment. The article written by [ITEM 2] is clearly an example of regulated editing and/or writing. Half a truth is half a lie.

Specifically, "[ITEM 3]," is sensationalist journalism. The coverage could have been made accurate by including [ITEM 4].

In the interest of fairness, [YOUR COMPANY NAME] demands that [COMPANY] print an immediate retraction or clarification of the aforementioned article. On behalf of [YOUR COMPANY NAME], I will be looking for justice and hoping that future dealings with [COMPANY] do not give me the Siberian chills.

Sincerely yours,

[YOUR NAME]
[YOUR TITLE]

[ITEM 1] = Date of publication
[ITEM 2] = First and last name of author
[ITEM 3] = Select what you consider the worst sentence from article
[ITEM 4] = Describe and list by number things that should have been included in article

[DATE]

[Mr./Mrs./Ms./Dr.] [FIRST AND LAST NAME]
[TITLE]
[COMPANY]
[ADDRESS]
[CITY], [STATE] [ZIP CODE]

Dear [Mr./Mrs./Ms./Dr.] [LAST NAME]:

The children's game of telephone is designed to demonstrate how rumors get started. In the game, a story is told to the first person, who tells it to the second, and so on, until the last person in line is asked to announce what he or she heard. The last person's version of the original story invariably causes laughter among the game's participants.

When paraphrased, any piece of information tends to lose accuracy. The story changes or is embellished; facts are left out as it moves from person to person. Having recently become aware of a rumor about [YOUR COMPANY NAME], I wish to stop it before the damage is too great to be repaired. There is absolutely no truth to the rumor that [ITEM 1]. As we both know, words carry many meanings, and rumors are often spread for selfish purposes. I hope that this letter makes it clear that the hearsay is not our say.

Sincerely yours,

[YOUR NAME]
[YOUR TITLE]

[ITEM 1] = Describe the obvious lie in the rumor

[DATE]

[Mr./Mrs./Ms./Dr.] [FIRST AND LAST NAME]
[TITLE]
[COMPANY]
[ADDRESS]
[CITY], [STATE] [ZIP CODE]

Dear [Mr./Mrs./Ms./Dr.] [LAST NAME]:

You have a tough job, and I do not want to make it any tougher. Everyone I know who is responsible for news, tells me that they dislike receiving unsolicited telephone calls about press releases. Therefore, I promise that we will never call you unless you call us first.

We would like, however, to send you releases about our advances in [ITEM 1]. Please complete the following and return this letter to my attention in the enclosed self-addressed, stamped envelope.

____ Yes, you can send them by mail.

____ Yes, but instead of mailing, fax the releases to my office at (_____) _____-_____.

_____ No thank you, that isn't the news area I specialize in.

Thank you for helping us give you only the news you can use. We know your day is hectic enough keeping the public up to date.

Sincerely yours,

[YOUR NAME]
[YOUR TITLE]

[ITEM 1] = Describe [YOUR COMPANY NAME]'s main business emphasis

[DATE]

[Mr./Mrs./Ms./Dr.] [FIRST AND LAST NAME]
[TITLE]
[COMPANY]
[ADDRESS]
[CITY], [STATE] [ZIP CODE]

Dear [Mr./Mrs./Ms./Dr.] [LAST NAME]:

The airline industry has benefited tremendously from a reward system for frequent flyers. "Travel with us now and you get free flights later," the advertisements proclaim. [YOUR COMPANY NAME]'s account with [COMPANY] clearly exhibits many long trips at first class fares.

As a dedicated customer, we have a special request of [COMPANY]. The current economy forces us to become lean and mean in our competitive stance. In cutting corners, we must limit expenditures that probably include future [COMPANY] purchases.

Based on our relationship, it is my hope that[COMPANY] will help us with our cost-saving measures. [YOUR COMPANY NAME] requests that future purchases be discounted by industry standards. Thank you for your consideration and reply. Think of it as a frequent flyer program rewarding us for the thousands of miles we have flown exclusively with [COMPANY].

Sincerely yours,

[YOUR NAME]
[YOUR TITLE]

[DATE]

[Mr./Mrs./Ms./Dr.] [FIRST AND LAST NAME]
[TITLE]
[COMPANY]
[ADDRESS]
[CITY], [STATE] [ZIP CODE]

Dear [Mr./Mrs./Ms./Dr.] [LAST NAME]:

Our lives are becoming increasingly globally oriented. It's routine to expect a package originating in Los Angeles to arrive at its London destination in no more than 48 hours. We are no longer amazed at such a display of coordination and advanced technology.

I am concerned that [YOUR COMPANY NAME]'s order placed on [ITEM 1] has not been received. Specifically, we requested shipment of [ITEM 2]. [COMPANY] promises timely delivery of all customer orders, and this situation is not consistent with your customer satisfaction commitments.

Believing that [COMPANY] may not be aware of this situation, I call it to your attention. Please advise me on the status of our order immediately. Thank you for your assistance and prompt reply. I would like to use the [ITEM 1] soon.

Sincerely yours,

[YOUR NAME]
[YOUR TITLE]

[ITEM 1] = Date order was placed
[ITEM 2] = Describe and list by number order's contents

[DATE]

[Mr./Mrs./Ms./Dr.] [FIRST AND LAST NAME]
[TITLE]
[COMPANY]
[ADDRESS]
[CITY], [STATE] [ZIP CODE]

Dear [Mr./Mrs./Ms./Dr.] [LAST NAME]:

From conglomerates to neighborhood shops, companies are required by law to represent products and pricing accurately. Falsifying advertisements or product claims either blatantly or in small print is not well-received. Consumer advocate groups work with government agencies to enforce truth in advertising.

On [ITEM 1], [YOUR COMPANY NAME] purchased [ITEM 2] from [COMPANY] based solely on the representations found in [ITEM 3], where it clearly states that the price is $[ITEM 4].

[YOUR COMPANY NAME] was charged $[ITEM 5], resulting in an overpayment of $[ITEM 6]. I presume that this is merely an oversight on [COMPANY]'s part. I harbor no harsh thoughts, but I do expect a refund in the immediate future. Thank you for your prompt attention and reply.

Sincerely yours,

[YOUR NAME]
[YOUR TITLE]

[ITEM 1] = Date [ITEM 2] was purchased from [COMPANY]
[ITEM 2] = Describe and list by number what [YOUR COMPANY NAME] purchased from [COMPANY]
[ITEM 3] = Publication showing lower price for [ITEM 2]
[ITEM 4] = Dollar amount of price advertised for [ITEM 2] in [ITEM 3]
[ITEM 5] = Dollar amount of price [YOUR COMPANY NAME] paid for [ITEM 2]
[ITEM 6] = Dollar amount of [ITEM 4] subtracted from [ITEM 5]

[DATE]

[Mr./Mrs./Ms./Dr.] [FIRST AND LAST NAME]
[TITLE]
[COMPANY]
[ADDRESS]
[CITY], [STATE] [ZIP CODE]

Dear [Mr./Mrs./Ms./Dr.] [LAST NAME]:

Business transactions may be ruled by contracts, but customers still need a certain amount of faith and trust. Employees, from the chairman of the board straight down the organizational chart, act as agents and voices representing the company. However, I have learned to expect a little puff-speak from a company's marketing staff.

I deal with many sales professionals regularly. [ITEM 1] from [COMPANY] was not the first to walk through our doors. Stretching the truth and telling a complete lie to close a sale are one in the same to me. [ITEM 1] did a lot of both, and I authorized the purchase of [ITEM 2] under the assumption it was [ITEM 3].

Today, our company suffers the effects of trusting [COMPANY]. [ITEM 1]'s statements were not accurate. I suggest you take immediate action. [YOUR COMPANY NAME] will not consider silencing this misrepresentation of the facts even with an immediate full refund in the amount of $[ITEM 4]. However, there is always the chance of rebuilding the relationship severed by [ITEM 1]. Hopefully, [ITEM 5] actions and unprofessional demeanor are not representative your entire organization.

Sincerely yours,

[YOUR NAME]
[YOUR TITLE]

[ITEM 1] = First and last name of [COMPANY] salesperson
[ITEM 2] = Product name of what [ITEM 1] sold you
[ITEM 3] = Describe and list by number [ITEM 1]'s misrepresentations
[ITEM 4] = Dollar amount of price paid for [ITEM 3]
[ITEM 5] = Pronoun referring to [ITEM 1]'s gender, i.e., "his" or "her"

[DATE]

[Mr./Mrs./Ms./Dr.] [FIRST AND LAST NAME]
[TITLE]
[COMPANY]
[ADDRESS]
[CITY], [STATE] [ZIP CODE]

Dear [Mr./Mrs./Ms./Dr.] [LAST NAME]:

Surveys suggest that people use about 10 percent of total purchases after six to twelve months of having the goods. This fact is easy to understand when we consider how quickly situations change and how inclined we are to impulse buying.

To limit [YOUR COMPANY NAME]'s participation in this statistic, we would like some hands-on time with [COMPANY]'s [ITEM 1]. [ITEM 2] presented the product's features well, and at first glance, it appears that the product would be beneficial to our operation. Yet, a [ITEM 3]-day, no-obligation, evaluation period would solidify our purchasing decision.

In addition to increasing our customer satisfaction level, granting the above request serves [COMPANY]'s purposes too. [YOUR COMPANY NAME]'s decision would be made during the trial period. Additional marketing efforts would be unnecessary, and [YOUR COMPANY NAME] would be less likely to return [ITEM 1] after purchase.

Be assured that our entire staff will treat [ITEM 1] as if it were our own, that is, with extreme care. I look forward to hearing your plan to provide [ITEM 1] for [YOUR COMPANY NAME]'s evaluation. Today's economy does not grant us the luxury of keeping 90 percent of our purchases in the closet.

Sincerely yours,

[YOUR NAME]
[YOUR TITLE]

[ITEM 1] = Name of product
[ITEM 2] = Name of [COMPANY]'s employee or documentation
[ITEM 3] = Number of days [YOUR COMPANY NAME] wants to evaluate [ITEM 1]

[DATE]

The Honorable [FIRST AND LAST NAME]
[TITLE]
[COMPANY]
[ADDRESS]
[CITY], [STATE] [ZIP CODE]

Dear [Mr./Mrs./Ms./Dr.] [LAST NAME]:

The truth is, the word "government" brings to mind scenes of officials caught too deep in bureaucracy's maze to accomplish much of anything. Paperwork and more paperwork leaves businesses like [YOUR COMPANY NAME] speechless except for the voices elected to represent us. Caught in government's quagmire, I seek your personal and professional involvement in resolving a specific problem.

So far, efforts to [ITEM 1] have resulted in nothing but frustration and obstruction. Moving from one department to another, [YOUR COMPANY NAME] has been repeatedly told, "I don't handle that. You need to talk to so-and-so." There appears to be nothing left to do but take both of our valuable time through this letter.

The bottom line is that I need your help to [ITEM 2]. From what I understand, the following actions must be taken: [ITEM 3]. Clearly, this problem is not insurmountable if we keep the channels of communication open.

[ITEM 4], I am confident that our request is quite reasonable when both sides of the story are fully understood. On behalf of [YOUR COMPANY NAME], I appreciate your assistance in settling the matter quickly. It is my hope that either you or a staff member can cut through the bureaucracy and speak loudly on our behalf.

Sincerely yours,

[YOUR NAME]
[YOUR TITLE]

[ITEM 1] = Describe the problem
[ITEM 2] = Describe the problem's resolution
[ITEM 3] = Describe and list by number steps needed for [ITEM 2] to occur
[ITEM 4] = First name of person receiving letter

[DATE]

[Mr./Mrs./Ms./Dr.] [FIRST AND LAST NAME]
[TITLE]
[COMPANY]
[ADDRESS]
[CITY], [STATE] [ZIP CODE]

Dear [Mr./Mrs./Ms./Dr.] [LAST NAME]:

    I understand that many professionals feel like puppets subject to the whims of customers, management, and suppliers. Everyone seems to want something—often at the most inopportune time. While I empathize, I still wonder why [YOUR COMPANY NAME]'s recent request for [ITEM 1] has not been acknowledged by [COMPANY].

    We handle our customer requests immediately to maintain high operating and satisfaction standards. As previously outlined, we are seeking [ITEM 2]. Given proper attention, this would seem to be a relatively easy task.

    Please take a break from the puppet show and fulfill our request. I look forward to receiving [COMPANY]'s reply or, at the very least, an update on the status of our request. Thank you for your assistance in the matter.

Sincerely yours,

[YOUR NAME]
[YOUR TITLE]

[ITEM 1] = Subject of request
[ITEM 2] = Describe and list by number what [YOUR COMPANY NAME] wants from [COMPANY]

[DATE]

[Mr./Mrs./Ms./Dr.] [FIRST AND LAST NAME]
[TITLE]
[COMPANY]
[ADDRESS]
[CITY], [STATE] [ZIP CODE]

Dear [Mr./Mrs./Ms./Dr.] [LAST NAME]:

We respect the copyright laws governing original works and request your permission use the following in [YOUR COMPANY NAME]'s [ITEM 1].

Author, Copyright Date, & Title: [ITEM 2]
Pages: [ITEM 3]

Please acknowledge that this permission is granted by completing the bottom portion of this letter and returning one copy to my attention. Your signature confirms that you control the rights to this work and that it does not infringe on any other copyrights. Should you grant permission, we will include a permission line: "Reprinted by courtesy of [COMPANY]."

If for some reason you do not control this copyright, I would appreciate knowing whom I should contact. Thank you for your professional assistance. I am sure the author spent much time on the work and deserves credit for the effort.

Sincerely yours,

[YOUR NAME]
[YOUR TITLE]

Accepted by:

_____   _____
Signature   Date

Copyright credit and/or notice as printed with material used:

_____

[ITEM 1] = Describe reason for obtaining copyright permission
[ITEM 2] = List the author, copyright date, title, and publication
[ITEM 3] = Provide the page numbers where [ITEM 2] can be found

[DATE]

[Mr./Mrs./Ms./Dr.] [FIRST AND LAST NAME]
[TITLE]
[COMPANY]
[ADDRESS]
[CITY], [STATE] [ZIP CODE]

Dear [Mr./Mrs./Ms./Dr.] [LAST NAME]:

People the world over are becoming increasingly aware of the importance of the environment in their lives. The preservation of our natural resources occupies an important place on the agendas of national and world leaders. Local efforts through commissions, such as [COMPANY], are also instrumental in achieving global goals.

As an environmentally conscious company, we lack patience with organizations that do not share our principles. Specifically, [ITEM 1] violates established regulations. The company has repeatedly allowed [ITEM 2].

As residents of [CITY], we cannot permit such practices to continue. A few violations here and there multiply until the cumulative effect becomes catastrophic. It is with hope that [YOUR COMPANY NAME] seeks [COMPANY]'s assistance in preserving our streets, community, and world. [ITEM 1] must be stopped before it's too late.

Sincerely yours,

[YOUR NAME]
[YOUR TITLE]

[ITEM 1] = Name of company violating planning and zoning regulations
[ITEM 2] = Describe and list by number what [ITEM 1] is doing

[DATE]

[Mr./Mrs./Ms./Dr.] [FIRST AND LAST NAME]
[TITLE]
[COMPANY]
[ADDRESS]
[CITY], [STATE] [ZIP CODE]

Dear [Mr./Mrs./Ms./Dr.] [LAST NAME]:

Where would America be without the determined few who seek to fulfill their dreams? Innovation and progress are not possible without futurists who visualize change and then make it happen. For years, the Small Business Administration (SBA) has assisted dreamers with practical professional support.

I provide an abstract of our fledgling organization with a special request. Apparently, your position demands knowledge of SBA operations that I could only hope to achieve. Because of your expertise, I ask you to read the following and make any suggestions you think we might find useful.

Briefly, [YOUR COMPANY NAME] is on the verge of an exciting venture to provide [ITEM 1]. Our company founders are [ITEM 2], [ITEM 3], and [ITEM 4], which may, or may not, place us in categories for which government sponsored grants and/or loans are available. Please forward to my attention any applications and materials that may be beneficial. Thank for your professionalism. We cannot achieve our dream without your assistance and SBA support.

Sincerely yours,

[YOUR NAME]
[YOUR TITLE]

[ITEM 1] = Describe [YOUR COMPANY NAME]'s main business emphasis
[ITEM 2] = Ethnic origin of all [YOUR COMPANY NAME]'s founders
[ITEM 3] = Race of all [YOUR COMPANY NAME]'s founders
[ITEM 4] = Gender of all [YOUR COMPANY NAME]'s founders

[DATE]

[Mr./Mrs./Ms./Dr.] [FIRST AND LAST NAME]
[TITLE]
[COMPANY]
[ADDRESS]
[CITY], [STATE] [ZIP CODE]

Dear [Mr./Mrs./Ms./Dr.] [LAST NAME]:

    Time management is a science. Glancing at my calendar each morning, I am reminded how much effort is required to squeeze 20 hours of labor into an 8- to 12-hour workday. Too much time spent in one place or too little in another upsets the balance.

    Knowing this should help you understand why I must decline your request for a meeting. I never make a commitment unless I am sure I can keep it. Broken promises damage professional reputations.

    Until we can set a time during which I can be certain that nothing will preempt our appointment, there is an alternative. I trust you had a specific purpose in mind when requesting the meeting. Therefore, feel free to send any documentation or literature you wanted to present in person. Thank you for your professional courtesy. I look forward to receiving the information.

Sincerely yours,

[YOUR NAME]
[YOUR TITLE]

BUSINESS \ Response
Résumé

[DATE]

[Mr./Mrs./Ms./Dr.] [FIRST AND LAST NAME]
[TITLE]
[COMPANY]
[ADDRESS]
[CITY], [STATE] [ZIP CODE]

Dear [Mr./Mrs./Ms./Dr.] [LAST NAME]:

    The reputation as a desirable employer is the highest honor the professional community can bestow on a company. [YOUR COMPANY NAME] considers our team family, and the strictest guidelines are followed regarding indoctrination of new members. Because of these rules, career and company developments have caused many to seek success within our walls.

    Choosing the few we will call when openings exist is a trying process. With so many qualified people competing for the same positions, résumés are reviewed only when jobs are available. Be assured, however, that yours was received and that we will be in contact when your skills match our company needs.

    If for some reason our paths do not cross during the next six months, please send us an updated résumé reflecting any recent accomplishments or changes in contact information. Thank you for your interest in [YOUR COMPANY NAME]. We consider it significant that you took the time to introduce yourself to us.

Sincerely yours,

[YOUR NAME]
[YOUR TITLE]

[DATE]

[Mr./Mrs./Ms./Dr.] [FIRST AND LAST NAME]
[TITLE]
[COMPANY]
[ADDRESS]
[CITY], [STATE] [ZIP CODE]

Dear [Mr./Mrs./Ms./Dr.] [LAST NAME]:

Sir Arthur Conan Doyle, creator of the detective Sherlock Holmes, gained fame by writing four novels and 56 stories about a man blessed with incredible reasoning capabilities. When presented with a perplexing situation, Sherlock Holmes, with the aid of his ingenious sidekick, Dr. Watson, found the solution. Your letter reminded me of the detective tactics we often use in getting a job done.

Think of me as your Dr. Watson, and I'll point you in the right direction. This is the right place, but I'm not the person to contact for [ITEM 1]. I suggest turning the corner and finding [ITEM 2], who is really the person you want, at [ITEM 3].

Interestingly, Sir Arthur Conan Doyle tried to kill Sherlock Holmes off in 1893. Public outcry led to *The Return of Sherlock Holmes* in 1904. In other words, don't give up the search. I extend my best wishes for your success.

Sincerely yours,

[YOUR NAME]
[YOUR TITLE]

[ITEM 1] = Describe what the person receiving letter requested from you
[ITEM 2] = First and last name of person to contact
[ITEM 3] = Telephone number or address of [ITEM 2]

BUSINESS \ Speakers
Confirmation

[DATE]

[Mr./Mrs./Ms./Dr.] [FIRST AND LAST NAME]
[TITLE]
[COMPANY]
[ADDRESS]
[CITY], [STATE] [ZIP CODE]

Dear [Mr./Mrs./Ms./Dr.] [LAST NAME]:

    Based on the tremendous response, our audience knows your reputation for engaging and entertaining, knowledge-filled presentations, so we look forward to filling the room with your voice and people eager to learn about [ITEM 1].

    As a confirmation, [YOUR COMPANY NAME]'s conference is on [ITEM 2] at [ITEM 3] beginning at [ITEM 4]. Your speech is scheduled from [ITEM 5] to [ITEM 6]. Let me know if you need any special equipment such as a projector or VCR. I am confident that your involvement will help make this our most successful and enlightening event yet.

Sincerely yours,

[YOUR NAME]
[YOUR TITLE]

[ITEM 1] = Topic of speech
[ITEM 2] = Date of conference
[ITEM 3] = Location of conference
[ITEM 4] = Time conference starts
[ITEM 5] = Time person receiving letter starts speech
[ITEM 6] = Time person receiving letter ends speech

[DATE]

[Mr./Mrs./Ms./Dr.] [FIRST AND LAST NAME]
[TITLE]
[COMPANY]
[ADDRESS]
[CITY], [STATE] [ZIP CODE]

Dear [Mr./Mrs./Ms./Dr.] [LAST NAME]:

Asking an audacious question of an admired person is uncomfortable. The biggest risk is offending the person and disrupting what could have been a business opportunity. There are times when it does hurt to ask.

I have given considerable thought to the predicament I now face. To say that we are merely impressed with your professional profile is an understatement. Your breadth of experience has sparked a sincere interest in confirming your attendance at [ITEM 1] on [ITEM 2].

Our staff has spent hours reworking the budget trying to find the funds for your standard fee. Frankly, no matter how many times the bottom line is erased, a positive number never appears. Pardon me for asking, but is there any way your fee could be reduced? Could you speak for a shorter time? Could we pay your expenses?

Please do not take our request as an insult; [YOUR COMPANY NAME] respects your talents immensely. We hope to reach a compromise so our audience can benefit from your experience. Let me know if you are still interested. Hopefully, I will hear from you soon.

Sincerely yours,

[YOUR NAME]
[YOUR TITLE]

[ITEM 1] = Name of conference
[ITEM 2] = Date of conference

[DATE]

[Mr./Mrs./Ms./Dr.] [FIRST AND LAST NAME]
[TITLE]
[COMPANY]
[ADDRESS]
[CITY], [STATE] [ZIP CODE]

Dear [Mr./Mrs./Ms./Dr.] [LAST NAME]:

A person of your expertise and stature has probably heard this story once or twice before. It starts out with an invitation to speak at a conference. Then you hear how you can help the audience, expand your contact base, increase your visibility, and improve your skills.

I am not disputing the validity of any of the above claims. You already know, probably better than I, that speaking engagements do all these things and more. You also know how often payment arrangements are made only to be canceled at the last minute when conference organizers discover that there is no money in the budget for your compensation.

[YOUR COMPANY NAME] is faced with wanting your skills at our [ITEM 1] on [ITEM 2] but not having any funds available. I see no need to give you a complete sales pitch that may insult your obvious intelligence. However, I do ask you to consider the advantages of spreading your message to so many people in such a setting. Please telephone me soon with a decision so that I can make alternate plans if you are unable to accommodate us. It would be an honor to have you participate in our event.

Sincerely yours,

[YOUR NAME]
[YOUR TITLE]

———————————————————◆———————————————————

[ITEM 1] = Name of conference
[ITEM 2] = Date of conference

[DATE]

[Mr./Mrs./Ms./Dr.] [FIRST AND LAST NAME]
[TITLE]
[COMPANY]
[ADDRESS]
[CITY], [STATE] [ZIP CODE]

Dear [Mr./Mrs./Ms./Dr.] [LAST NAME]:

The voices of influential people have commanded attention throughout history. From the first entertainers to present-day politicians, a few special people have the unique ability to spark enthusiasm in their audiences. Everything I have heard about your talents confirms that you share this ability with some of our great leaders.

Fortunately, our paths have crossed. I am pleased to extend a formal invitation to you to use your professional talents at [YOUR COMPANY NAME]'s [ITEM 1] on [ITEM 2]. As agreed, we will pay you $[ITEM 3].

To help you tailor your speech, responses received thus far suggest that the attendee profile is as follows: [ITEM 4]. While your knowledge of [ITEM 5] is a definite advantage, extra emphasis on [ITEM 6] would be also well-received. Thank you for calling with confirmation and for giving us the honor of placing your name on our agenda.

Sincerely yours,

[YOUR NAME]
[YOUR TITLE]

[ITEM 1] = Name of conference
[ITEM 2] = Date of conference
[ITEM 3] = Amount speaker will be paid
[ITEM 4] = Describe and list by number average attendee's professional characteristics
[ITEM 5] = Topic of speech
[ITEM 6] = Describe and list by number additional ideas to incorporate in [ITEM 5]

[DATE]

[Mr./Mrs./Ms./Dr.] [FIRST AND LAST NAME]
[TITLE]
[COMPANY]
[ADDRESS]
[CITY], [STATE] [ZIP CODE]

Dear [Mr./Mrs./Ms./Dr.] [LAST NAME]:

Fulfilling people's expectations can be a real challenge. When launching a seminar, much thought is given to the background and knowledge of the audience. Our goal with [ITEM 1] on [ITEM 2] is to provide such a fulfilling experience that each person walks away confident that the time could not have been better spent.

The decision committee has reviewed your impressive professional speaking credentials. From the overview, it appears that we may have an exact fit between your expertise and our expectations. However, we need just a little more information before reaching a decision.

An outline detailing and highlighting specific points you might cover would be helpful. If at all possible, please ensure delivery to my attention before the committee's next meeting on [ITEM 3]. Thank you in advance for your help in enabling us to make our decision in the most efficient manner. People with your outstanding credentials are few and far between.

Sincerely yours,

[YOUR NAME]
[YOUR TITLE]

[ITEM 1] = Name of conference
[ITEM 2] = Date of conference
[ITEM 3] = Date outline is required

[DATE]

[Mr./Mrs./Ms./Dr.] [FIRST AND LAST NAME]
[TITLE]
[COMPANY]
[ADDRESS]
[CITY], [STATE] [ZIP CODE]

Dear [Mr./Mrs./Ms./Dr.] [LAST NAME]:

Applause is just fleeting recognition of a good job. After the crowds have left and the auditorium is silent, professionals move on to the next achievement with added confidence and higher expectations. The applause for your impressive display of knowledge at our [ITEM 1] on [ITEM 2] still echoes.

The comments and evaluations gathered from your audience were outstanding. In fact, several members have requested copies of your slides.

If possible, please forward one original set to my attention. I will deliver copies to the people who request them. Thank you for a very informative, professional presentation. I look forward to revisiting the topics myself through the slides.

Sincerely yours,

[YOUR NAME]
[YOUR TITLE]

[ITEM 1] = Name of conference
[ITEM 2] = Date of conference

[DATE]

[Mr./Mrs./Ms./Dr.] [FIRST AND LAST NAME]
[TITLE]
[COMPANY]
[ADDRESS]
[CITY], [STATE] [ZIP CODE]

Dear [Mr./Mrs./Ms./Dr.] [LAST NAME]:

Where there is unity, there is victory. [YOUR COMPANY NAME]'s triumph could not have occurred without support in and out of our headquarters halls. I extend my personal invitation to you to make an investment in our future and join [YOUR COMPANY NAME]'s visionary team at our forthcoming annual meeting of shareholders.

On [ITEM 1], at [ITEM 2], beginning promptly at [ITEM 3], you will hear firsthand [YOUR COMPANY NAME]'s strategies for increased growth and income to promote higher returns on shareholder investment. I encourage your participation in this event, because there are many important issues under discussion and review. Those who are unable to join in this meeting can voice their opinions with the enclosed proxy.

Your completion of the proxy ensures an accurate reflection of our shareholders' thoughts regarding future moves. Should this be your method of participation, please sign, date, and mail the proxy promptly in the envelope provided. Otherwise, complete the information confirming attendance and let your voice be heard at the meeting. On behalf of the Board of Directors and [YOUR COMPANY NAME] employees, I thank you for your assistance in the direction of our company.

Sincerely yours,

[YOUR NAME]
[YOUR TITLE]

[ITEM 1] = Date of annual meeting
[ITEM 2] = Location of annual meeting
[ITEM 3] = Time annual meeting begins

[DATE]

[Mr./Mrs./Ms./Dr.] [FIRST AND LAST NAME]
[TITLE]
[COMPANY]
[ADDRESS]
[CITY], [STATE] [ZIP CODE]

Dear [Mr./Mrs./Ms./Dr.] [LAST NAME]:

There is much more to a company's success than earnings ratios. The numbers are simply a by-product of the time and effort expended taking a proactive stance in this dynamic marketplace. [YOUR COMPANY NAME]'s most valuable asset is not inscribed on our balance sheet; it is the teamwork of knowledgeable and talented people dedicated to excellence.

Last year was both challenging and exciting. We progressed steadily toward achieving our goal to [ITEM 1]. These accomplishments facilitated maturation and growth, enabling the implementation of plans that include [ITEM 2]. All of these actions enhance the value of our company.

Even in a highly competitive marketplace and uncertain economy, we controlled variables resulting in [ITEM 3]. Our financial future holds endless possibilities as advancements lead to success. On behalf of [YOUR COMPANY NAME], I thank you for your support as we approach the next year together, confident in our company's imminent prosperity.

Sincerely yours,

[YOUR NAME]
[YOUR TITLE]

[ITEM 1] = Describe the most important goal achieved
[ITEM 2] = Describe and list by number future goals based on [ITEM 1]'s completion
[ITEM 3] = Provide financial overview

[DATE]

[Mr./Mrs./Ms./Dr.] [FIRST AND LAST NAME]
[TITLE]
[COMPANY]
[ADDRESS]
[CITY], [STATE] [ZIP CODE]

Dear [Mr./Mrs./Ms./Dr.] [LAST NAME]:

    With each ending, there is a beginning. Identifying accomplishments within time-based constraints provides knowledge that can influence future directions. As this [ITEM 1] draws to a close, I report that [YOUR COMPANY NAME]'s financial results clearly indicate the attainment of past objectives.

    Propelled by our executive team's commitment to success, steady progress was reported in all operational areas. In summary, net sales were $[ITEM 2] reflecting a [ITEM 3] percent [ITEM 4] due to [ITEM 5]. The attached statements provide a detailed analysis of [YOUR COMPANY NAME]'s financial profile.

    Increasing market presence and new developments promise financial growth. I take this opportunity to pay tribute to our loyal employees and stockholders for their dedication. Together, we have the knowledge, skills, and talents we need to approach the coming [ITEM 1] confident in our continued prosperity.

Sincerely yours,

[YOUR NAME]
[YOUR TITLE]

[ITEM 1] = Time the earnings reflect, i.e., "quarter" or "year"
[ITEM 2] = Dollar amount of net sales for [ITEM 1]
[ITEM 3] = Percentage of decrease or increase as compared to previous [ITEM 1]
[ITEM 4] = Movement of [ITEM 3], i.e., "decrease" or "increase"
[ITEM 5] = Describe reason(s) for [ITEM 4]

[DATE]

[Mr./Mrs./Ms./Dr.] [FIRST AND LAST NAME]
[TITLE]
[COMPANY]
[ADDRESS]
[CITY], [STATE] [ZIP CODE]

Dear [Mr./Mrs./Ms./Dr.] [LAST NAME]:

 The vision of democracy set forth by our founding fathers endures today in the opportunity to voice opinions by casting votes. Preservation of freedom is our responsibility, and I hope that you, as a [YOUR COMPANY NAME] stockholder, do not take it lightly. Although you are unable to attend our Annual Meeting on [ITEM 1], you can still voice your opinion with this proxy statement.

 Please appoint [YOUR COMPANY NAME]'s Corporate Secretary as your representative and complete the following:

 This vote covers [ITEM 2].

_____ I VOTE FOR   _____ I VOTE AGAINST

_____
Signature

_____   _____
Printed Name   Date

 It is imperative that this document be received before the Annual Meeting on [ITEM 1]. Thank you for your voice and participation in [YOUR COMPANY NAME]'s future directions.

Sincerely yours,

[YOUR NAME]
[YOUR TITLE]

_____

[ITEM 1] = Date of Annual Meeting
[ITEM 2] = Describe the issue voted on

[DATE]

[Mr./Mrs./Ms./Dr.] [FIRST AND LAST NAME]
[TITLE]
[COMPANY]
[ADDRESS]
[CITY], [STATE] [ZIP CODE]

Dear [Mr./Mrs./Ms./Dr.] [LAST NAME]:

We can control only the next few seconds of our lives. After that, so many variables come into play that even the most formidable plans are subject to change. On [ITEM 1], [YOUR COMPANY NAME] placed an order for [ITEM 2] based on information available at the time.

Unfortunately, new information makes it necessary for us to cancel the order immediately. The details surrounding cancellation are confidential. I have personally checked your cancellation policies and confirmed that we are in compliance with them.

Believe me, if I were at liberty to provide a full explanation, I would. Thank you for processing this cancellation promptly to obviate any additional work for either of our companies. This action is under [COMPANY]'s complete control.

Sincerely yours,

[YOUR NAME]
[YOUR TITLE]

[ITEM 1] = Date order was made
[ITEM 2] = Describe and list by number what the order contained

[DATE]

[Mr./Mrs./Ms./Dr.] [FIRST AND LAST NAME]
[TITLE]
[COMPANY]
[ADDRESS]
[CITY], [STATE] [ZIP CODE]

Dear [Mr./Mrs./Ms./Dr.] [LAST NAME]:

The word "watch" originated in England when town watchmen were common sights. These watchmen, who walked through town crying out the hour, were among the first to carry portable timepieces. Glancing at my date-and time-equipped 20th century watch in a recent staff meeting, I became aware of a situation requiring [COMPANY]'s assistance.

Under normal conditions, I would not ask for special arrangements in order delivery. Circumstances beyond my control, however, demand that [ITEM 1], ordered on [ITEM 2], be in our possession no later than the close of business on [ITEM 3].

Before shipment, please obtain my approval on any additional [COMPANY] charges required to accommodate our request. My clock is ticking, and pressures are mounting. I look forward to receiving confirmation that our request is being handled. Your professional assistance in ensuring delivery within these time limitations is greatly appreciated.

Sincerely yours,

[YOUR NAME]
[YOUR TITLE]

------------------◆------------------

[ITEM 1] = Name of product
[ITEM 2] = Date [ITEM 1] ordered
[ITEM 3] = Date [ITEM 1] is required

BUSINESS \ Suppliers
Money-Back Guarantee Return

[DATE]

[Mr./Mrs./Ms./Dr.] [FIRST AND LAST NAME]
[TITLE]
[COMPANY]
[ADDRESS]
[CITY], [STATE] [ZIP CODE]

Dear [Mr./Mrs./Ms./Dr.] [LAST NAME]:

Today, what you buy is not as important as who you buy from. Customer satisfaction and operational goals are intertwined in companies of high ethical standing. I write in the hope that [COMPANY] recognizes the value of a customer as [YOUR COMPANY NAME] returns [ITEM 1].

Based upon [COMPANY]'s claims of 100 percent satisfaction through a money-back guarantee, we willingly purchased [ITEM 1] for $[ITEM 2] on [ITEM 3]. Simply stated, it does not meet our performance or quality expectations. The [ITEM 1] is enclosed with this letter.

[YOUR COMPANY NAME] has already spent much time and effort acquiring [ITEM 1]. It is my hope that no more of either will be required to receive our rightful 100 percent refund of the purchase price. Thank you for your prompt attention. We find reassurance in the fulfillment of supplier claims.

Sincerely yours,

[YOUR NAME]
[YOUR TITLE]

[ITEM 1] = Name of product purchased
[ITEM 2] = Dollar amount paid for [ITEM 1]
[ITEM 3] = Date [ITEM 1] was purchased

[DATE]

[Mr./Mrs./Ms./Dr.] [FIRST AND LAST NAME]
[TITLE]
[COMPANY]
[ADDRESS]
[CITY], [STATE] [ZIP CODE]

Dear [Mr./Mrs./Ms./Dr.] [LAST NAME]:

New customers and increasing revenues enhance security for an entire company. It is important for every employee to realize that his or her individual actions contribute to everyone's welfare. I know [COMPANY]'s team knows the significance of maintaining customer satisfaction.

Therefore, I expect that professional attention will be given to our order for [ITEM 1]. [YOUR COMPANY NAME]'s decision was not made frivolously, as exhibited by the time required for our research. The price of $[ITEM 2] is a bit high, but I believe additional value will ultimately be gained through consumer confidence.

I assume that you have specific requirements for payment and scheduling. Please contact me to discuss these in the immediate future. [ITEM 3], I look forward to a long, professional relationship. Thank you for getting us off to a great start.

Sincerely yours,

[YOUR NAME]
[YOUR TITLE]

[ITEM 1] = Name of product(s) ordered
[ITEM 2] = Dollar amount of price quoted for [ITEM 1]
[ITEM 3] = First name of person receiving letter

[DATE]

[Mr./Mrs./Ms./Dr.] [FIRST AND LAST NAME]
[TITLE]
[COMPANY]
[ADDRESS]
[CITY], [STATE] [ZIP CODE]

Dear [Mr./Mrs./Ms./Dr.] [LAST NAME]:

   In New York City, it is estimated that a person can dine out every night for 65 years without visiting the same restaurant twice. The trendy places come and go, but certain establishments stand the test of time.

   The ambiance and food are important, but so is the customer service orientation. [YOUR COMPANY NAME] obviously has options when purchasing [ITEM 1]. Based upon our past relationship with [COMPANY], which has always demonstrated the highest professional standards, the alternatives are just names in the telephone directory.

   [COMPANY]'s entire staff deserves commendation for their unrelenting efforts and commitment to customers. Repeatedly, they anticipate our needs and increase our operational efficiency. They also know that their best critics are not newspaper restaurant reviewers. [ITEM 2], thank you for building such a strong team of customer-oriented employees. [COMPANY]'s stability makes our lives easier.

Sincerely yours,

[YOUR NAME]
[YOUR TITLE]

[ITEM 1] = Describe main product sold by [COMPANY]
[ITEM 2] = First name of person receiving letter

[DATE]

[Mr./Mrs./Ms./Dr.] [FIRST AND LAST NAME]
[TITLE]
[COMPANY]
[ADDRESS]
[CITY], [STATE] [ZIP CODE]

Dear [Mr./Mrs./Ms./Dr.] [LAST NAME]:

In this competitive business world, an unselfish helping hand is rare indeed. Fighting the tendency to self-absorption is difficult as pressures escalate. Yet, there is much gratification in knowing that your actions were beneficial to another's life.

Because of your assistance, I was able to [ITEM 1]. While it's up to me now, the initial results would not have been possible without your support. [ITEM 2], thank you for making me more aware of ways in which I can help others and for reaffirming my belief in the goodness of human nature.

Sincerely yours,

[YOUR NAME]
[YOUR TITLE]

––––––––––––––––––––––––––––––––

[ITEM 1] = Describe results from assistance
[ITEM 2] = First name of person receiving letter

BUSINESS \ Thank You
Endorsement

[DATE]

[Mr./Mrs./Ms./Dr.] [FIRST AND LAST NAME]
[TITLE]
[COMPANY]
[ADDRESS]
[CITY], [STATE] [ZIP CODE]

Dear [Mr./Mrs./Ms./Dr.] [LAST NAME]:

   Turning aspirations into realities is easier when quality people are supportive of your efforts. Thank you for sharing your knowledge and time with me as I worked on [ITEM 1]. Our conversation is with me still as I transcribe mental notes in preparation for the future.

   It was reassuring to know that a person like you shared my vision. I am putting your recommendations into action and am confident that the results will be positive. I extend my utmost appreciation and thanks for your professional endorsement. You really have had an influence on my life.

Respectfully yours,

[YOUR NAME]
[YOUR TITLE]

[ITEM 1] = Describe the subject of endorsement

[DATE]

[Mr./Mrs./Ms./Dr.] [FIRST AND LAST NAME]
[TITLE]
[COMPANY]
[ADDRESS]
[CITY], [STATE] [ZIP CODE]

Dear [Mr./Mrs./Ms./Dr.] [LAST NAME]:

It has been estimated there are more than 200,000 useless words in the English language. Many times, conversations are full of them; they waste our time and accomplish nothing. Our meeting today was exceptional in that we were able to achieve much without wasting time on gibberish.

I found your breadth of experience and apparent knowledge enlightening. There are many avenues for us to pursue based on our mutual interests. Because of this, I propose [ITEM 1]. Thank you for taking time out of your busy schedule. I look forward to seeing you again and sharing another engaging conversation.

Sincerely yours,

[YOUR NAME]
[YOUR TITLE]

[ITEM 1] = Describe and list by number actions resulting from meeting

[DATE]

[Mr./Mrs./Ms./Dr.] [FIRST AND LAST NAME]
[TITLE]
[COMPANY]
[ADDRESS]
[CITY], [STATE] [ZIP CODE]

Dear [Mr./Mrs./Ms./Dr.] [LAST NAME]:

Many of the best telephone calls we receive start with, "I was referred to you by…" Knowing that someone believes in us reinforces our ideals and goals. Thank you for initiating [ITEM 1]'s interest in [YOUR COMPANY NAME] for a potential business affiliation.

I realize that much more than time is involved in making a referral. Your reputation as a credible source is on the line too. Be assured that I will treat [ITEM 2] with the utmost respect. Again, thank you for the referral, and when the opportunity arises, please know I will return your gracious extension of support.

Sincerely yours,

[YOUR NAME]
[YOUR TITLE]

[ITEM 1] = First and last name of person referred
[ITEM 2] = First name of [ITEM 1]

[DATE]

[Mr./Mrs./Ms./Dr.] [FIRST AND LAST NAME]
[TITLE]
[COMPANY]
[ADDRESS]
[CITY], [STATE] [ZIP CODE]

Dear [Mr./Mrs./Ms./Dr.] [LAST NAME]:

    Expertise is achieved through continuous education and proficiency. We rely on your judgment and knowledge in reviewing the enclosed records and statements for accuracy and compliance as dictated by the Financial Accounting Standards Board (F.A.S.B.). Therefore, herewith are [ITEM 1]'s accounting records covering the year(s) [ITEM 2].

    [YOUR COMPANY NAME]'s goal in requesting your services is to reach an intelligent decision regarding [ITEM 3]. Time is of the essence, so we must have this information no later than [ITEM 4]. After examining the project's scope, please call with an estimated charge for [COMPANY]'s services. Thank you for your assistance in this matter. I always hold your opinions in the highest regard.

Sincerely yours,

[YOUR NAME]
[YOUR TITLE]

[ITEM 1] = Name of company
[ITEM 2] = Year(s) of the accounting records
[ITEM 3] = Describe why **[YOUR COMPANY NAME]** is reviewing accounting records
[ITEM 4] = Date information is required

[DATE]

[Mr./Mrs./Ms./Dr.] [FIRST AND LAST NAME]
[TITLE]
[COMPANY]
[ADDRESS]
[CITY], [STATE] [ZIP CODE]

Dear [Mr./Mrs./Ms./Dr.] [LAST NAME]:

    Experience is often gained in the pursuit of something else. Seasoned professionals know that lessons must be remembered and applied to be of use. Respecting you as I do, I hope to limit any harm to [YOUR COMPANY NAME] by offering the following for your feedback.

    Briefly, our company is contemplating a move that appears worthy of a complete investigation. Your impressions would help us decide whether to pursue this further. Our particular interest lies in [ITEM 1].

    I realize that your own projects take priority, and I appreciate your effort. Be assured that your constructive criticism will weigh heavily in our analysis. I look forward to hearing your professional opinion. [ITEM 2], thank you.

Sincerely yours,

[YOUR NAME]
[YOUR TITLE]

[ITEM 1] = Describe your interest in project
[ITEM 2] = First name of person receiving letter

[DATE]

[Mr./Mrs./Ms./Dr.] [FIRST AND LAST NAME]
[TITLE]
[COMPANY]
[ADDRESS]
[CITY], [STATE] [ZIP CODE]

Dear [Mr./Mrs./Ms./Dr.] [LAST NAME]:

Making a mutually beneficial business deal requires a great deal of time and effort. Thank you for the professionalism that has resulted in the agreement between [YOUR COMPANY NAME] and [COMPANY]. The executed contracts for [ITEM 1], signed by [ITEM 2], are enclosed.

After verifying that all [ITEM 3] pages have been received, please retain the document for your files. [YOUR COMPANY NAME] looks forward to a long and prosperous relationship with [COMPANY] under the terms and conditions of the contract. Again, my thanks for your assistance. We could not have gotten this far without your support.

Sincerely yours,

[YOUR NAME]
[YOUR TITLE]

[ITEM 1] = Describe and list by number the contract's purposes
[ITEM 2] = First and last name of person who signed contract
[ITEM 3] = Total number of pages in contract

FACSIMILE COMMUNICATION
COVER SHEET

DATE: _____   SHEET 1 OF_____TOTAL PAGES

TO: _____

FROM: _____

IMPORTANT NOTES:

    If you do not receive complete pages or legible copy, please call [ITEM 1] immediately. The information contained in this facsimile is intended only for the use of the individual or entity named above. If you receive this fax in error, please notify us by telephone immediately at the number listed above and return the facsimile to us via First Class mail at the following address: [ITEM 2]. We will, of course, be happy to reimburse you for the cost. Thank you.

[ITEM 1] = Telephone number of your office
[ITEM 2] = [YOUR COMPANY NAME] address

[DATE]

[Mr./Mrs./Ms./Dr.] [FIRST AND LAST NAME]
[TITLE]
[COMPANY]
[ADDRESS]
[CITY], [STATE] [ZIP CODE]

Dear [Mr./Mrs./Ms./Dr.] [LAST NAME]:

Laws are intended to promote good conduct and minimize contempt. Written by people to serve people, governing principles are subject to interpretation. As expected, agreements generated by one company for another's signature are tainted with obvious bias.

This is why I forward the agreement drafted by [ITEM 1] for your analysis and review. The agreement serves to solidify the terms and conditions of [YOUR COMPANY NAME]'s relationship with [ITEM 1] to [ITEM 2]. My primary concern with the agreement as it stands is [ITEM 3].

Before you start, I would appreciate some idea of how many hours you expect to spend reviewing the agreement and an anticipated completion date. Should you have any questions or require supporting documentation, let me know. Thank you for your assistance. Your expertise guarantees that our present and future interests will be protected.

Sincerely yours,

[YOUR NAME]
[YOUR TITLE]

[ITEM 1] = Name of company that provided legal agreement
[ITEM 2] = Describe and list by number purposes of agreement
[ITEM 3] = Describe your main concern in agreement

SECTION 2

Business-to-Customer Correspondence

Every business and profession has customers. Every letter sent to your customers should reinforce your professional skills and your company's reputation. Far too many executives neglect the opportunity to promote a positive image under the most seemingly trivial circumstances. They fail to ask such important questions as, "How can I give them another reason to buy in a letter telling them we made a mistake?"

Examine the next section and learn how to constantly remind your customer that your company is the best choice. You believe in the importance of customer satisfaction, and your employees put that belief into practice. You understand that customers have alternatives. You prove time after time just how hard you work to earn their business. Don't just tell them in person; tell them in all your letters.

People Buy from People. Customers buy from a person, not from a company. A customer is a person just like you and me; only the hats we wear are different. Make the lives of your customers easier and tell them that you understand the stresses of their jobs. Strive to form solid relationships that turn buyers into friends. We like to buy from people we know.

In this section, you will find letters dealing with everything from credit refusal to apologies to asking why they have not bought lately. Use the pronoun "I" as often as possible, and share a personal story with the customer. The chances are good that the customer can relate to your story, and the customer-vendor affiliation will be strengthened.

Unforgettable You. Each letter is an advertisement for you and your company. Promote, promote, promote your level of expertise, your professionalism, and your company's attributes in that order. A customer pays much more attention to a letter than to any four-color advertisement.

You have an unparalleled opportunity to place your message right before their eyes. Take advantage of the profit potential by stressing that each customer is important and that product and service quality are top priorities.

Power Selling. These letters are designed for positive reader appeal. In a perfect world, all customers would be happy. Since this is not the case, let them know that you try your best. Be sure to check out the facsimile response sheet. Fax machines have made this the response medium of the late 20th century. The common matters of deal closings, orders, payments, returns, and thank yous are covered too.

Finally, remember that a letter is not an interruption, like a telephone call. Keep your name and your company name in front of the customer. Why waste any opportunity with, "Enclosed please find"?

[DATE]

[Mr./Mrs./Ms./Dr.] [CUSTOMER'S FULL NAME]
[CUSTOMER'S TITLE]
[COMPANY]
[ADDRESS]
[CITY], [STATE] [ZIP CODE]

Dear [Mr./Mrs./Ms./Dr.] [CUSTOMER'S LAST NAME]:

Policies govern companies and allow customers to buy with confidence. Policies cannot be so rigid, however, that they cause us to be unresponsive to the needs of a dynamic world.

[COMPANY]'s experience with [ITEM 1] is very unusual. Having recently become aware of the circumstances surrounding [ITEM 1], I understand your disappointment. There is no precedent worth invoking when our relationship with a customer is at stake.

You have [YOUR COMPANY NAME]'s promise that we will [ITEM 2]. In the face of life's uncertainties, there remains something [COMPANY] can rely on. Day after day, [YOUR COMPANY NAME] dedicates itself to customer satisfaction. Thank you for allowing [YOUR COMPANY NAME] to participate in [COMPANY]'s future.

Sincerely yours,

[YOUR NAME]
[YOUR TITLE]

[ITEM 1] = Describe [COMPANY]'s adjustment request
[ITEM 2] = Describe actions taken by [YOUR COMPANY NAME] to do [ITEM 1]

[DATE]

[Mr./Mrs./Ms./Dr.] [CUSTOMER'S FULL NAME]
[CUSTOMER'S TITLE]
[COMPANY]
[ADDRESS]
[CITY], [STATE] [ZIP CODE]

Dear [Mr./Mrs./Ms./Dr.] [CUSTOMER'S LAST NAME]:

A decision founded on fact rather than hearsay is optimum. This does not imply, however, that we ignore another's perspective before making a final judgment. For our mutual benefit, [YOUR COMPANY NAME] follows rigorous decision-making standards that include customer input.

Upon reviewing [COMPANY]'s file and your correspondence requesting an adjustment on [ITEM 1], I find that we need more information.

We are missing facts and documentation that are essential to our prompt resolution of your problem. Specifically, [ITEM 2] would substantiate [COMPANY]'s adjustment request and might facilitate a decision in your favor. Thank you for working with us to reach a resolution. You can anticipate a response within [ITEM 3] of my receipt of the information.

Sincerely yours,

[YOUR NAME]
[YOUR TITLE]

[ITEM 1] = Describe the adjustment request
[ITEM 2] = Describe the information needed from [COMPANY]
[ITEM 3] = Length of time needed by [YOUR COMPANY NAME] to make decision

[DATE]

[Mr./Mrs./Ms./Dr.] [CUSTOMER'S FULL NAME]
[CUSTOMER'S TITLE]
[COMPANY]
[ADDRESS]
[CITY], [STATE] [ZIP CODE]

Dear [Mr./Mrs./Ms./Dr.] [CUSTOMER'S LAST NAME]:

A customer's concern is our concern. Thank you for informing [YOUR COMPANY NAME] of a possible discrepancy regarding [COMPANY]'s [ITEM 1]. We encourage customers to contact us when such situations arise.

However, an extensive review of [COMPANY]'s records indicates that no mistakes were made and the [ITEM 1] is correct as stated. If you have discovered additional information about the situation, by all means, call or write again; your input will help us serve you better. We are always here when you need us, and we thank you for your past and future business.

Sincerely yours,

[YOUR NAME]
[YOUR TITLE]

_____◆_____

[ITEM 1] = Describe the issue on which [COMPANY] requested an adjustment

CUSTOMER \ Adjustment
Positive Response

[DATE]

[Mr./Mrs./Ms./Dr.] [CUSTOMER'S FULL NAME]
[CUSTOMER'S TITLE]
[COMPANY]
[ADDRESS]
[CITY], [STATE] [ZIP CODE]

Dear [Mr./Mrs./Ms./Dr.] [CUSTOMER'S LAST NAME]:

No defense exists for a situation that jeopardizes customer satisfaction. Companies like [COMPANY] are [YOUR COMPANY NAME]'s link with prosperity. Thank you for apprising us of an error in [COMPANY]'s [ITEM 1].

We have made an immediate change to reflect the correct [ITEM 2] as [ITEM 3]. Thank you for bringing this matter to our attention. [YOUR COMPANY NAME] always considers it beneficial when customers feel comfortable pointing out areas in which we fall below our high operational standards.

Sincerely yours,

[YOUR NAME]
[YOUR TITLE]

[ITEM 1] = Describe the mistake
[ITEM 2] = Describe the area where [ITEM 1] was made
[ITEM 3] = Describe result of [YOUR COMPANY NAME]'s actions that fixed [ITEM 1]

[DATE]

[Mr./Mrs./Ms./Dr.] [CUSTOMER'S FULL NAME]
[CUSTOMER'S TITLE]
[COMPANY]
[ADDRESS]
[CITY], [STATE] [ZIP CODE]

Dear [Mr./Mrs./Ms./Dr.] [CUSTOMER'S LAST NAME]:

Looking around our old offices, we see that we underestimated the effort required to move to a location from which we could better serve our customers. The time was well spent. Now [YOUR COMPANY NAME]'s friendly staff is improving on the superior service standards our customers have come to expect over the years.

Whether you keep important contacts in a card file, on a computer, in a pocket organizer, or on scraps of paper in your desk drawer, please be sure [YOUR COMPANY NAME]'s is correct. Our new address and telephone number are:

Address: [ITEM 1]
City, State, Zip Code: [ITEM 2]
Telephone Number: [ITEM 3]
Facsimile Number: [ITEM 4]

As always, we appreciate [COMPANY]'s business, and if you're ever in the area, do stop by. I don't know whether it's the extra space or just the increased enthusiasm, but I think the coffee is better here too!

Sincerely yours,

[YOUR NAME]
[YOUR TITLE]

[ITEM 1] = [YOUR COMPANY NAME]'s street address
[ITEM 2] = [YOUR COMPANY NAME]'s city, state, and zip code
[ITEM 3] = [YOUR COMPANY NAME]'s telephone number
[ITEM 4] = [YOUR COMPANY NAME]'s facsimile number

[DATE]

[Mr./Mrs./Ms./Dr.] [CUSTOMER'S FULL NAME]
[CUSTOMER'S TITLE]
[COMPANY]
[ADDRESS]
[CITY], [STATE] [ZIP CODE]

Dear [Mr./Mrs./Ms./Dr.] [CUSTOMER'S LAST NAME]:

Successful personal and professional relationships are cooperative endeavors. This fine day at [YOUR COMPANY NAME] would not be possible without companies like [COMPANY]. I am proud that over the past [ITEM 1] years, our operation has helped people appreciate the true meaning of customer satisfaction and quality management.

We look forward with confidence; our past success merely hints at the accomplishments we expect to see in the future. Speaking for the entire [YOUR COMPANY NAME] team, we thank you for your support and participation in our growth. The encouragement of [COMPANY] and other fine companies has made it possible for us to mark this momentous occasion.

Sincerely yours,

[YOUR NAME]
[YOUR TITLE]

————————————————◆————————————————

[ITEM 1] = Length of time of [YOUR COMPANY NAME] has been in business

[DATE]

[Mr./Mrs./Ms./Dr.] [CUSTOMER'S FULL NAME]
[CUSTOMER'S TITLE]
[COMPANY]
[ADDRESS]
[CITY], [STATE] [ZIP CODE]

Dear [Mr./Mrs./Ms./Dr.] [CUSTOMER'S LAST NAME]:

Is there ever enough time in a day? [YOUR COMPANY NAME] is relentless in our quest to outperform the competition. Therefore, we've extended our hours to accommodate almost everyone's schedule.

[YOUR COMPANY NAME]'s offices are now ready to serve you from [ITEM 1] to [ITEM 2]. As always, you'll find our professional staff ready to help at all times.

This change in hours resulted from customer recommendations. If you have other suggestions, please let us know. We're known as the people's choice for a good reason. Simply stated, [YOUR COMPANY NAME]'s business is helping [COMPANY]'s business.

Sincerely yours,

[YOUR NAME]
[YOUR TITLE]

[ITEM 1] = Time [YOUR COMPANY NAME]'s offices open
[ITEM 2] = Time [YOUR COMPANY NAME]'s offices close

CUSTOMER \ Announcement
Merger/Acquisition

[DATE]

[Mr./Mrs./Ms./Dr.] [CUSTOMER'S FULL NAME]
[CUSTOMER'S TITLE]
[COMPANY]
[ADDRESS]
[CITY], [STATE] [ZIP CODE]

Dear [Mr./Mrs./Ms./Dr.] [CUSTOMER'S LAST NAME]:

Survival in this business-driven and time-oriented world requires a proactive competitive stance. Reactive moves are often too late and can result in losses. Taking the initiative, [YOUR COMPANY NAME] has found a perfect complement to our company. Joining forces with this company is destined to benefit operations and, more important, our customers.

[ITEM 1] has been in the [ITEM 2] business for some time now, and we believe that the combination of our companies will enable us to exceed market demands. This move does change our relationship—for the better.

The additional products and support offered by [ITEM 1] are the answer to all [COMPANY]'s [ITEM 3] needs. Should you require information or just have a question, please do not hesitate to call. I am here whenever you need me.

Sincerely yours,

[YOUR NAME]
[YOUR TITLE]

[ITEM 1] = Name of company merged with or bought by [YOUR COMPANY NAME]
[ITEM 2] = Name of [ITEM 1]'s industry segment
[ITEM 3] = Describe the main products sold by [YOUR COMPANY NAME] and [ITEM 1]

[DATE]

[Mr./Mrs./Ms./Dr.] [CUSTOMER'S FULL NAME]
[CUSTOMER'S TITLE]
[COMPANY]
[ADDRESS]
[CITY], [STATE] [ZIP CODE]

Dear [Mr./Mrs./Ms./Dr.] [CUSTOMER'S LAST NAME]:

Philosophers have for centuries contemplated the question, "What is a name?" What a name is, however, is not as important as what stands behind it. Therefore, we doubt that a name change from [YOUR COMPANY NAME] to [ITEM 1] will mean very much to valued customers like [COMPANY].

Our business relationship has given you an insider's appreciation of our customer-oriented attitude and outstanding ethics. The new name merely serves as a better reflection of our successful positioning in the [ITEM 2] industry. We know [COMPANY] stands behind us. After all, it does not really matter what we call ourselves. The inside, not the outside, is what counts.

Sincerely yours,

[YOUR NAME]
[YOUR TITLE]

[ITEM 1] = New name of [YOUR COMPANY NAME]
[ITEM 2] = Describe [ITEM 1]'s main business emphasis

[DATE]

[Mr./Mrs./Ms./Dr.] [CUSTOMER'S FULL NAME]
[CUSTOMER'S TITLE]
[COMPANY]
[ADDRESS]
[CITY], [STATE] [ZIP CODE]

Dear [Mr./Mrs./Ms./Dr.] [CUSTOMER'S LAST NAME]:

Every year, the National Football League commands much attention as teams pick their superstars and starting line-ups for the new season. We haven't hired a football star, but we have come very close with our newest marketing team member, [ITEM 1].

[ITEM 2]'s extensive background and experience promotes excellence for our company, customers, and fans. [YOUR COMPANY NAME] has confidence in [ITEM 2]'s ability to serve you in the most competent and professional manner possible. Soon, [ITEM 3] will visit [COMPANY]'s offices, and I am sure you'll approve of [YOUR COMPANY NAME]'s newest first string choice. We searched long and hard for this all-star player.

Sincerely yours,

[YOUR NAME]
[YOUR TITLE]

[ITEM 1] = First and last name of new salesperson
[ITEM 2] = First name of new salesperson
[ITEM 3] = Pronoun referring to [ITEM 1]'s gender, i.e., "he" or "she"

[DATE]

[Mr./Mrs./Ms./Dr.] [CUSTOMER'S FULL NAME]
[CUSTOMER'S TITLE]
[COMPANY]
[ADDRESS]
[CITY], [STATE] [ZIP CODE]

Dear [Mr./Mrs./Ms./Dr.] [CUSTOMER'S LAST NAME]:

A prosperity-bound company modifies operations the moment it recognizes an area of weakness. [YOUR COMPANY NAME] appreciates [COMPANY]'s diligence in pointing out an error in your billing statement. I am embarrassed by this failure of our accounting controls and have taken immediate steps to prevent similar errors in the future.

We have rectified the situation with actions rather than words. The statement was corrected to reflect [ITEM 1]. Please accept my apologies for any inconvenience we may have caused. [YOUR COMPANY NAME] believes that customers are the ultimate directors of our future. Thank you for taking the time to give us some guidance.

Sincerely yours,

[YOUR NAME]
[YOUR TITLE]

[ITEM 1] = Describe how statement was corrected

[DATE]

[Mr./Mrs./Ms./Dr.] [CUSTOMER'S FULL NAME]
[CUSTOMER'S TITLE]
[COMPANY]
[ADDRESS]
[CITY], [STATE] [ZIP CODE]

Dear [Mr./Mrs./Ms./Dr.] [CUSTOMER'S LAST NAME]:

Imagine a world without computer technology. From ordinary appliances to sophisticated satellite systems, computers are everywhere. As business relies on technology for more and more of its everyday operations, we begin to presume that the machines are infallible.

Recently, [YOUR COMPANY NAME] was reminded that this presumption can be dangerous. You may have noticed this on [ITEM 1]. Although the problem was corrected immediately, my concern is [COMPANY]'s impression of [YOUR COMPANY NAME].

Our expert staff has spent many hours working to eliminate the possibility of any future system mishaps. I appreciate your understanding. We've pledged to work harder than ever.

Sincerely yours,

[YOUR NAME]
[YOUR TITLE]

[ITEM 1] = Describe how [COMPANY] was affected by computer error

[DATE]

[Mr./Mrs./Ms./Dr.] [CUSTOMER'S FULL NAME]
[CUSTOMER'S TITLE]
[COMPANY]
[ADDRESS]
[CITY], [STATE] [ZIP CODE]

Dear [Mr./Mrs./Ms./Dr.] [CUSTOMER'S LAST NAME]:

There is absolutely no excuse for rudeness in the home or workplace. A little kindness goes a long way. We at [YOUR COMPANY NAME] pride ourselves on the good customer relations that allow companies like [COMPANY] to turn to us with confidence.

To say that I am disturbed about the incident regarding [ITEM 1] is an understatement. The situation was examined thoroughly, and the strictest reprimands enforced. [ITEM 2], I ask you to remember that the actions of one person do not reflect the attitude of our entire company. Thank you for your tolerance in the matter. Hopefully, we can move forward and put the past far behind us.

Sincerely yours,

[YOUR NAME]
[YOUR TITLE]

[ITEM 1] = Describe what [COMPANY] was doing when incident happened
[ITEM 2] = First name of person receiving letter

CUSTOMER \ Apology
General Mix-Up

[DATE]

[Mr./Mrs./Ms./Dr.] [CUSTOMER'S FULL NAME]
[CUSTOMER'S TITLE]
[COMPANY]
[ADDRESS]
[CITY], [STATE] [ZIP CODE]

Dear [Mr./Mrs./Ms./Dr.] [CUSTOMER'S LAST NAME]:

Often, when things go wrong, far too much energy is wasted in finger-pointing. We are better served using those resources to solve the problem than worrying about who is to blame. [YOUR COMPANY NAME]'s standards do not permit game playing.

It really doesn't matter where the fault lies in [COMPANY]'s disappointment regarding [ITEM 1]. A disgruntled customer is always right. Steps have been taken to [ITEM 2].

Please accept my apologies and suggestion that we move forward and put this situation behind us. Thank you for your patience. [YOUR COMPANY NAME] doesn't waste time with games; we just work for 100 percent customer confidence.

Sincerely yours,

[YOUR NAME]
[YOUR TITLE]

[ITEM 1] = Describe what happened
[ITEM 2] = Describe actions [YOUR COMPANY NAME] is taking to fix [ITEM 1]

[DATE]

[Mr./Mrs./Ms./Dr.] [CUSTOMER'S FULL NAME]
[CUSTOMER'S TITLE]
[COMPANY]
[ADDRESS]
[CITY], [STATE] [ZIP CODE]

Dear [Mr./Mrs./Ms./Dr.] [CUSTOMER'S LAST NAME]:

Quality is the responsibility of every member of the organization. Long before [YOUR COMPANY NAME]'s shipping department ever emerged, management developed a comprehensive quality assurance handbook. The overriding goal is customer satisfaction from start to finish.

Shipping department training takes place regularly. As our business expands, additional employees are assimilated into the system. Frankly, they were doing a good job shipping customer orders until, on one specific day last [ITEM 1], a few forgot the handbook's cast-in-stone quality assurance lessons.

Error crept in. Unfortunately, our records show that [COMPANY] was shipped [ITEM 2] in place of the requested [ITEM 3]. I would like to make the merchandise exchange with the least inconvenience to [COMPANY]. Therefore, I propose [ITEM 4]. Please let me know if this is convenient for you. Thank you for your patience and understanding. We have taken steps to prevent this distressing incident from recurring.

Sincerely yours,

[YOUR NAME]
[YOUR TITLE]

———————————————◆———————————————

[ITEM 1] = Time from when error occurred to when this letter is sent, i.e., "week" or "month"
[ITEM 2] = Describe merchandise received by [COMPANY]
[ITEM 3] = Describe merchandise requested by [COMPANY]
[ITEM 4] = Describe how [YOUR COMPANY NAME] wants to exchange [ITEM 2] for [ITEM 3]

[DATE]

[Mr./Mrs./Ms./Dr.] [CUSTOMER'S FULL NAME]
[CUSTOMER'S TITLE]
[COMPANY]
[ADDRESS]
[CITY], [STATE] [ZIP CODE]

Dear [Mr./Mrs./Ms./Dr.] [CUSTOMER'S LAST NAME]:

Isn't it better to spend a little more now than a lot more later? Experienced business professionals like you appreciate the value of responsiveness and customer satisfaction. Too many executives tell horror stories about problems caused by vendors who neglected them after the sale.

Supplier qualifications and price structures are both important buying criteria. Although [YOUR COMPANY NAME]'s response to bid number [ITEM 1], for [ITEM 2], was quite competitive, additional discount solicitations from customers are given priority. [COMPANY]'s request for [YOUR COMPANY NAME]'s best and final offer demanded top management intervention.

The final pricing structure review pinpointed areas in which discounts could be delivered without compromising our standards. These are as follows: [ITEM 3].

In selecting [YOUR COMPANY NAME]'s proposal, [COMPANY] is assured of both a fair price and our pledge to provide immediate and long-term operational advantages. Other companies try to imitate us; none even compares. Give us a chance, and you will join the other [YOUR COMPANY NAME] customers who loudly proclaim, "They give the best product value, quality, and service while keeping costs quite competitive."

Sincerely yours,

[YOUR NAME]
[YOUR TITLE]

[ITEM 1] = Provide [COMPANY]'s bid tracking number for [ITEM 2]
[ITEM 2] = Describe what the bid was for
[ITEM 3] = Describe the price reduction

[DATE]

[Mr./Mrs./Ms./Dr.] [CUSTOMER'S FULL NAME]
[CUSTOMER'S TITLE]
[COMPANY]
[ADDRESS]
[CITY], [STATE] [ZIP CODE]

Dear [Mr./Mrs./Ms./Dr.] [CUSTOMER'S LAST NAME]:

It is a little known fact that for hundreds of years, the Chinese used gunpowder for fireworks. Wars were frequent, but the Chinese soldiers had no idea of the incredible power within their reach. Although they were familiar with gunpowder, they did not envision using that funny gray dust as a strategic weapon until China lay in ruins.

Business is a marketing war of bigger and better manufacturer claims. Vendor is pitted against vendor. While I am confident that there is no other choice in [COMPANY]'s bid request for [ITEM 1], number [ITEM 2], than the enclosed, I admit to being biased by past success.

My professional experience advising clients just like [COMPANY] is marked by a long history of satisfied organizations. [YOUR COMPANY NAME] has the gunpowder; let's get together and use it as a strategic operational weapon. Joining forces with us is probably the best decision you can make for [COMPANY]'s future. We are the shortcut to prosperity and peace of mind.

Sincerely yours,

[YOUR NAME]
[YOUR TITLE]

[ITEM 1] = Describe what the bid is for
[ITEM 2] = Provide [COMPANY]'s bid tracking number for [ITEM 1]

[DATE]

[Mr./Mrs./Ms./Dr.] [CUSTOMER'S FULL NAME]
[CUSTOMER'S TITLE]
[COMPANY]
[ADDRESS]
[CITY], [STATE] [ZIP CODE]

Dear [Mr./Mrs./Ms./Dr.] [CUSTOMER'S LAST NAME]:

Preserving a reputation for excellence is demanding. After reviewing [COMPANY]'s bid for [ITEM 1], number [ITEM 2], we were faced with a difficult decision. Of course, we want the opportunity, but we are not sure that we can adhere to our usual high quality standards.

It is a painstaking process to turn down potential business. Unfortunately, this letter is formal notification that [YOUR COMPANY NAME] is not responding to the aforementioned bid. Please do not interpret this as a lack of desire to establish a long-term relationship with [COMPANY].

[YOUR COMPANY NAME] hopes that other opportunities more in line with our areas of expertise and specialization will materialize. Then, we have the chance to demonstrate our unparalleled dedication and profession-alism. I look forward to those opportunities and extend our entire company's thanks for keeping us in your future. [YOUR COMPANY NAME] is the most trusted name in the [ITEM 3] business. We are committed to staying that way even if it means forsaking an opportunity.

Sincerely yours,

[YOUR NAME]
[YOUR TITLE]

[ITEM 1] = Describe what the bid was for
[ITEM 2] = Provide [COMPANY]'s bid tracking number for [ITEM 1]
[ITEM 3] = Describe [YOUR COMPANY NAME]'s main business emphasis

[DATE]

[Mr./Mrs./Ms./Dr.] [CUSTOMER'S FULL NAME]
[CUSTOMER'S TITLE]
[COMPANY]
[ADDRESS]
[CITY], [STATE] [ZIP CODE]

Dear [Mr./Mrs./Ms./Dr.] [CUSTOMER'S LAST NAME]:

[COMPANY] has presented us with a unique challenge. I have spent much time formulating a time-based action plan to be used in completing the bid for [ITEM 1], number [ITEM 2]. Resources have been distributed with the obvious goal of winning your business.

[YOUR COMPANY NAME] has a reputation for delivering superb bid responses to its customers. I fear that submitting anything less may jeopardize my, and the company's, professional standing. In order for us to uphold this standard, [YOUR COMPANY NAME] requests an extension of the due date from [ITEM 3] to [ITEM 4].

The extra time will permit us to deliver a document worthy of your business and praise. If possible, please confirm this extension in writing at your earliest convenience. Thank you for your professional courtesy in this matter. I consider a bid response more than a document; it is a direct reflection of [YOUR COMPANY NAME]'s customer commitment.

Sincerely yours,

[YOUR NAME]
[YOUR TITLE]

[ITEM 1] = Describe what the bid is for
[ITEM 2] = Provide [COMPANY]'s bid tracking number for [ITEM 1]
[ITEM 3] = Date [COMPANY]'s bid is due
[ITEM 4] = Date [YOUR COMPANY NAME] wants to submit the bid response

[DATE]

[Mr./Mrs./Ms./Dr.] [CUSTOMER'S FULL NAME]
[CUSTOMER'S TITLE]
[COMPANY]
[ADDRESS]
[CITY], [STATE] [ZIP CODE]

Dear [Mr./Mrs./Ms./Dr.] [CUSTOMER'S LAST NAME]:

When all is said and done, there can be only one winner of [COMPANY]'s bid for [ITEM 1], number [ITEM 2]. I am positive that the decision committee has already formulated their evaluation criteria, among which, I am sure, is accuracy. [YOUR COMPANY NAME]'s primary goal in answering [COMPANY]'s bid request is to provide the information completely and clearly, according to your specifications.

We want your business without doubt or hesitation. But before we can provide a bid, we require the following additional information: [ITEM 3].

Please either call or forward your interpretation of the above areas as soon as possible. Only then, will we be confident that our answers match your questions. Thank you for your prompt assistance. The [YOUR COMPANY NAME]-[COMPANY] account team is eager to finish the winning proposal.

Sincerely yours,

[YOUR NAME]
[YOUR TITLE]

[ITEM 1] = Describe what the bid is for
[ITEM 2] = Provide [COMPANY]'s bid tracking number for [ITEM 1]
[ITEM 3] = Describe [YOUR COMPANY NAME]'s questions

[DATE]

[Mr./Mrs./Ms./Dr.] [CUSTOMER'S FULL NAME]
[CUSTOMER'S TITLE]
[COMPANY]
[ADDRESS]
[CITY], [STATE] [ZIP CODE]

Dear [Mr./Mrs./Ms./Dr.] [CUSTOMER'S LAST NAME]:

It makes sound business sense to evaluate all available sources before selecting a vendor. [YOUR COMPANY NAME] recently became aware that [COMPANY] has released a bid for [ITEM 1], number [ITEM 2], requesting that potential vendors provide product and pricing information. We hope to be included in this, and all future, bid opportunities.

Please send complete bid specifications to my attention at: [ITEM 3]. I have a special request because of your expertise in [COMPANY] operational needs. For some time, [YOUR COMPANY NAME] has built a solid foundation providing superior service and [ITEM 4] products for companies just like yours.

Should there be any other outstanding bids you believe might complement our business, I would appreciate the opportunity to give these my professional attention as well. Thank you for your assistance. [YOUR COMPANY NAME] is everything you always wanted in a vendor, and we have the track record to prove it.

Sincerely yours,

[YOUR NAME]
[YOUR TITLE]

[ITEM 1] = Describe what the bid is for
[ITEM 2] = Provide [COMPANY]'s bid tracking number for [ITEM 1]
[ITEM 3] = [YOUR COMPANY NAME]'s address
[ITEM 4] = Describe [YOUR COMPANY NAME]'s main business emphasis

[DATE]

[Mr./Mrs./Ms./Dr.] [CUSTOMER'S FULL NAME]
[CUSTOMER'S TITLE]
[COMPANY]
[ADDRESS]
[CITY], [STATE] [ZIP CODE]

Dear [Mr./Mrs./Ms./Dr.] [CUSTOMER'S LAST NAME]:

Life can be so hectic at times that even our habits fall by the wayside. We neglect the simple things like eating lunch or reading the paper. Many times, people call with requests, and we must drop everything to meet their expectations.

[COMPANY] has an obligation to [YOUR COMPANY NAME] too. Your credit history suggests that simple neglect is the reason for your lack of promptness in remitting payment to [YOUR COMPANY NAME]. Our records indicate that the amount of $[ITEM 1] is currently past due by [ITEM 2].

It is never too late to make payment on the account. If this letter crossed paths with your check, please accept my apologies for this friendly reminder. We simply want to revive [COMPANY]'s good habits before the situation has a chance to get out of control. Thank you for your assistance.

Sincerely yours,

[YOUR NAME]
[YOUR TITLE]

[ITEM 1] = Dollar amount of payment needed from [COMPANY]
[ITEM 2] = Length of time [ITEM 1] is past due

[DATE]

[Mr./Mrs./Ms./Dr.] [CUSTOMER'S FULL NAME]
[CUSTOMER'S TITLE]
[COMPANY]
[ADDRESS]
[CITY], [STATE] [ZIP CODE]

Dear [Mr./Mrs./Ms./Dr.] [CUSTOMER'S LAST NAME]:

Far too often, companies take credit extensions lightly, failing to consider that suppliers must carry the burden for late-paying customers. Both vendors and customers have obligations. Vendors provide high-quality goods and services; customers, in return, pay for those goods and services under the agreed upon terms.

[YOUR COMPANY NAME] has lived up to our side of the bargain; [COMPANY] has fallen behind. Because of [COMPANY]'s credit rating, we extended ourselves to the point of providing references when [COMPANY] applied for credit with other companies.

By sending $[ITEM 1] immediately, you will make your account current and protect your credit rating. If this is not possible or extenuating circumstances prevent [COMPANY] from complying with our request for payment, please call me today. Good credit ratings take years to establish and only months to destroy. Thank you for your prompt attention. Professionals like us know that bad credit is very difficult to conceal. Don't let another day go by without addressing this issue.

Sincerely yours,

[YOUR NAME]
[YOUR TITLE]

———————————————◆———————————————

[ITEM 1] = Dollar amount of payment needed from [COMPANY]

[DATE]

[Mr./Mrs./Ms./Dr.] [CUSTOMER'S FULL NAME]
[CUSTOMER'S TITLE]
[COMPANY]
[ADDRESS]
[CITY], [STATE] [ZIP CODE]

Dear [Mr./Mrs./Ms./Dr.] [CUSTOMER'S LAST NAME]:

Time is money. Unfortunately, we have been wasting much of both in trying to collect [COMPANY]'s debt to [YOUR COMPANY NAME]. In every management meeting, we discuss with disbelief the fact that [COMPANY] continues to shirk its obligations. The outstanding balance of $[ITEM 1] is overdue by an excessive [ITEM 2].

I am responsible for our company's accounting, and your lack of action has forced me to cancel all future extensions of credit. Because [YOUR COMPANY NAME] is a fair company, management has developed two options that will allow [COMPANY] to fulfill its obligations:

1. Remit the full amount of $[ITEM 1]; or
2. Remit a partial payment of $[ITEM 3] with the understanding that the balance is to be paid by [ITEM 4].

If given the opportunity, I will help [COMPANY]. Your immediate response is imperative. [YOUR COMPANY NAME] is not going away, and I would like our business affiliation to continue. However, only your actions can allow this to happen, and time is running out.

Sincerely yours,

[YOUR NAME]
[YOUR TITLE]

[ITEM 1] = Dollar amount of payment needed from [COMPANY]
[ITEM 2] = Length of time [ITEM 1] is past due
[ITEM 3] = Dollar amount of partial payment needed from [COMPANY]
[ITEM 4] = Date [ITEM 3] is due

[DATE]

[Mr./Mrs./Ms./Dr.] [CUSTOMER'S FULL NAME]
[CUSTOMER'S TITLE]
[COMPANY]
[ADDRESS]
[CITY], [STATE] [ZIP CODE]

Dear [Mr./Mrs./Ms./Dr.] [CUSTOMER'S LAST NAME]:

When things are going badly, we tend to turn our backs on the world and refuse to deal with the issues that haunt us. [COMPANY] has always been a valued [YOUR COMPANY NAME] customer, and we are confused by the change in your payment history. I have checked the files for any circumstances that might explain such unprofessionalism.

There are none. The file is, however, full of our requests for an explanation or partial payment. I also see a fair number of unfulfilled [COMPANY] promises. The account is $[ITEM 1] overdue, which means that it will soon be turned over to a collection agency.

To date, I have personally gone out of my way to see that such action is not taken with [COMPANY]. Why? Because a careful review of your payment history suggests that this is not your normal business practice.

I must know what is going on and what type of payment, if any, [COMPANY] will remit on the account immediately. Why can't we discuss this issue before I am forced to turn the account over for collection? One action taken by [COMPANY] could prevent [YOUR COMPANY NAME] from taking any. I am not your enemy; I hope to hear from you soon.

Sincerely yours,

[YOUR NAME]
[YOUR TITLE]

[ITEM 1] = Dollar amount of payment needed from [COMPANY]

[DATE]

[Mr./Mrs./Ms./Dr.] [CUSTOMER'S FULL NAME]
[CUSTOMER'S TITLE]
[COMPANY]
[ADDRESS]
[CITY], [STATE] [ZIP CODE]

Dear [Mr./Mrs./Ms./Dr.] [CUSTOMER'S LAST NAME]:

[COMPANY] has brought this on itself. On several occasions, [YOUR COMPANY NAME] has politely asked that the debt of $[ITEM 1] owed to our company be satisfied. Because payment is long overdue, our choices for resolution are severely limited.

Take this notice as a warning, and use your imagination. Think how you would handle this situation if the roles were reversed. Would [COMPANY] continue saying, "Please"? I don't think so.

I do not have to educate you on the importance of credit checks. They are truly an organization's calling card. I recommend that [COMPANY] give the matter immediate attention. If [YOUR COMPANY NAME] has not heard from you by [ITEM 2], I will have no choice but to pursue more serious measures. It is my hope that [COMPANY]'s blatant disregard of its debts ends today.

Sincerely yours,

[YOUR NAME]
[YOUR TITLE]

[ITEM 1] = Dollar amount of payment needed from [COMPANY]
[ITEM 2] = Date [COMPANY] must contact [YOUR COMPANY NAME] by

[DATE]

[Mr./Mrs./Ms./Dr.] [CUSTOMER'S FULL NAME]
[CUSTOMER'S TITLE]
[COMPANY]
[ADDRESS]
[CITY], [STATE] [ZIP CODE]

Dear [Mr./Mrs./Ms./Dr.] [CUSTOMER'S LAST NAME]:

    Demand is hereby made upon [COMPANY] for the total amount of $[ITEM 1] to satisfy all debts incurred for purchases made from our company. It is expected that [COMPANY] will remit full payment of $[ITEM 1] on, or before, [ITEM 2]. In accordance with the law, [YOUR COMPANY NAME] has notified the proper entities of [COMPANY]'s overdue debt, and we are prepared to take immediate action.

    Although [YOUR COMPANY NAME] is reluctant to pursue such measures, we will have no choice if payment is not received before [ITEM 2]. We hope for an immediate reconciliation in receiving what is rightfully ours before being forced to seek a harsher remedy.

Sincerely yours,

[YOUR NAME]
[YOUR TITLE]

[ITEM 1] = Dollar amount of payment needed from [COMPANY]
[ITEM 2] = Date [COMPANY] must pay [ITEM 1] by

CUSTOMER \ Complaint Response
Customer Misunderstood Delivery Terms

(26.1)

[DATE]

[Mr./Mrs./Ms./Dr.] [CUSTOMER'S FULL NAME]
[CUSTOMER'S TITLE]
[COMPANY]
[ADDRESS]
[CITY], [STATE] [ZIP CODE]

Dear [Mr./Mrs./Ms./Dr.] [CUSTOMER'S LAST NAME]:

No matter what, where, or how we buy, it takes time and energy. Business is pressure-filled enough without vendors adding to the stress. [YOUR COMPANY NAME] is committed to making buying from us effortless—not just the first time, but every time.

Our total quality assurance program safeguards all customer commitments. From initial sale to final delivery, rules are in place and printed on the literature all customers receive. Your recent letter expressed disappointment regarding the delivery of our products.

I understand your position. However, our [ITEM 1] clearly states that goods are delivered by [ITEM 2] within [ITEM 3]. [COMPANY]'s transaction meets these criteria. Enclosed is a copy of [ITEM 1] for your review and to eliminate any future misunderstanding. If you still question whether the policy was followed, do not hesitate to call. You can depend on me to put your best interest ahead of mine.

Sincerely yours,

[YOUR NAME]
[YOUR TITLE]

[ITEM 1] = Name of [YOUR COMPANY NAME] literature enclosed with letter, i.e., "brochure," "catalog," etc. that specifies delivery terms
[ITEM 2] = Describe means and method by which orders are delivered
[ITEM 3] = Length of time [YOUR COMPANY NAME] guarantees delivery by

Business-to-Customer Correspondence   145

[DATE]

[Mr./Mrs./Ms./Dr.] [CUSTOMER'S FULL NAME]
[CUSTOMER'S TITLE]
[COMPANY]
[ADDRESS]
[CITY], [STATE] [ZIP CODE]

Dear [Mr./Mrs./Ms./Dr.] [CUSTOMER'S LAST NAME]:

Tell a child a secret, and watch his or her eyes light up with joy. In business though, secrecy can severely damage customer relationships. For as long as [YOUR COMPANY NAME] has been in business, ethical practices have guided our dealings with both customers and employees.

Sometimes in our buying enthusiasm and desire to act quickly, we overlook details. [YOUR COMPANY NAME] takes extra time to describe company policies that relate to purchases. Our [ITEM 1] exemplifies our commitment to ethical business practices. Included in it are the following statements: [ITEM 2].

I have enclosed a copy of [ITEM 1] for your review. [YOUR COMPANY NAME] is a trustworthy company in a sometimes untrustworthy world. If any doubts remain, please do not hesitate one moment in contacting me. [YOUR COMPANY NAME] is proud of the honorable reputation that keeps customers coming back.

Sincerely yours,

[YOUR NAME]
[YOUR TITLE]

[ITEM 1] = Name of [YOUR COMPANY NAME] literature enclosed with letter, i.e., "brochure," "catalog," etc. that specifies sale terms
[ITEM 2] = Describe buying terms as related to [COMPANY]'s complaint

[DATE]

[Mr./Mrs./Ms./Dr.] [CUSTOMER'S FULL NAME]
[CUSTOMER'S TITLE]
[COMPANY]
[ADDRESS]
[CITY], [STATE] [ZIP CODE]

Dear [Mr./Mrs./Ms./Dr.] [CUSTOMER'S LAST NAME]:

Jumping to conclusions often lands one in the slough of regret. On rare occasions, a customer presents [YOUR COMPANY NAME] with a problem to which an immediate response is not possible. Your criticism regarding [ITEM 1] is my responsibility, and you should know that our company is not ignoring it.

However, I need additional time to assure a thorough evaluation. I am starting at the beginning to uncover the conditions that placed a valued customer in such a situation.

You can be confident that I will move quickly, because customer satisfaction is one of our greatest priorities. You demand and deserve nothing less than the best. Thank you for your patience. I look forward to an amicable resolution.

Sincerely yours,

[YOUR NAME]
[YOUR TITLE]

———————————————————————————

[ITEM 1] = Describe [COMPANY]'s complaint

[DATE]

[Mr./Mrs./Ms./Dr.] [CUSTOMER'S FULL NAME]
[CUSTOMER'S TITLE]
[COMPANY]
[ADDRESS]
[CITY], [STATE] [ZIP CODE]

Dear [Mr./Mrs./Ms./Dr.] [CUSTOMER'S LAST NAME]:

The simplest transaction becomes complex when a misunderstanding clouds the issue. Words are so easily taken out of context. After thoroughly reviewing your criticism about [ITEM 1], I gathered my findings and presented them at our internal quality assurance meeting.

I realize the results are not what you want to hear. However, we reaffirm [YOUR COMPANY NAME]'s commitment to excellence in customer service. In addition, because no wrongful acts were done, I cannot offer restitution in the matter.

This decision was based primarily on [ITEM 2]. Although we cannot accept responsibility, we want you to understand that all transactions are important to us. Thank you for taking [YOUR COMPANY NAME]'s word as honorable. We value good customers like [COMPANY] and hope this response does not impair our business affiliation.

Sincerely yours,

[YOUR NAME]
[YOUR TITLE]

[ITEM 1] = Describe [COMPANY]'s complaint
[ITEM 2] = Describe the major reason [ITEM 1] is not [YOUR COMPANY NAME]'s fault

CUSTOMER \ Complaint Response
Referred to Another

[DATE]

[Mr./Mrs./Ms./Dr.] [CUSTOMER'S FULL NAME]
[CUSTOMER'S TITLE]
[COMPANY]
[ADDRESS]
[CITY], [STATE] [ZIP CODE]

Dear [Mr./Mrs./Ms./Dr.] [CUSTOMER'S LAST NAME]:

In the 1930s, 30 cents created and mailed a letter. This cost has risen to nearly 18 dollars over last 60 years. The hidden and obvious costs of sending a letter add up quickly.

Not the least of these costs is the time of the person who writes the letter. Thank you for taking the time to inform [YOUR COMPANY NAME] of your recent displeasure concerning [ITEM 1].

Like most organizations, [YOUR COMPANY NAME] is divided by responsibilities. Addressing your situation properly requires expert handling by someone more qualified than I. I have briefed [ITEM 2] on the situation and left our meeting confident that your complaint is in good hands.

Thank you again for writing and letting us know that [YOUR COMPANY NAME] failed to live up to the expectations of [COMPANY]. With [ITEM 2] on your side, your next letter will surely be one of praise.

Sincerely yours,

[YOUR NAME]
[YOUR TITLE]

[ITEM 1] = Describe [COMPANY]'s complaint
[ITEM 2] = First and last name of person handling [ITEM 1]

[DATE]

[Mr./Mrs./Ms./Dr.] [CUSTOMER'S FULL NAME]
[CUSTOMER'S TITLE]
[COMPANY]
[ADDRESS]
[CITY], [STATE] [ZIP CODE]

Dear [Mr./Mrs./Ms./Dr.] [CUSTOMER'S LAST NAME]:

Customer appraisals carry more weight than management appraisals. You are who we ultimately serve and, therefore, the best source of feedback. Thank you for taking time from your busy schedule to let us know that we are earning high marks with [COMPANY].

Your letter praising [ITEM 1] was a gracious acknowledgment of our stringent standards and commitment to 100 percent customer satisfaction. I guarantee that your letter will not be sitting on my desk much longer. [ITEM 2] will receive [YOUR COMPANY NAME] accolades for exemplifying a first rate professional image. Again, thank you for bringing such good news into our company. Your comments prove that hard work and quality never go out of style.

Sincerely yours,

[YOUR NAME]
[YOUR TITLE]

[ITEM 1] = First and last name of person who received compliment
[ITEM 2] = First name of [ITEM 1]

[DATE]

[Mr./Mrs./Ms./Dr.] [CUSTOMER'S FULL NAME]
[CUSTOMER'S TITLE]
[COMPANY]
[ADDRESS]
[CITY], [STATE] [ZIP CODE]

Dear [Mr./Mrs./Ms./Dr.] [CUSTOMER'S LAST NAME]:

It takes ability, knowledge, and talent to express ideas in a way that is both informative and entertaining. I feel fortunate to have had the opportunity to hear your recent speech about [ITEM 1]. From the introduction to the closing remarks, the content was helpful and right on the money.

An audience's reaction is a speaker's best indicator of success. In addition to keeping our attention, your thoughts stimulated further thinking on the subject. You must find great satisfaction in being revered so highly.

Congratulations on your apparent success, and please let me know when and where you speak next. Other professionals in my contact circle would definitely enjoy your presentation as much as I did. I wish you continued success in all your endeavors!

Sincerely yours,

[YOUR NAME]
[YOUR TITLE]

[ITEM 1] = Describe the subject of the speech

[DATE]

[Mr./Mrs./Ms./Dr.] [CUSTOMER'S FULL NAME]
[CUSTOMER'S TITLE]
[COMPANY]
[ADDRESS]
[CITY], [STATE] [ZIP CODE]

Dear [Mr./Mrs./Ms./Dr.] [CUSTOMER'S LAST NAME]:

A crew is only as good as its captain. From shore to shore, the crew must be compelled and motivated to go beyond the call of duty for the captain, the ship, and themselves. Your crew's commitment to a tip-top ship is evident.

In my profession, I see many operations unlike [COMPANY] that are full of discontent and disregard for corporate goals. Seeing your staff truly teaming efforts in a pleasant atmosphere is my welcome mat for every visit. This says much about your leadership abilities.

I salute you, the captain, for your professionalism in creating an organization full of enthusiastic and talented people. Please accept my commendations and congratulations on your prosperity. With you at the helm, [COMPANY] is destined to be the best [ITEM 1] from port to port.

Sincerely yours,

[YOUR NAME]
[YOUR TITLE]

[ITEM 1] = Describe the business focus of [COMPANY]

[DATE]

[Mr./Mrs./Ms./Dr.] [CUSTOMER'S FULL NAME]
[CUSTOMER'S TITLE]
[COMPANY]
[ADDRESS]
[CITY], [STATE] [ZIP CODE]

Dear [Mr./Mrs./Ms./Dr.] [CUSTOMER'S LAST NAME]:

Like any worthwhile relationship, a customer-vendor affiliation brings together ideas and common goals. Striking the delicate balance between likes and dislikes can sometimes be difficult. Two traits I hold in high regard personally and professionally are integrity and respect.

Consequently, I am compelled to tell you that working with you is an absolute pleasure. Everything is upbeat and upfront. Business is tough, but not with people like you.

Our relationship confirms that win-win situations occur when two people desire a positive result. Thank you for being a model customer. You make the reason I chose this profession obvious.

Sincerely yours,

[YOUR NAME]
[YOUR TITLE]

[DATE]

[Mr./Mrs./Ms./Dr.] [CUSTOMER'S FULL NAME]
[CUSTOMER'S TITLE]
[COMPANY]
[ADDRESS]
[CITY], [STATE] [ZIP CODE]

Dear [Mr./Mrs./Ms./Dr.] [CUSTOMER'S LAST NAME]:

Putting what you believe into words is a real art. Expressing a belief, taking a position, or teaching a particular subject through the written word alone is a creative, demanding process. Limited editorial space makes the ability to get to the point a writer's best friend.

There is a fine line between saying too much and saying too little. Apparently, walking that line comes naturally to you. I thoroughly enjoyed your article on [ITEM 1], which appeared in [ITEM 2]. I cannot imagine a clearer or more concise depiction of [ITEM 3].

Your words struck a responsive chord within me. I shared the article with my associates so that they too might reap the benefits of your knowledge. Keep up the great work. I wish you continued success in your publishing career. I have a premonition that I'll be saying someday, "I knew [ITEM 4] when..."

Sincerely yours,

[YOUR NAME]
[YOUR TITLE]

———————————————————◆———————————————————

[ITEM 1] = Describe the subject of article
[ITEM 2] = Name of publication in which [ITEM 1] appeared
[ITEM 3] = Describe the major point of article
[ITEM 4] = First and last name of person receiving letter

[DATE]

[Mr./Mrs./Ms./Dr.] [CUSTOMER'S FULL NAME]
[CUSTOMER'S TITLE]
[COMPANY]
[ADDRESS]
[CITY], [STATE] [ZIP CODE]

Dear [Mr./Mrs./Ms./Dr.] [CUSTOMER'S LAST NAME]:

Like a child, a business begins to mature the moment those first baby steps are taken. Lessons are learned, directions become focused, and in time, strength coupled with determination makes a marathon runner. For both individuals and enterprises, the road to adulthood is simultaneously rocky and rewarding.

Congratulations on paving a prosperous path for your company, your employees, and their families. As your expansion demonstrates, [COMPANY] has developed the attributes that help companies win awards. I extend my wishes for your continued success, and when time allows, I would like to discuss how [YOUR COMPANY NAME] might be of assistance in [COMPANY]'s explosive growth.

Sincerely yours,

[YOUR NAME]
[YOUR TITLE]

[DATE]

[Mr./Mrs./Ms./Dr.] [CUSTOMER'S FULL NAME]
[CUSTOMER'S TITLE]
[COMPANY]
[ADDRESS]
[CITY], [STATE] [ZIP CODE]

Dear [Mr./Mrs./Ms./Dr.] [CUSTOMER'S LAST NAME]:

Business stresses and successes harden many people to the problems of the less fortunate. I, for example, used to view the homeless with disgust, thinking, "They could get jobs." Then I came to realize that something had happened in their lives that made them give up on their dreams.

We all have ambitions; some are simply more grandiose than others. In moving toward our goals, challenges either make us stronger or weaken the pursuit. Because we have not relinquished our dreams, it is our responsibility to help those who may have given up.

I respect you for understanding the benefits of helping the underprivileged. Your compassionate efforts to [ITEM 1] are commendable. No doubt, the time you have spent has had far-reaching effects on their lives. Please let me know if I can help with the program in any way. It would be my pleasure.

Sincerely yours,

[YOUR NAME]
[YOUR TITLE]

[ITEM 1] = Describe the community program's goal

[DATE]

[Mr./Mrs./Ms./Dr.] [CUSTOMER'S FULL NAME]
[CUSTOMER'S TITLE]
[COMPANY]
[ADDRESS]
[CITY], [STATE] [ZIP CODE]

Dear [Mr./Mrs./Ms./Dr.] [CUSTOMER'S LAST NAME]:

Many fear change and choose comfort over challenge. After all, it is easier to plod along in the familiar than to explore the unknown. I extend my congratulations to you for moving forward in your new position as [ITEM 1].

You have both the knowledge and the skills to excel. While the title may be nothing new to [COMPANY], your professionalism makes this position a corporate asset. If there is any way I can support you in this transition, just say the word.

Again, congratulations on the new job! I would wish you good luck, but I know it isn't necessary. Your talents already have things well-covered.

Sincerely yours,

[YOUR NAME]
[YOUR TITLE]

[ITEM 1] = Title of the new job

[DATE]

[Mr./Mrs./Ms./Dr.] [CUSTOMER'S FULL NAME]
[CUSTOMER'S TITLE]
[COMPANY]
[ADDRESS]
[CITY], [STATE] [ZIP CODE]

Dear [Mr./Mrs./Ms./Dr.] [CUSTOMER'S LAST NAME]:

    Onward and upward you go! Congratulations on your recent promotion and continuing success with [COM-PANY]. I meet many professionals in my job, and I can honestly say that you are one of the few I admire for their level of expertise and "get up and go" attitude.

    It's encouraging for me to participate in your success. Seeing your determination, skills, and talents pushes me to further achievements. I extend my best wishes for your future and, again, my congratulations.

Sincerely yours,

[YOUR NAME]
[YOUR TITLE]

[DATE]

[Mr./Mrs./Ms./Dr.] [CUSTOMER'S FULL NAME]
[CUSTOMER'S TITLE]
[COMPANY]
[ADDRESS]
[CITY], [STATE] [ZIP CODE]

Dear [Mr./Mrs./Ms./Dr.] [CUSTOMER'S LAST NAME]:

Eloquence and speech are not the same. Expressing one's ideas is easy; expressing them with style requires forethought. Please do not think your insightful quotation on [ITEM 1] in [ITEM 2] went unnoticed.

On the contrary, your discerning vision left readers with a well-founded reference point. Congratulations on being recognized for your expertise. I hope to be reading your name more often. Your eloquence is rare and admirable; it reflects the confidence and knowledge reserved for people with a winning attitude. We have enough chatter in our lives.

Sincerely yours,

[YOUR NAME]
[YOUR TITLE]

[ITEM 1] = Describe the subject of the quotation
[ITEM 2] = Name of publication in which [ITEM 1] appeared

[DATE]

[Mr./Mrs./Ms./Dr.] [CUSTOMER'S FULL NAME]
[CUSTOMER'S TITLE]
[COMPANY]
[ADDRESS]
[CITY], [STATE] [ZIP CODE]

Dear [Mr./Mrs./Ms./Dr.] [CUSTOMER'S LAST NAME]:

The demands of our chosen professions often exhaust us as we strive to create opportunities from challenges. The personal satisfaction found in a job done well, however, prepares us for the next goal.

Outside professional recognition and respect are equally important. I am pleased to hear that [COMPANY] has honored your achievements with its prestigious [ITEM 1] award. It really could not be bestowed on a more deserving recipient. Management and peer appreciation of your unrelenting efforts to [ITEM 2] must give you a great sense of satisfaction.

Congratulations on a well-earned tribute; I extend my best wishes for continued success and additional trophies.

Sincerely yours,

[YOUR NAME]
[YOUR TITLE]

[ITEM 1] = Name of [COMPANY]'s award
[ITEM 2] = Describe why person receiving letter got [ITEM 1]

[DATE]

[Mr./Mrs./Ms./Dr.] [CUSTOMER'S FULL NAME]
[CUSTOMER'S TITLE]
[COMPANY]
[ADDRESS]
[CITY], [STATE] [ZIP CODE]

Dear [Mr./Mrs./Ms./Dr.] [CUSTOMER'S LAST NAME]:

Contracts serve as confirmation that verbal commitments will be honored throughout a business relationship. [YOUR COMPANY NAME] wants every agreement made with our customers to be a positive experience. We want you to sign with enthusiasm and without reservation.

Therefore, [COMPANY]'s request to modify [ITEM 1] on our contract for [ITEM 2] is approved. Enclosed are the revised contracts for your review and signature. Please let me know the quickest way to obtain the executed agreements so [YOUR COMPANY NAME] can get started as soon as possible. Thank you for your assistance and confidence. I guarantee [COMPANY]'s complete satisfaction as we fulfill our commitments.

Sincerely yours,

[YOUR NAME]
[YOUR TITLE]

[ITEM 1] = Describe the changes approved
[ITEM 2] = Describe what the contract is for

[DATE]

[Mr./Mrs./Ms./Dr.] [CUSTOMER'S FULL NAME]
[CUSTOMER'S TITLE]
[COMPANY]
[ADDRESS]
[CITY], [STATE] [ZIP CODE]

Dear [Mr./Mrs./Ms./Dr.] [CUSTOMER'S LAST NAME]:

Good companies welcome the opportunity to put their commitments in writing. Agreements protect the interests of both parties. Thank you for your help in preparing the contract for [ITEM 1] being executed between [COMPANY] and [YOUR COMPANY NAME]. I know it took a lot of time and patience.

Although the enclosed documents are direct results of our previous discussions, please review them thoroughly. I have verified that the contract contains your primary concerns of [ITEM 2]. Just sign on page [ITEM 3], and your long-awaited solution for [ITEM 4] is within reach.

On behalf of [YOUR COMPANY NAME], thank you again for your assistance in making our business relationship possible. I look forward to getting started on meeting [COMPANY]'s requirements.

Sincerely yours,

[YOUR NAME]
[YOUR TITLE]

[ITEM 1] = Describe what the contract is for
[ITEM 2] = Describe highlights of contract
[ITEM 3] = Page number of contract [COMPANY] must sign
[ITEM 4] = Describe the contract's purpose

[DATE]

[Mr./Mrs./Ms./Dr.] [CUSTOMER'S FULL NAME]
[CUSTOMER'S TITLE]
[COMPANY]
[ADDRESS]
[CITY], [STATE] [ZIP CODE]

Dear [Mr./Mrs./Ms./Dr.] [CUSTOMER'S LAST NAME]:

We form relationships gradually. One action alone does not create an enduring business affiliation. [COMPANY] has waited long enough for [YOUR COMPANY NAME] to prove that no competition surpasses us.

Perhaps our contract is in that pile of things you have been meaning to do. Certainly, we all get overwhelmed at times. We need your help, though, before [YOUR COMPANY NAME] can move forward with our plan to improve [COMPANY]'s operations.

The contracts for [ITEM 1] are necessary to our business. Thank you in advance for the speedy return of the signed contract. I am eager to turn those words into actions that will further strengthen our business relationship.

Sincerely yours,

[YOUR NAME]
[YOUR TITLE]

———————————————————————————

[ITEM 1] = Describe what the contract is for

[DATE]

[Mr./Mrs./Ms./Dr.] [CUSTOMER'S FULL NAME]
[CUSTOMER'S TITLE]
[COMPANY]
[ADDRESS]
[CITY], [STATE] [ZIP CODE]

Dear [Mr./Mrs./Ms./Dr.] [CUSTOMER'S LAST NAME]:

Sometimes in the daily hustle and bustle of business, the big picture gets our undivided attention. Occasionally, even an intelligent, influential individual like you will overlook a minor detail or two. We received the contract for [COMPANY]'s [ITEM 1], but one very critical item is missing.

Before we can proceed, page [ITEM 2] requires your signature. I know this is simply an oversight, and we'll be on our way just as soon as I receive the signed contract.

[COMPANY] has a reputation for never letting people down. However, should you foresee a problem in returning the contract within the next five days, please notify me of your plans. I'll need to undo the preparations I have made and the work already in progress to meet [COMPANY]'s needs. Thank you for your prompt attention.

Sincerely yours,

[YOUR NAME]
[YOUR TITLE]

[ITEM 1] = Describe the contract's purpose
[ITEM 2] = Page number of contract [COMPANY] must sign

[DATE]

[Mr./Mrs./Ms./Dr.] [CUSTOMER'S FULL NAME]
[CUSTOMER'S TITLE]
[COMPANY]
[ADDRESS]
[CITY], [STATE] [ZIP CODE]

Dear [Mr./Mrs./Ms./Dr.] [CUSTOMER'S LAST NAME]:

Doesn't it seem like the days move quicker as we get older? Count it in the strange but true category that the time has come for us to renew our contract for [ITEM 1] with [COMPANY]. We have enjoyed doing business with your company and need concurrence on our future dealings.

To prevent any interruption in service, please sign page [ITEM 2] and then return the entire document to my attention at your earliest convenience. The entire [YOUR COMPANY NAME] staff thanks you in advance for your continued business. Before the coming days turn quickly into weeks, we ask you to follow Benjamin Franklin's advice, "Don't put off until tomorrow what you can do today!"

Sincerely yours,

[YOUR NAME]
[YOUR TITLE]

[ITEM 1] = Describe contract's purpose
[ITEM 2] = Page number of contract [COMPANY] must sign

[DATE]

[Mr./Mrs./Ms./Dr.] [CUSTOMER'S FULL NAME]
[CUSTOMER'S TITLE]
[COMPANY]
[ADDRESS]
[CITY], [STATE] [ZIP CODE]

Dear [Mr./Mrs./Ms./Dr.] [CUSTOMER'S LAST NAME]:

There is no way around it. Credit applications are a necessary evil in business. Our last thought is to burden you with additional paperwork, but we require certain information before establishing a credit account for [COMPANY].

Enclosed is [YOUR COMPANY NAME]'s standard credit application. Evaluating your credit request is easier when the application is printed or typed. If you run out of room on any item, simply use a blank page on which you reference the item number(s) to which the details pertain and attach it to the application. One last thing, the signature on the application must be by an authorized [COMPANY] representative.

Please allow us [ITEM 1] days to process your request. Thank you for your interest in the payment alternatives offered by our company. This is another example of [YOUR COMPANY NAME]'s dedication to tailoring our operations to unique customer requirements.

Sincerely yours,

[YOUR NAME]
[YOUR TITLE]

[ITEM 1] = Length of time [YOUR COMPANY NAME] needs before responding to [COMPANY]

[DATE]

[Mr./Mrs./Ms./Dr.] [CUSTOMER'S FULL NAME]
[CUSTOMER'S TITLE]
[COMPANY]
[ADDRESS]
[CITY], [STATE] [ZIP CODE]

Dear [Mr./Mrs./Ms./Dr.] [CUSTOMER'S LAST NAME]:

Good habits encourage personal and professional growth. It is important to [YOUR COMPANY NAME] that our customers exhibit admirable business practices. We prefer to deal with companies whose rigorous operational standards match our own.

Thank you for allowing us to verify your credit history. After thoroughly reviewing [COMPANY]'s request, we are pleased to grant your organization credit terms and establish a monthly billing cycle.

[COMPANY]'s account credit limit is $[ITEM 1] subject to the following terms and conditions: [ITEM 2]. The individual responsible for expert handling of [COMPANY]'s account, [ITEM 3], should be available at all times to answer any questions. Speaking for our entire company, I thank you again for giving us the opportunity to serve [COMPANY]. We never compromise on our standards, and we look forward to a long business relationship.

Sincerely yours,

[YOUR NAME]
[YOUR TITLE]

[ITEM 1] = Dollar amount of credit on [COMPANY]'s account
[ITEM 2] = Describe all terms and conditions of credit extension
[ITEM 3] = First and last name of [YOUR COMPANY NAME]'s credit representative

[DATE]

[Mr./Mrs./Ms./Dr.] [CUSTOMER'S FULL NAME]
[CUSTOMER'S TITLE]
[COMPANY]
[ADDRESS]
[CITY], [STATE] [ZIP CODE]

Dear [Mr./Mrs./Ms./Dr.] [CUSTOMER'S LAST NAME]:

Extending credit is a demonstration of good faith. A business exchanges goods and services for promises of payment. When a debt goes unpaid, both the business and the customer suffer a loss.

Customers forfeit the convenience credit offers by not upholding their commitments. [YOUR COMPANY NAME]'s records indicate that [COMPANY]'s account is overdue by [ITEM 1] on an outstanding balance of $[ITEM 2]. At this point, it is in our mutual best interest to cancel your credit effective [ITEM 3].

Not that this is the case with [COMPANY], but credit has led companies and people into financial trouble. We cannot extend ourselves or [COMPANY]'s credit line any further. If you believe our calculations are in error or there are mitigating circumstances delaying your payment, contact me immediately.

Please know that this is not my decision; I am merely the enforcer of the company policies that keep our operation running smoothly. I want to help [COMPANY] get back in our good graces in any way possible. Let's talk about how we can work toward this goal. I hope to hear from you soon.

Sincerely yours,

[YOUR NAME]
[YOUR TITLE]

———————————————◆———————————————

[ITEM 1] = **Length of time payment is overdue**
[ITEM 2] = **Dollar amount of [COMPANY]'s overdue balance**
[ITEM 3] = **Date [COMPANY]'s credit will be canceled**

[DATE]

[Mr./Mrs./Ms./Dr.] [CUSTOMER'S FULL NAME]
[CUSTOMER'S TITLE]
[COMPANY]
[ADDRESS]
[CITY], [STATE] [ZIP CODE]

Dear [Mr./Mrs./Ms./Dr.] [CUSTOMER'S LAST NAME]:

Saying no to a customer is not easy, but [YOUR COMPANY NAME]'s formal guidelines governing credit extensions must be followed to maintain equitable treatment for all our customers.

Unfortunately, we cannot comply with [COMPANY]'s request for credit. [YOUR COMPANY NAME] does its best to promote, not inhibit, business affiliations. If you believe there has been an error or omission in the information provided on your credit application, please bring this to our immediate attention. We may be able to reverse our decision.

The application can be reprocessed here in the office without starting from scratch. [YOUR COMPANY NAME] appreciates your understanding that our company is committed to service. Please feel free to reapply in another [ITEM 1] months. Today, based on the information we have in hand, we have no choice in the matter.

Sincerely yours,

[YOUR NAME]
[YOUR TITLE]

———————————————◆———————————————

[ITEM 1] = Length of time before [COMPANY] can reapply for credit

[DATE]

[Mr./Mrs./Ms./Dr.] [CUSTOMER'S FULL NAME]
[CUSTOMER'S TITLE]
[COMPANY]
[ADDRESS]
[CITY], [STATE] [ZIP CODE]

Dear [Mr./Mrs./Ms./Dr.] [CUSTOMER'S LAST NAME]:

Business rulebooks are necessary to fair play. [YOUR COMPANY NAME]'s credit policies are applicable to new and existing customers without exception. Besides the terms and conditions governing payments, established guidelines extend into other areas.

One rule requires credit limitations when a customer's account indicates [ITEM 1]. Therefore, [COMPANY]'s account is restricted in the following manner: [ITEM 2]. To resume normal credit allowances, [ITEM 3] must occur by [ITEM 4].

We appreciate your immediate attention in rectifying the situation and for understanding that rules benefit everyone. Thank you for your professionalism in this very important matter. Please remember, customer satisfaction is important to me, and I will help in any way possible.

Sincerely yours,

[YOUR NAME]
[YOUR TITLE]

———————————————————◄►———————————————————

[ITEM 1] = Describe problem causing restriction
[ITEM 2] = Describe restriction
[ITEM 3] = Describe how to remove restriction
[ITEM 4] = Date [ITEM 3] must happen

[DATE]

[Mr./Mrs./Ms./Dr.] [CUSTOMER'S FULL NAME]
[CUSTOMER'S TITLE]
[COMPANY]
[ADDRESS]
[CITY], [STATE] [ZIP CODE]

Dear [Mr./Mrs./Ms./Dr.] [CUSTOMER'S LAST NAME]:

Franz Schubert's masterpiece, his Sixth Symphony, was rejected by the Paris Symphony Orchestra. The London Philharmonic laughed. The piece was not played in public until 30 years after it was written. Now experts consider Schubert's Sixth Symphony one of the greatest works of all time.

While things have undoubtedly changed since Schubert's day, it still takes time to gain confidence and trust in business relationships. Yet, [YOUR COMPANY NAME] can't sing our song without your decision to serve as the ultimate conductor of our moves.

Our company's symphony has many parts, and the best critics are applauding the high-quality [ITEM 1] they receive. Don't let another moment pass; let's get started. [YOUR COMPANY NAME] is a masterpiece hidden in the sea of merchants. Call me and make today a turning point in your company's future.

Sincerely yours,

[YOUR NAME]
[YOUR TITLE]

[ITEM 1] = Describe [YOUR COMPANY NAME]'s main business emphasis and what you are trying to market to [COMPANY]

[DATE]

[Mr./Mrs./Ms./Dr.] [CUSTOMER'S FULL NAME]
[CUSTOMER'S TITLE]
[COMPANY]
[ADDRESS]
[CITY], [STATE] [ZIP CODE]

Dear [Mr./Mrs./Ms./Dr.] [CUSTOMER'S LAST NAME]:

Of all the wonders of the deep, I am especially fond of the relationship between the clown fish and the sea anemone. The bright orange clown fish lives inside the waving, stinging tentacles of the sea anemone.

The clown fish and the sea anemone have no chance for survival separately. Therefore, they have formed a partnership that allows them to live side by side. The bright orange color attracts prey into the tentacles, and the two organisms share the meal.

We have the makings of a similarly beneficial partnership. In keeping with our customer satisfaction goals, [YOUR COMPANY NAME] has competitively priced [ITEM 1]. [COMPANY] needs excellent service and product quality to remain competitive.

Today, it is a mystery to me why [COMPANY] would select any company but [YOUR COMPANY NAME]. Thank you in advance for letting me know what I can do to reinforce our future. If given the chance, we could survive as a team against all competitive odds.

Sincerely yours,

[YOUR NAME]
[YOUR TITLE]

[ITEM 1] = Describe [YOUR COMPANY NAME]'s main business emphasis and what you are trying to market to [COMPANY]

[DATE]

[Mr./Mrs./Ms./Dr.] [CUSTOMER'S FULL NAME]
[CUSTOMER'S TITLE]
[COMPANY]
[ADDRESS]
[CITY], [STATE] [ZIP CODE]

Dear [Mr./Mrs./Ms./Dr.] [CUSTOMER'S LAST NAME]:

This morning's office commute was very typical of most days. The coffee, traffic, and radio disk jockey reminded me that another day had begun. Between traffic lights, I thought of our business relationship, which ended for no apparent reason.

In my mind, I replayed our conversations and meetings looking for clues. Was it price? Was it service? Maybe they just found a better deal elsewhere.

Whatever the reason, I write to let you know that I want to win back your confidence in our company. Let's talk about what happened and the things we can do to reestablish the relationship. I look forward to receiving your call, and I hope to be driving to your office some morning soon.

Sincerely yours,

[YOUR NAME]
[YOUR TITLE]

[DATE]

[Mr./Mrs./Ms./Dr.] [CUSTOMER'S FULL NAME]
[CUSTOMER'S TITLE]
[COMPANY]
[ADDRESS]
[CITY], [STATE] [ZIP CODE]

Dear [Mr./Mrs./Ms./Dr.] [CUSTOMER'S LAST NAME]:

Have you ever really thought about a fruit? Even with artificial light and stimulants, fruit ripens at its own pace. All the efforts of modern science have failed to shorten significantly the growth cycle of a shiny red apple.

We have planted the seeds, watched our business relationship grow, and now the time has arrived for you to reap the harvest. Our fruit is ready for picking. Fruit selected at the wrong time is not of the highest grade.

Left too long in the market, it perishes. Management advised me recently that [COMPANY]'s decision is crucial. I fear time is running out and our prime offer for [ITEM 1] will soon have been on the tree too long. The fruit is available to everyone, but obviously, I want [COMPANY] to have first choice. Please let me know what I can do to help you act quickly. It would be a shame for you to miss this golden opportunity.

Sincerely yours,

[YOUR NAME]
[YOUR TITLE]

[ITEM 1] = Describe what the deal is for and terms

[DATE]

[Mr./Mrs./Ms./Dr.] [CUSTOMER'S FULL NAME]
[CUSTOMER'S TITLE]
[COMPANY]
[ADDRESS]
[CITY], [STATE] [ZIP CODE]

Dear [Mr./Mrs./Ms./Dr.] [CUSTOMER'S LAST NAME]:

I'm not naive when it comes to business. But, I have trouble understanding what happened. We've called, sent literature, and addressed your concerns, and still you decline to do business with our company. Is there something [YOUR COMPANY NAME] has done wrong?

Many of our customers are just like [COMPANY]. They need [ITEM 1] with excellent service, and we provide both in the most professional manner. In fact, we've been doing this for our customers for some time now.

There may be other reasons you haven't bought from our company. Perhaps it's just that you're busy and haven't had time to think about how we could work together. If this isn't the case and there are other facts you think I should be aware of, please let me know. It would only help make our respective companies even better.

Sincerely yours,

[YOUR NAME]
[YOUR TITLE]

[ITEM 1] = Describe [YOUR COMPANY NAME]'s main business emphasis and what you are trying to market to [COMPANY]

[DATE]

[Mr./Mrs./Ms./Dr.] [CUSTOMER'S FULL NAME]
[CUSTOMER'S TITLE]
[COMPANY]
[ADDRESS]
[CITY], [STATE] [ZIP CODE]

Dear [Mr./Mrs./Ms./Dr.] [CUSTOMER'S LAST NAME]:

There are few holidays that people forget. Christmas, New Year's Day, and Independence Day are all occasions for celebration. Yet, there is another day that is probably not marked on your calendar, but which holds great significance for [YOUR COMPANY NAME].

This month marks the [ITEM 1] year we have been doing business together. Our goals of excellence are being met. Sending flowers is an anniversary tradition, but we extend something far more meaningful—our entire organization's sincerest thanks for making this anniversary date possible. We all look forward to many more.

Sincerely yours,

[YOUR NAME]
[YOUR TITLE]

———————————————————————

[ITEM 1] = Number of year(s) marking anniversary

[DATE]

[Mr./Mrs./Ms./Dr.] [CUSTOMER'S FULL NAME]
[CUSTOMER'S TITLE]
[COMPANY]
[ADDRESS]
[CITY], [STATE] [ZIP CODE]

Dear [Mr./Mrs./Ms./Dr.] [CUSTOMER'S LAST NAME]:

There was a friendly face missing in the crowd! Our event on [ITEM 1] went well, and those who attended walked away with an armful of beneficial literature and a mind full of ideas. It is unfortunate that you were not able to attend and missed this opportunity to learn more about [ITEM 2].

At your convenience of course, it would be my pleasure to go over the highlights of the event with you. While I can't promise to be as effective as our expert presenters, I will do my very best. We have not scheduled another presentation like this for some time.

I will phone to set a time for a brief, informal presentation in the near future. Thank you in advance for sharing my excitement over [ITEM 2]. A recap of the cutting-edge advancements would surely be beneficial to both of us.

Sincerely yours,

[YOUR NAME]
[YOUR TITLE]

———————————◆   ◆———————————

[ITEM 1] = Date event was held
[ITEM 2] = Describe most significant topic of [ITEM 1]

[DATE]

[Mr./Mrs./Ms./Dr.] [CUSTOMER'S FULL NAME]
[CUSTOMER'S TITLE]
[COMPANY]
[ADDRESS]
[CITY], [STATE] [ZIP CODE]

Dear [Mr./Mrs./Ms./Dr.] [CUSTOMER'S LAST NAME]:

There are 170,000,000,000,000,000,000,000,000 ways to play the opening ten moves in a game of chess. Whether by pawns or knights, the first moves have an enormous impact on the remainder of the match. The same holds true for beginning a business relationship.

I want to make sure our first moves set the stage for mutual respect and trust. It's no secret that you can buy just about anything from someone. We're different, and we're prepared to prove it to you.

It remains my hope that over time, you will recognize how important our business affiliation is to me personally and professionally. Business has been likened many times to a game in which both parties win. I look forward to working together and making the right moves throughout our relationship.

Sincerely yours,

[YOUR NAME]
[YOUR TITLE]

[DATE]

[Mr./Mrs./Ms./Dr.] [CUSTOMER'S FULL NAME]
[CUSTOMER'S TITLE]
[COMPANY]
[ADDRESS]
[CITY], [STATE] [ZIP CODE]

Dear [Mr./Mrs./Ms./Dr.] [CUSTOMER'S LAST NAME]:

Moving into a new area is a tough transition. Any change is filled with both apprehension and excitement. It usually has a fresh but sometimes foreign appeal. On behalf of [YOUR COMPANY NAME], I welcome you to this growing community, where our company has prospered and our employees have raised their families for [ITEM 1] years.

[YOUR COMPANY NAME] is filled with friendly faces eager to help with your move. You may be new to our community, but our company's longstanding reputation for superior quality is not. Say [ITEM 2] around here, and you'll probably hear [YOUR COMPANY NAME].

We are proud of our accomplishments and look forward to welcoming you into our family of customers. Enjoy your new surroundings, and please remember we are here if you ever need [ITEM 2]. You will be pleased to learn what our customers already know. [YOUR COMPANY NAME] is a reputable company that pays close attention to details and service.

Sincerely yours,

[YOUR NAME]
[YOUR TITLE]

[ITEM 1] = Number of years [YOUR COMPANY NAME] has been in business
[ITEM 2] = Describe [YOUR COMPANY NAME]'s main business emphasis and what you are trying to market to [COMPANY]

[DATE]

[Mr./Mrs./Ms./Dr.] [CUSTOMER'S FULL NAME]
[CUSTOMER'S TITLE]
[COMPANY]
[ADDRESS]
[CITY], [STATE] [ZIP CODE]

Dear [Mr./Mrs./Ms./Dr.] [CUSTOMER'S LAST NAME]:

Success will never make us so aloof that we forget our manners and fail to extend a welcome. After all, [COMPANY]'s influx of new talent allows our entire community to prosper. [YOUR COMPANY NAME] has been a leading source for [ITEM 1] in the metropolitan area for years.

Our latest [ITEM 2], which is enclosed, provides an excellent overview of who and what we are. There's much more to the [YOUR COMPANY NAME] story. I could go on for pages listing the numerous ways in which we maintain high levels of customer satisfaction. For now, let's say I would like the opportunity to prove to you what we have proved to others about our company.

Please take a few minutes to examine this information about our company and its offerings. Once you do, I am confident that we will be welcoming you into much more than our community. We will be welcoming you into a family of customers who have found the right source for all their [ITEM 1] needs.

Sincerely yours,

[YOUR NAME]
[YOUR TITLE]

[ITEM 1] = Describe [YOUR COMPANY NAME]'s main business emphasis and what you are trying to
market to [COMPANY]
[ITEM 2] = Name of [YOUR COMPANY NAME] literature enclosed with letter, i.e., "brochure," "catalog," etc.

[DATE]

[Mr./Mrs./Ms./Dr.] [CUSTOMER'S FULL NAME]
[CUSTOMER'S TITLE]
[COMPANY]
[ADDRESS]
[CITY], [STATE] [ZIP CODE]

Dear [Mr./Mrs./Ms./Dr.] [CUSTOMER'S LAST NAME]:

In 1875, the director of the United States Patent Office resigned from his position, recommending that the department be closed. Why? He believed that there was nothing left to invent.

Just imagine for a moment how [COMPANY] would operate if no one had the determination and stamina to bring to life [ITEM 1]. Many companies like [COMPANY] have enhanced their image and performance with this simple idea. As the market continues to expand, [YOUR COMPANY NAME] is prepared to deliver this and more to you.

Our company portfolio is full of proven inventions certainly brought to market since 1875. I would be happy to stop by at your earliest convenience and tell you more about them. Until then, please feel free to examine the [ITEM 2], which I have enclosed for your review. Seeing is believing.

Sincerely yours,

[YOUR NAME]
[YOUR TITLE]

[ITEM 1] = Describe [YOUR COMPANY NAME]'s main business emphasis and what you are trying to market to [COMPANY]
[ITEM 2] = Name of [YOUR COMPANY NAME] literature enclosed with letter, i.e., "brochure," "catalog," etc.

[DATE]

[Mr./Mrs./Ms./Dr.] [CUSTOMER'S FULL NAME]
[CUSTOMER'S TITLE]
[COMPANY]
[ADDRESS]
[CITY], [STATE] [ZIP CODE]

Dear [Mr./Mrs./Ms./Dr.] [CUSTOMER'S LAST NAME]:

"Men wanted for a hazardous journey. Small wages, bitter cold, long months of complete darkness, constant danger, safe return doubtful." Surprisingly, this advertisement that appeared in London papers around the turn of the 20th century received numerous responses.

Many companies treat their customers the same way; you just don't see them apply such blatant truth in advertising. For some reason, buyers still follow these companies into uncharted territories. Our best advertising is intelligent people like you who would never even consider doing business with a company other than [YOUR COMPANY NAME] for [ITEM 1] needs.

They know we make the journey pleasant and safe. Our pricing climate is temperate. Our business light always shines on customer satisfaction. And with money-back guarantees, returns are always possible.

In my quest to offer the best possible service to my customers, I have asked them what they don't like about business. And heeding their responses has made me better than most. When you become my customer, I go the extra mile because I have a genuine interest in your company. You work hard and deserve the best. Please call me today, because purchasing should be a pleasure, not a hazardous journey into the unknown.

Sincerely yours,

[YOUR NAME]
[YOUR TITLE]

[ITEM 1] = Describe [YOUR COMPANY NAME]'s main business emphasis and what you are trying to market to [COMPANY]

THE CUSTOMER FAST FACTS
FAX RESPONSE

[YOUR COMPANY NAME] wants to help our customers quickly. Please complete this sheet and transmit it to [ITEM 1]. This is our customer-dedicated facsimile machine, which is checked throughout the day. We'll respond A.S.A.P.

I'm _____

_____
Company

_____
Telephone Number

_____
Facsimile Number

1. You got my attention and I'd like to know more about:

_____

_____

2. Please have a company representative:

_____Call me   _____Fax the information

3. You have the right place, but I'm not the right person. You really should talk to:

_____

4. I'm interested, but this isn't a good time. Try back in:

_____1 week   _____1 month   _____2 weeks   _____2 months

[ITEM 1] = [YOUR COMPANY NAME]'s facsimile number

[DATE]

[Mr./Mrs./Ms./Dr.] [CUSTOMER'S FULL NAME]
[CUSTOMER'S TITLE]
[COMPANY]
[ADDRESS]
[CITY], [STATE] [ZIP CODE]

Dear [Mr./Mrs./Ms./Dr.] [CUSTOMER'S LAST NAME]:

The year was 1876. Three days had passed since Alexander Graham Bell received the patent for a device that used electricity to transmit speech. Mr. Bell was working in his laboratory when he dropped acid from a battery on himself. He called to his assistant on a primitive telephone, "Mr. Watson. Come at once. I want you."

If Mr. Bell were around today, I would thank him for allowing us to meet via technology based on his invention. The breadth of your responsibilities was interesting and quite complementary to my professional career. As a follow-up to our conversation, the [ITEM 1] enclosed outlines the information we discussed.

Clearly, you have high standards to maintain at [COMPANY], and I look for that characteristic in customers. It makes for the best business relationships. I extend my thanks for an enjoyable conversation. I'll be in touch to check on your interest level and, if appropriate, set a time for us to meet in person.

Sincerely yours,

[YOUR NAME]
[YOUR TITLE]

———————————————◆———————————————

[ITEM 1] = Name of [YOUR COMPANY NAME] literature enclosed with letter, i.e., "brochure," "catalog," etc.

[DATE]

[Mr./Mrs./Ms./Dr.] [CUSTOMER'S FULL NAME]
[CUSTOMER'S TITLE]
[COMPANY]
[ADDRESS]
[CITY], [STATE] [ZIP CODE]

Dear [Mr./Mrs./Ms./Dr.] [CUSTOMER'S LAST NAME]:

A person in a prestigious position such as yours must be tired of vendors squeezing in 500 words per minute about low prices and great customer service. They can help you run your business. They want your business. They will work hard for you.

Enough already, as you tactfully interrupt and say, "Thank you, but I'm not interested." Honestly, I want your business too, but I am not going to show disrespect by barging into your life unannounced at an inopportune time.

Yes, [YOUR COMPANY NAME] gives customers a full line of competitively priced [ITEM 1] and prides itself on its thorough understanding of the word "service." Yes, we know our clients are our most valuable asset, and we are willing to work for your business. And yes, I hope to have the opportunity to demonstrate this to you in the near future. I will telephone soon, and if I call at a bad time, just say the word. I'll try back at another time. I want you to be my customer on your terms, not mine.

Sincerely yours,

[YOUR NAME]
[YOUR TITLE]

[ITEM 1] = Describe [YOUR COMPANY NAME]'s main business emphasis and what you are trying to market
 to [COMPANY]

[DATE]

[Mr./Mrs./Ms./Dr.] [CUSTOMER'S FULL NAME]
[CUSTOMER'S TITLE]
[COMPANY]
[ADDRESS]
[CITY], [STATE] [ZIP CODE]

Dear [Mr./Mrs./Ms./Dr.] [CUSTOMER'S LAST NAME]:

    Ever since my childhood, Sundays have been a special day in my home. I especially enjoy getting up early before everyone else's day begins and reading the paper. Have you noticed how many advertisements fill the pages lately?

    It's hard to find the news anymore. No wonder people are confused about buying [ITEM 1]. I think many companies want to see just how much they can squeeze into an advertisement.

    You don't have to look at the advertisements anymore. Just scan the enclosed [ITEM 2], and check out our carnival of savings. If you're not careful, you could end up wasting your hard-earned money shopping any place else but [YOUR COMPANY NAME]. We won't be undersold any day of the week. You have my personal guarantee.

Sincerely yours,

[YOUR NAME]
[YOUR TITLE]

[ITEM 1] = Describe [YOUR COMPANY NAME]'s main business emphasis and what you are trying to market to [COMPANY]
[ITEM 2] = Name of [YOUR COMPANY NAME] literature enclosed with letter, i.e., "brochure," "catalog," etc.

[DATE]

[Mr./Mrs./Ms./Dr.] [CUSTOMER'S FULL NAME]
[CUSTOMER'S TITLE]
[COMPANY]
[ADDRESS]
[CITY], [STATE] [ZIP CODE]

Dear [Mr./Mrs./Ms./Dr.] [CUSTOMER'S LAST NAME]:

During a recent committee meeting, my colleagues told me, "[YOUR FIRST NAME], people don't care about service like they used to. They just want the best price." I don't believe them. I want service when I shop.

And, I bet you still do too, and maybe you're willing to pay a little more to be treated with respect. If you have ever been slighted by a waiter or forced to run after a salesperson in a department store to take your money, you know what I mean.

So, [YOUR COMPANY NAME]'s prices are a little—not much—higher. Don't you deserve first class service? Isn't there comfort in knowing that the extra money you pay means that you'll never be disappointed? Browse through the enclosed [ITEM 1] highlighting our [ITEM 2] products.

If my colleagues are right, you'll do that because it doesn't cost anything. I need your help to prove them wrong about service not being important too. Call us today with your order, and thank you for being the type of person who does not settle for second best.

Sincerely yours,

[YOUR NAME]
[YOUR TITLE

[ITEM 1] = Name of [YOUR COMPANY NAME] literature enclosed with letter, i.e., "brochure," "catalog," etc.
[ITEM 2] = Describe [YOUR COMPANY NAME]'s main business emphasis and what you are trying to market to [COMPANY]

[DATE]

[Mr./Mrs./Ms./Dr.] [CUSTOMER'S FULL NAME]
[CUSTOMER'S TITLE]
[COMPANY]
[ADDRESS]
[CITY], [STATE] [ZIP CODE]

Dear [Mr./Mrs./Ms./Dr.] [CUSTOMER'S LAST NAME]:

Trade shows bring on information overload. They are an excellent way to view the latest and greatest under one roof. The problem is remembering who was showing what when you get back in the office. However, I remember our conversation and thank you for taking time to stop by [YOUR COMPANY NAME]'s showcase.

Having strolled the floor myself, I realize that our company has spawned a host of imitators. Therefore, I have outlined a few ways in which our [ITEM 1] is unlike the others. The benefits our customers get include: [ITEM 2].

Don't settle for imitations. This quick overview of [YOUR COMPANY NAME]'s business should be sufficient to pique your curiosity about what lies behind our trade show exhibit. Sheer floor space limits our ability to tell all. Again, thanks for stopping by. I look forward to speaking with you soon. In the interim, I have enclosed our [ITEM 3] just in case yours got lost in the trade show brochure bag.

Sincerely yours,

[YOUR NAME]
[YOUR TITLE]

[ITEM 1] = Describe [YOUR COMPANY NAME]'s main business emphasis and what you are trying to market to [COMPANY]
[ITEM 2] = Describe the main features and benefits of [ITEM 1] and [YOUR COMPANY NAME]
[ITEM 3] = Name of [YOUR COMPANY NAME] literature enclosed with letter, i.e., "brochure," "catalog," etc.

CUSTOMER \ Invitation
Company-Sponsored Event

[DATE]

[Mr./Mrs./Ms./Dr.] [CUSTOMER'S FULL NAME]
[CUSTOMER'S TITLE]
[COMPANY]
[ADDRESS]
[CITY], [STATE] [ZIP CODE]

Dear [Mr./Mrs./Ms./Dr.] [CUSTOMER'S LAST NAME]:

Isn't it time you took a break? While listening to the radio or reading the paper, you may have become aware of an exciting event coming to town. In getting the news out about [ITEM 1], the media occasionally neglect to mention the sponsors making this calendar item possible.

[YOUR COMPANY NAME] is proud to be a corporate sponsor of [ITEM 1] on [ITEM 2] at [ITEM 3]. We invite you to be our special guest at this event, and it is my honor to arrange your guest passes. Knowing how hard you work, I suspect that this will be a welcome break in your daily routine. Just reach for your telephone and tell me you'll be there, and it'll be a done deal.

Sincerely yours,

[YOUR NAME]
[YOUR TITLE]

[ITEM 1] = Name of event
[ITEM 2] = Date of event
[ITEM 3] = Specific location of [ITEM 1]

[DATE]

[Mr./Mrs./Ms./Dr.] [CUSTOMER'S FULL NAME]
[CUSTOMER'S TITLE]
[COMPANY]
[ADDRESS]
[CITY], [STATE] [ZIP CODE]

Dear [Mr./Mrs./Ms./Dr.] [CUSTOMER'S LAST NAME]:

I looked at the calendar recently and thought, "Has it been that long?" For what seems like both a minute and year, we have been working toward this special day. Visions changed quickly, and now the grand opening of [YOUR COMPANY NAME]'s [ITEM 1] is a reality.

We extend this personal invitation to a special few. Please join our celebration on [ITEM 2] from [ITEM 3] to [ITEM 4] at [ITEM 5]. It's our way of thanking our clients and friends for their encouragement and support. If for only five minutes, please stop by and allow the entire family of [YOUR COMPANY NAME] professionals to express our appreciation in person. It would be our honor.

Sincerely yours,

[YOUR NAME]
[YOUR TITLE]

[ITEM 1] = Describe what is being opened, i.e., "new offices," "another location," or "remodeled store"
[ITEM 2] = Date of grand opening
[ITEM 3] = Time grand opening begins
[ITEM 4] = Time grand opening ends
[ITEM 5] = Location of grand opening

[DATE]

[Mr./Mrs./Ms./Dr.] [CUSTOMER'S FULL NAME]
[CUSTOMER'S TITLE]
[COMPANY]
[ADDRESS]
[CITY], [STATE] [ZIP CODE]

Dear [Mr./Mrs./Ms./Dr.] [CUSTOMER'S LAST NAME]:

Customer opinion is the pulse of the marketplace. It is imperative that the leaders of [YOUR COMPANY NAME] maintain close contact with our most vital asset, our customers. In-person briefings give top customers, like [COMPANY], an inside look at our company, too.

For this reason, you are among the valued customers who are being invited to meet our [ITEM 1], [ITEM 2], who has a long history of understanding both company and customer priorities. [ITEM 3] would like the opportunity to discuss the needs and offerings of our respective organizations.

As you can imagine, [ITEM 2]'s position requires that meetings be scheduled in advance. Therefore, I will be phoning with some suggested times. [COMPANY] is one of our esteemed corporate assets serving as the heartbeat of our operations. Your presence and opinions are important to us.

Sincerely yours,

[YOUR NAME]
[YOUR TITLE]

[ITEM 1] = Title of [ITEM 2]
[ITEM 2] = First and last name of [YOUR COMPANY NAME]'s executive
[ITEM 3] = Pronoun referring to [ITEM 2]'s gender, i.e., "He" or "She"

[DATE]

[Mr./Mrs./Ms./Dr.] [CUSTOMER'S FULL NAME]
[CUSTOMER'S TITLE]
[COMPANY]
[ADDRESS]
[CITY], [STATE] [ZIP CODE]

Dear [Mr./Mrs./Ms./Dr.] [CUSTOMER'S LAST NAME]:

We blink our eyes about 84,000,000 times every year. Because it happens so fast, we see just about everything that falls within our field of vision. However, there are many more facets to [YOUR COMPANY NAME] than meet the eye.

From the highest executive ranks to the invaluable operational staff, we are separately and collectively proud of our efficient corporation. On [ITEM 1] beginning at [ITEM 2], we are opening the doors to our most treasured customers.

I hope you will accept our invitation and share our vision. Please R.S.V.P. by [ITEM 3] no later than [ITEM 4]. We want you to see us up close and personal.

Sincerely yours,

[YOUR NAME]
[YOUR TITLE]

[ITEM 1] = Date of open house
[ITEM 2] = Time open house begins
[ITEM 3] = Describe how and who to contact to R.S.V.P.
[ITEM 4] = Date person receiving letter should [ITEM 3] by

[DATE]

[Mr./Mrs./Ms./Dr.] [CUSTOMER'S FULL NAME]
[CUSTOMER'S TITLE]
[COMPANY]
[ADDRESS]
[CITY], [STATE] [ZIP CODE]

Dear [Mr./Mrs./Ms./Dr.] [CUSTOMER'S LAST NAME]:

Do we ever reach a point in our lives when there is nothing new to learn? Absolutely not; we do, indeed, learn something new every day. Although [ITEM 1]'s story is not a complete secret, a wide range of fallacies and facts have been described in articles, advertisements, and rumors.

Having the right information is key to decision making. To provide this, we are hosting an exciting seminar on [ITEM 2] from [ITEM 3] to [ITEM 4] at [ITEM 5]. Any person interested in [ITEM 1] must learn how to distinguish the valid from the unsubstantiated claims.

Although the seminar carries a $[ITEM 6] charge, one cannot put a price on intellectual power. Rather than simply reading about [ITEM 1], take the first step today to increase your knowledge. Call [ITEM 7] and reserve your place among the decision makers who want the facts. You'll be glad you did.

Sincerely yours,

[YOUR NAME]
[YOUR TITLE]

[ITEM 1] = Topic of the seminar
[ITEM 2] = Date of the seminar
[ITEM 3] = Time seminar begins
[ITEM 4] = Time seminar ends
[ITEM 5] = Location of seminar
[ITEM 6] = Price of seminar
[ITEM 7] = Telephone number to reserve a seat at seminar

[DATE]

[Mr./Mrs./Ms./Dr.] [CUSTOMER'S FULL NAME]
[CUSTOMER'S TITLE]
[COMPANY]
[ADDRESS]
[CITY], [STATE] [ZIP CODE]

Dear [Mr./Mrs./Ms./Dr.] [CUSTOMER'S LAST NAME]:

When entering foreign territory, it's natural for a person to proceed cautiously. We've all learned to test the water before jumping in with both feet. The temperature has to be just right, or at the very least comfortable, to avoid assaulting our senses.

After giving it some thought, I believe this must be the reason [COMPANY] has not given our other superior products a chance. You simply want to be sure [COMPANY] is satisfied with its initial purchases. It's a completely natural thing to do.

Now that you are, I would like to point out some complementary products offered by [YOUR COMPANY NAME]. Have you ever considered how [ITEM 1] would be beneficial to your operations? Or what about [ITEM 2]? This is merely a small sampling of [YOUR COMPANY NAME]'s portfolio. Enclosed is [ITEM 3] for your browsing pleasure, and additional information is a phone call away. So dive in and take a look; [YOUR COMPANY NAME] has already proven that the water is absolutely perfect!

Sincerely yours,

[YOUR NAME]
[YOUR TITLE]

[ITEM 1] = Name of a [YOUR COMPANY NAME] product
[ITEM 2] = Name of a [YOUR COMPANY NAME] product different from [ITEM 1]
[ITEM 3] = Name of [YOUR COMPANY NAME] literature enclosed with letter, i.e., "brochure," "catalog," etc.

[DATE]

[Mr./Mrs./Ms./Dr.] [CUSTOMER'S FULL NAME]
[CUSTOMER'S TITLE]
[COMPANY]
[ADDRESS]
[CITY], [STATE] [ZIP CODE]

Dear [Mr./Mrs./Ms./Dr.] [CUSTOMER'S LAST NAME]:

When I was a child, I sometimes had trouble mastering things others picked up with ease. I remember always offering an excuse when I dropped the ball or received a low test score. One day all that changed when my father sat me down on his knee and in a burly tone said, "An excuse is just a statement you make when you know you could have done better."

Today, many years later, I am reminded of his wisdom as I offer no excuse for missing our meeting. I have chastised myself repeatedly for such a display of unprofessionalism. There is no reason good enough, and to give one would be an insult to your intelligence.

I only hope this has not reflected poorly on me or our company. Please accept my apologies and know I would like another chance to set a convenient time for us to meet. Thank you for understanding. You have my promise that this will never happen again.

Sincerely yours,

[YOUR NAME]
[YOUR TITLE]

[DATE]

[Mr./Mrs./Ms./Dr.] [CUSTOMER'S FULL NAME]
[CUSTOMER'S TITLE]
[COMPANY]
[ADDRESS]
[CITY], [STATE] [ZIP CODE]

Dear [Mr./Mrs./Ms./Dr.] [CUSTOMER'S LAST NAME]:

Time is a precious commodity. Every tick of the clock marks another moment spent either fruitfully or frivolously. Considering how valuable your time is, I plan not to waste any of it.

It would be in your best interest if we waited until the appropriate resources were available for our meeting regarding [ITEM 1]. The information we will discuss is still being gathered, and I do not want to present you with half the story. Therefore, I find it necessary to postpone the meeting scheduled on [ITEM 2] at [ITEM 3].

Given an additional [ITEM 4], we can give [COMPANY] all the attention it deserves. I apologize for any inconvenience and hope that this notice is sufficient to allow you to reschedule the time. Thank you for understanding. I want our time together to be spent wisely.

Sincerely yours,

[YOUR NAME]
[YOUR TITLE]

[ITEM 1] = Topic of meeting
[ITEM 2] = Date of meeting
[ITEM 3] = Time of meeting
[ITEM 4] = Amount of time needed before meeting occurs

[DATE]

[Mr./Mrs./Ms./Dr.] [CUSTOMER'S FULL NAME]
[CUSTOMER'S TITLE]
[COMPANY]
[ADDRESS]
[CITY], [STATE] [ZIP CODE]

Dear [Mr./Mrs./Ms./Dr.] [CUSTOMER'S LAST NAME]:

Professionals can spend as much as half of every day in meetings. Sometimes it feels as if we live in the conference room. And, that doesn't count the time we spend preparing for those meetings.

I have worked hard to ensure that our meeting on [ITEM 1] at [ITEM 2] will be 100 percent effective. I have structured the agenda to provide optimum efficiency by presenting as much information about [ITEM 3] as possible in the time allotted. This is one meeting you should not miss. I look forward to showing you my formula for success.

Sincerely yours,

[YOUR NAME]
[YOUR TITLE]

[ITEM 1] = Date of meeting
[ITEM 2] = Time of meeting
[ITEM 3] = Topic of meeting

[DATE]

[Mr./Mrs./Ms./Dr.] [CUSTOMER'S FULL NAME]
[CUSTOMER'S TITLE]
[COMPANY]
[ADDRESS]
[CITY], [STATE] [ZIP CODE]

Dear [Mr./Mrs./Ms./Dr.] [CUSTOMER'S LAST NAME]:

Each of us is the product of our experiences. We travel different routes that mold who we are and what we become. No matter where we have been, I believe we all have something to contribute to others' lives.

While my name may be foreign to you, our language is the same and our backgrounds are similar. I have traveled highways that have taken me into businesses just like [COMPANY]; I have experiences that you can learn from. My record shows a strong commitment to keeping customers ahead in the race for success.

In one short meeting, I would like to show you a map that could put [COMPANY] on the road to cost containment and prosperity. I hope you accept the phone call that will open new channels of information.

Sincerely yours,

[YOUR NAME]
[YOUR TITLE]

[DATE]

[Mr./Mrs./Ms./Dr.] [CUSTOMER'S FULL NAME]
[CUSTOMER'S TITLE]
[COMPANY]
[ADDRESS]
[CITY], [STATE] [ZIP CODE]

Dear [Mr./Mrs./Ms./Dr.] [CUSTOMER'S LAST NAME]:

When ideas are exchanged freely, different interpretations are a likely result. This seems especially true in dynamic and thought-provoking meetings like the one we had on [ITEM 1]. At times, I found myself not taking notes for fear of missing the next comment.

My understanding of our discussion regarding [ITEM 2] is as follows: [ITEM 3].

I want to feel confident that we came away from the meeting with the same conclusions. Take a look and let me know if you see anything that might lead us in the wrong direction. Thank you in advance for the feedback.

Sincerely yours,

[YOUR NAME]
[YOUR TITLE]

———————————————————————

[ITEM 1] = Date of meeting
[ITEM 2] = Topic of meeting
[ITEM 3] = Describe the results of the meeting

[DATE]

[Mr./Mrs./Ms./Dr.] [CUSTOMER'S FULL NAME]
[CUSTOMER'S TITLE]
[COMPANY]
[ADDRESS]
[CITY], [STATE] [ZIP CODE]

Dear [Mr./Mrs./Ms./Dr.] [CUSTOMER'S LAST NAME]:

There is absolutely no reason to leave anything to chance. A little extra effort now decreases the chance that an error will occur later. My unwillingness to take unnecessary chances means that I must take direct responsibility for all my customer orders.

Therefore, I am confirming your order for [ITEM 1] placed on [ITEM 2]. [YOUR COMPANY NAME] expects this order to be received by [COMPANY] no later than [ITEM 3] from today's date.

After double-checking with our department managers, I do not anticipate any changes that would delay the shipment. It has been a pleasure serving you. I look forward to working with [COMPANY] again to meet your [ITEM 4] needs.

Sincerely yours,

[YOUR NAME]
[YOUR TITLE]

─────────────◆─────────────

[ITEM 1] = Describe the order
[ITEM 2] = Date order was placed
[ITEM 3] = Number of days from the date the letter is sent [COMPANY] will receive order
[ITEM 4] = General noun referring to [ITEM 1], i.e., "advertising," "equipment," or "supplies"

[DATE]

[Mr./Mrs./Ms./Dr.] [CUSTOMER'S FULL NAME]
[CUSTOMER'S TITLE]
[COMPANY]
[ADDRESS]
[CITY], [STATE] [ZIP CODE]

Dear [Mr./Mrs./Ms./Dr.] [CUSTOMER'S LAST NAME]:

Imagine getting absorbed in an action-packed novel only to discover that it was missing a few chapters? The story would lack the continuity and flow needed to create an engaging plot. [YOUR COMPANY NAME]'s order form does not lend much creativity, but it does provide the whole story.

[COMPANY]'s order placed on [ITEM 1] for [ITEM 2] is missing a few character sketches. Specifically, we need to know [ITEM 3].

For your convenience, just [ITEM 4] the information to our order department. We want to have the required materials in your hands as soon as possible. Only then will every chapter be complete, allowing us to reach the end of this story and start a new one.

Sincerely yours,

[YOUR NAME]
[YOUR TITLE]

[ITEM 1] = Date order was placed
[ITEM 2] = Describe what the order was for
[ITEM 3] = Describe the information needed to complete order
[ITEM 4] = Manner in which the information can be sent to [YOUR COMPANY NAME], i.e., "fax," "mail,"
  or "telephone"

[DATE]

[Mr./Mrs./Ms./Dr.] [CUSTOMER'S FULL NAME]
[CUSTOMER'S TITLE]
[COMPANY]
[ADDRESS]
[CITY], [STATE] [ZIP CODE]

Dear [Mr./Mrs./Ms./Dr.] [CUSTOMER'S LAST NAME]:

Have you ever gone to the grocery store for just a handful of things and returned with more than one full grocery bag? If you're like most people, you frequently spend more than you plan to. Based on [COMPANY]'s recent order activity, it may be time to raise your credit with [YOUR COMPANY NAME].

[COMPANY]'s order placed on [ITEM 1], for [ITEM 2], exceeded the $[ITEM 3] charge authorization level on your account by $[ITEM 4]. The easiest and quickest way to work around this problem is to remit $[ITEM 5] immediately.

In no time at all, the order will be on its way. I would, however, like to prevent any future inconvenience. I recommend updating your credit profile so our accounting department can evaluate the possibility of increasing your credit line. The application can be processed when [COMPANY]'s outstanding balance is $[ITEM 6]. Please let me know as soon as possible what you would like us to do. We want smooth sailing now and in the future.

Sincerely yours,

[YOUR NAME]
[YOUR TITLE]

[ITEM 1] = Date order was placed
[ITEM 2] = Describe what the order was for
[ITEM 3] = Dollar amount of [COMPANY]'s maximum allowable credit
[ITEM 4] = Dollar amount [COMPANY] is over [ITEM 3]
[ITEM 5] = Dollar amount [COMPANY] must pay to resume credit privileges
[ITEM 6] = Dollar amount of [COMPANY]'s outstanding balance that [YOUR COMPANY NAME] wants
      before considering an increase in [ITEM 3]

[DATE]

[Mr./Mrs./Ms./Dr.] [CUSTOMER'S FULL NAME]
[CUSTOMER'S TITLE]
[COMPANY]
[ADDRESS]
[CITY], [STATE] [ZIP CODE]

Dear [Mr./Mrs./Ms./Dr.] [CUSTOMER'S LAST NAME]:

Surprises have no place in business. Whether a handshake or a contract seals a deal, unanticipated events lower credibility. Once that's gone, the odds of a beneficial affiliation are slim.

[YOUR COMPANY NAME] takes pride in being the most trusted name in the [ITEM 1] business. Therefore, any order requiring product substitution is handled promptly and directly. We wouldn't want you to think you ordered X and were mistakenly sent Y.

[ITEM 2], recently ordered by [COMPANY], is currently unavailable. However, [ITEM 3], which we recommend as a substitute, has been very well received by customers. The price difference of $[ITEM 4] can be handled by [ITEM 5]. While we are confident that you will find [ITEM 3] acceptable, we require your confirmation before shipping. Just call [ITEM 6], and we'll handle the rest. This way when your order arrives, there won't be any surprises.

Sincerely yours,

[YOUR NAME]
[YOUR TITLE]

[ITEM 1] = Describe [YOUR COMPANY NAME]'s major business emphasis
[ITEM 2] = Describe what the order was for
[ITEM 3] = Describe the replacement
[ITEM 4] = Dollar amount of price difference between [ITEM 2] and [ITEM 3]
[ITEM 5] = Actions [COMPANY] should take to receive [ITEM 3]
[ITEM 6] = Telephone number at [YOUR COMPANY NAME] to handle replacement

[DATE]

[Mr./Mrs./Ms./Dr.] [CUSTOMER'S FULL NAME]
[CUSTOMER'S TITLE]
[COMPANY]
[ADDRESS]
[CITY], [STATE] [ZIP CODE]

Dear [Mr./Mrs./Ms./Dr.] [CUSTOMER'S LAST NAME]:

Does it ever seem to you that identification numbers control our world? We have driver's license, social security, telephone, and credit card numbers. Recently, [YOUR COMPANY NAME] tried to process [COMPANY]'s order for [ITEM 1], and there was a slight problem with the credit card number you provided.

Because it's so easy to transpose numbers, please take a moment to confirm the following:

Name on the Account: [ITEM 2]
Issuer: [ITEM 3]
Credit Card Number: [ITEM 4]
Expiration Date: [ITEM 5]

If we have made an error or you would like us to charge another credit card, please telephone [ITEM 6] at your earliest convenience. That's all it takes to speed [ITEM 1] on its way to [COMPANY]. Thank you for helping us serve you.

Sincerely yours,

[YOUR NAME]
[YOUR TITLE]

[ITEM 1] = Name of product order
[ITEM 2] = Name provided for [COMPANY]'s credit card
[ITEM 3] = Issuer of [COMPANY]'s credit card
[ITEM 4] = Number provided for [COMPANY]'s credit card
[ITEM 5] = Expiration date provided for [COMPANY]'s credit card
[ITEM 6] = First and last name of person to call at [YOUR COMPANY NAME] with the telephone number

[DATE]

[Mr./Mrs./Ms./Dr.] [CUSTOMER'S FULL NAME]
[CUSTOMER'S TITLE]
[COMPANY]
[ADDRESS]
[CITY], [STATE] [ZIP CODE]

Dear [Mr./Mrs./Ms./Dr.] [CUSTOMER'S LAST NAME]:

   Textbook budgeting theories are difficult to implement in business. Especially in a growth company like [COMPANY], emergency expenditures can create havoc in money management. Although I am not positive, I suspect that this may be happening at your company.

   The [COMPANY] check [YOUR COMPANY NAME] received as payment for [ITEM 1] was returned to us by the bank on [ITEM 2] because of insufficient funds. For your records, the draft posing the problem is check number [ITEM 3], in the amount of $[ITEM 4], written on [ITEM 5].

   Based on [COMPANY]'s previous professional practices, I assume that maintaining an honorable reputation is just as important to you as it is to us. We want to put this embarrassing situation behind us and move forward in our business relationship. Before this can happen, however, [YOUR COMPANY NAME] must have $[ITEM 4] by [ITEM 6]. Thank you, and please remember that if there are extenuating circumstances, we will work with you.

Sincerely yours,

[YOUR NAME]
[YOUR TITLE]

[ITEM 1] = Describe what the check was for
[ITEM 2] = Date [YOUR COMPANY NAME] received check back
[ITEM 3] = Number on [COMPANY]'s check
[ITEM 4] = Amount of [COMPANY]'s check
[ITEM 5] = Date the check was written
[ITEM 6] = Date [COMPANY] must resubmit payment to [YOUR COMPANY NAME]

[DATE]

[Mr./Mrs./Ms./Dr.] [CUSTOMER'S FULL NAME]
[CUSTOMER'S TITLE]
[COMPANY]
[ADDRESS]
[CITY], [STATE] [ZIP CODE]

Dear [Mr./Mrs./Ms./Dr.] [CUSTOMER'S LAST NAME]:

Several prominent psychologists contend that our signatures reveal things about our personalities. Fine-tuned letters reflect a precise character; extending lines mark an extrovert. Unfortunately, even if we wanted to, we would be unable to analyze your personality on the check sent as payment for [ITEM 1].

The check was received without the required signature. Therefore, [YOUR COMPANY NAME] is sending the check back to you. We expect a replacement, properly completed and signed, within the next [ITEM 2] business days. [YOUR COMPANY NAME] assumes this was an oversight rather than a reflection of [COMPANY]'s true character. Thank you for your prompt attention in this matter.

Sincerely yours,

[YOUR NAME]
[YOUR TITLE]

[ITEM 1] = Describe the check's purpose
[ITEM 2] = Date by which [COMPANY] must resubmit check to [YOUR COMPANY NAME]

[DATE]

[Mr./Mrs./Ms./Dr.] [CUSTOMER'S FULL NAME]
[CUSTOMER'S TITLE]
[COMPANY]
[ADDRESS]
[CITY], [STATE] [ZIP CODE]

Dear [Mr./Mrs./Ms./Dr.] [CUSTOMER'S LAST NAME]:

An error is not a mistake unless it's not corrected. As a well-respected company, [YOUR COMPANY NAME] appreciates opportunities to correct its infrequent errors. We know you follow similar leadership principles.

Unfortunately, the last payment on [COMPANY]'s account was $[ITEM 1] short of the outstanding balance. To prevent finance charges from accruing on the account, please remit $[ITEM 1] no later than [ITEM 2]. Should there be any questions, please do not hesitate to contact us. It will take just a moment to review [COMPANY]'s account activity.

We look forward to the speedy remittance of the outstanding balance. Thank you in advance for your professional handling of this matter. [YOUR COMPANY NAME] assumes that this is merely an oversight.

Sincerely yours,

[YOUR NAME]
[YOUR TITLE]

[ITEM 1] = Dollar amount payment was short
[ITEM 2] = Date by which [COMPANY] must resubmit payment to [YOUR COMPANY NAME]

[DATE]

[Mr./Mrs./Ms./Dr.] [CUSTOMER'S FULL NAME]
[CUSTOMER'S TITLE]
[COMPANY]
[ADDRESS]
[CITY], [STATE] [ZIP CODE]

Dear [Mr./Mrs./Ms./Dr.] [CUSTOMER'S LAST NAME]:

Throughout the world, budding artists study technique in the towns where renowned masters lived and worked. However, some of today's students are doing much more than painting. They are creating Monets, da Vincis, Picassos, and Van Goghs in a fraction of the time it took the artists to create the originals.

By studying brushstrokes with a magnifying glass, today's artists can produce reproductions that create havoc in the art market. Aging techniques are applied to further increase the apparent authenticity of the counterfeits. The results are copies even the experts have trouble identifying.

[YOUR COMPANY NAME] is the leader in [ITEM 1]; we regularly receive awards for our continuing excellence. Our best honors do not adorn our office walls, however; they are our repeat customers.

Don't be swayed by second-rate reproductions. If you have any questions about our works, I would be happy to show you some critical reviews and provide a magnifying glass with which you can make your own examination. No other company even comes close to [YOUR COMPANY NAME]. We're number one now and will remain so for many years to come.

Sincerely yours,

[YOUR NAME]
[YOUR TITLE]

————————————◆————————————

[ITEM 1] =Describe [YOUR COMPANY NAME]'s main business emphasis and what you are trying to market to [COMPANY] that has competition

[DATE]

[Mr./Mrs./Ms./Dr.] [CUSTOMER'S FULL NAME]
[CUSTOMER'S TITLE]
[COMPANY]
[ADDRESS]
[CITY], [STATE] [ZIP CODE]

Dear [Mr./Mrs./Ms./Dr.] [CUSTOMER'S LAST NAME]:

It's easy to say, "plan for the future or be doomed to live in the past." Forecasting customer needs in today's dynamic marketplace is a complex science. While we know that [ITEM 1]'s quality and price are superior, the volume of customer orders surprised us and exceeded our in-stock supply.

Moving quickly, we have taken every action possible to limit any inconvenience to our customers. It is our intention to complete your order for [ITEM 1] by [ITEM 2].

[YOUR COMPANY NAME] is confident that our future forecasts, now based on past success, will be more accurate. Thank you for your understanding and making our success possible with your ongoing support. We plan to continue being the undisputed leader in [ITEM 3], but now we are smarter and better than ever before.

Sincerely yours,

[YOUR NAME]
[YOUR TITLE]

[ITEM 1] = Name of product ordered
[ITEM 2] = Date [YOUR COMPANY NAME] plans to ship [ITEM 1]
[ITEM 3] = Describe [YOUR COMPANY NAME]'s main business emphasis

[DATE]

[Mr./Mrs./Ms./Dr.] [CUSTOMER'S FULL NAME]
[CUSTOMER'S TITLE]
[COMPANY]
[ADDRESS]
[CITY], [STATE] [ZIP CODE]

Dear [Mr./ Mrs./Ms./Dr.] [CUSTOMER'S LAST NAME]:

A company that catches its errors is just about as perfect as a company can be. Even [YOUR COMPANY NAME]'s commitment to total quality management has not made us faultless. Our routine checks found an error in the invoice for [COMPANY]'s recent purchase of [ITEM 1].

The [ITEM 2] on invoice number [ITEM 3] should have been [ITEM 4], not [ITEM 5]. To correct this mistake, we ask you to call [ITEM 6] at the earliest convenience. Thank you for your patience and cooperation in this matter. No one can declare perfection in every arena; we can only continue to strive for it. The only things that [YOUR COMPANY NAME] can guarantee are honesty and customer satisfaction.

Sincerely yours,

[YOUR NAME]
[YOUR TITLE]

[ITEM 1] = Describe purchase(s) invoice represents
[ITEM 2] = Describe the place where error is on invoice
[ITEM 3] = Number on invoice used for tracking purposes
[ITEM 4] = Describe the correction for [ITEM 2]
[ITEM 5] = Describe the error in detail
[ITEM 6] = First and last name of [YOUR COMPANY NAME]'s credit representative

[DATE]

[Mr./Mrs./Ms./Dr.] [CUSTOMER'S FULL NAME]
[CUSTOMER'S TITLE]
[COMPANY]
[ADDRESS]
[CITY], [STATE] [ZIP CODE]

Dear [Mr./Mrs./Ms./Dr.] [CUSTOMER'S LAST NAME]:

Accept no substitutes. These words reverberate through my mind as I recall the last [YOUR COMPANY NAME] product meeting. Management did not have to think long about what to do with orders for [ITEM 1].

Selling an inferior product definitely was out of the question. Continuing to be straightforward with our customers was the only answer. Therefore, I regret to report that [COMPANY]'s order for [ITEM 1], placed on [ITEM 2], cannot be filled at this time.

We all wish [YOUR COMPANY NAME] could change manufacturing's decision. Until there is a product comparable in quality and price, all we can do is be honest and do everything we can to uphold our reputation. I appreciate these characteristics in my business dealings. [YOUR COMPANY NAME] hopes you do too. Thank you for understanding. When we do find another [ITEM 1], you'll be the first to receive a telephone call.

Sincerely yours,

[YOUR NAME]
[YOUR TITLE]

[ITEM 1] = Describe the unavailable product
[ITEM 2] = Date [COMPANY] placed order for [ITEM 1]

[DATE]

[Mr./Mrs./Ms./Dr.] [CUSTOMER'S FULL NAME]
[CUSTOMER'S TITLE]
[COMPANY]
[ADDRESS]
[CITY], [STATE] [ZIP CODE]

Dear [Mr./Mrs./Ms./Dr.] [CUSTOMER'S LAST NAME]:

Would it help if I reminded you that these are inflationary times and the economy is tricky? Surely, [COMPANY] is feeling the pinch as much as [YOUR COMPANY NAME]. You know that, although sales may be increasing, profit margins are not keeping up.

In the past, we have done a fine job of shielding customers from economic concerns. Costs are rising at an unprecedented rate, however, leaving [YOUR COMPANY NAME] no alternative but to raise the price of [ITEM 1] by [ITEM 2].

Unlike other companies, we won't cut corners on product quality. [YOUR COMPANY NAME] never settles for second best, and we know you don't either. Thank you for understanding that this is not our choice; it is the economy's upper hand.

Sincerely yours,

[YOUR NAME]
[YOUR TITLE]

———————————————————————◆———————————————————————

[ITEM 1] = Describe product/service with price increase
[ITEM 2] = Dollar amount or percentage of price increase

[DATE]

[Mr./Mrs./Ms./Dr.] [CUSTOMER'S FULL NAME]
[CUSTOMER'S TITLE]
[COMPANY]
[ADDRESS]
[CITY], [STATE] [ZIP CODE]

Dear [Mr./Mrs./Ms./Dr.] [CUSTOMER'S LAST NAME]:

Our company's golden rule is simple: treat every customer with the same dignity and respect you would expect if you were the customer. Once a year, we randomly select customers from our files and ask them to tell us how we are doing. This equips our organization to meet the most significant of standards—our customers' standards.

Using a 1 to 10 rating scale, where 1 represents total disagreement and 10 total accord, please answer the seven questions below. Your answers will give us insight into our own operations. When completed, simply drop this letter in the mail using the enclosed self-addressed, stamped envelope.

1. Your staff is always pleasant and helpful.   _____
2. Promised delivery schedules are adhered.   _____
3. Your products are superior in performance and quality.   _____
4. Your pricing is competitive.   _____
5. It's easy to buy from your company.   _____
6. Your company is responsive to our needs.   _____
7. We plan to be your customer in the future.   _____

In tallying the results, we may contact you for additional information that will help us heed our golden rule. Thank you for taking the time to help us learn how to serve you better.

Sincerely yours,

[YOUR NAME]
[YOUR TITLE]

[DATE]

[Mr./Mrs./Ms./Dr.] [CUSTOMER'S FULL NAME]
[CUSTOMER'S TITLE]
[COMPANY]
[ADDRESS]
[CITY], [STATE] [ZIP CODE]

Dear [Mr./Mrs./Ms./Dr.] [CUSTOMER'S LAST NAME]:

You probably thought that we had forgotten about you, that your business could not be all that important to a big company like [YOUR COMPANY NAME]. I have news for you; you and your business are important to us. There must be a good reason to explain why [COMPANY] has not purchased from us for some time.

I work hard at customer relationships, and when one ends, I take it personally. I know I shouldn't, but I can't help it. Would you please take a moment to answer a few questions?

1. What is the main reason you haven't ordered from us?

_____

2. What could we have done differently in handling your account?

_____

3. On a scale of 1 to 10, where 1 is the lowest possible score and 10 the highest, please rate the followings:

    The courtesy and knowledge of our staff.   _____
    The overall customer service efforts.   _____
    The competitive pricing of our products.   _____
    The quality of our operations.   _____

4. What can we do to welcome you back as our customer?

_____

Just drop this letter in the mail using the enclosed self-addressed, stamped envelope. You have my promise that your answers will be held in strictest confidence. Thank you for your time. Your ideas and responses will help us learn how to serve you better.

Sincerely yours,

[YOUR NAME]
[YOUR TITLE]

[DATE]

[Mr./Mrs./Ms./Dr.] [CUSTOMER'S FULL NAME]
[CUSTOMER'S TITLE]
[COMPANY]
[ADDRESS]
[CITY], [STATE] [ZIP CODE]

Dear [Mr./Mrs./Ms./Dr.] [CUSTOMER'S LAST NAME]:

Walking into any trade show, you see them positioned in the doorways. They are the people holding program directories and looking through the index to find a particular company. On the trade show floor, companies are often overshadowed by the banners, booths, crowds, and general hoopla.

Shows such as the one you recently attended, the [ITEM 1] on [ITEM 2], offer a panoramic view. We hope you'll help us make our next public appearance more beneficial by answering a few short questions.

1. What booth impressed you most at the trade show?

_____

2. Why did you stop there?

_____

3. What do you remember about our booth?

_____

4. Which of the products you saw impressed you most?

_____

Please return this letter in the enclosed self-addressed, stamped envelope. Thank you for your valuable help in placing our booth in a class by itself. We want every visitor to seek out [YOUR COMPANY NAME]'s company showcase first and last.

Sincerely yours,

[YOUR NAME]
[YOUR TITLE]

———————————————◆◆———————————————

[ITEM 1] = Name of trade show
[ITEM 2] = Date [ITEM 1] was held

[DATE]

[Mr./Mrs./Ms./Dr.] [CUSTOMER'S FULL NAME]
[CUSTOMER'S TITLE]
[COMPANY]
[ADDRESS]
[CITY], [STATE] [ZIP CODE]

Dear [Mr./Mrs./Ms./Dr.] [CUSTOMER'S LAST NAME]:

There is a big difference between market intelligence and market research. Getting the facts through market research is only half the job; market intelligence is putting them to good use. Thank you for giving us the whole picture as we continually strive to evaluate and improve our performance.

Your cooperation and participation in our recent customer survey yielded valuable insight. We do not underestimate the value of the objective views shared by [COMPANY]. Frankly, your honesty helps us improve our operations for all of our customers. There appears to be no limit to either intelligence or ignorance in our lives; either can make or break any situation. Thank you again for your assistance in helping us grow smarter.

Sincerely yours,

[YOUR NAME]
[YOUR TITLE]

[DATE]

[Mr./Mrs./Ms./Dr.] [CUSTOMER'S FULL NAME]
[CUSTOMER'S TITLE]
[COMPANY]
[ADDRESS]
[CITY], [STATE] [ZIP CODE]

Dear [Mr./Mrs./Ms./Dr.] [CUSTOMER'S LAST NAME]:

Some people believe life would be easier if we all had the same likes and dislikes. Communication would be all but unnecessary, and marketing a snap. But we are all different. Communication sometimes breaks down, mass marketing sometimes fails to do its job, and merchandise is occasionally returned.

We recently received [ITEM 1], which apparently did not meet [COMPANY]'s requirements. Therefore, we are posting to your account a credit for $[ITEM 2], the amount paid.

Please accept our apologies for your apparent lack of satisfaction with this one product. Although we try to give our customers the best of all worlds, uniqueness challenges these efforts. [YOUR COMPANY NAME] looks forward to having the opportunity to fulfill other [COMPANY] needs.

Sincerely yours,

[YOUR NAME]
[YOUR TITLE]

[ITEM 1] = Name of product returned
[ITEM 2] = Amount [COMPANY] paid for [ITEM 1]

[DATE]

[Mr./Mrs./Ms./Dr.] [CUSTOMER'S FULL NAME]
[CUSTOMER'S TITLE]
[COMPANY]
[ADDRESS]
[CITY], [STATE] [ZIP CODE]

Dear [Mr./Mrs./Ms./Dr.] [CUSTOMER'S LAST NAME]:

Because business needs do not come in shrink-wrapped boxes, every product is not exactly right for everyone. We do our best to achieve general appeal in satisfying a wide range of requirements. However, I understand that the [ITEM 1] purchased from us does not meet [COMPANY]'s criteria.

After giving this situation much thought, I have concluded that a viable alternative is [ITEM 2]. To complete the exchange, all [COMPANY] must do is [ITEM 3].

I am confident you will be pleased with the exchange offered. Thank you for giving us another chance.

Sincerely yours,

[YOUR NAME]
[YOUR TITLE]

———————————————◆———————————————

[ITEM 1] = Name of product purchased
[ITEM 2] = Describe the exchange offered
[ITEM 3] = Describe the actions necessary to perform exchange

[DATE]

[Mr./Mrs./Ms./Dr.] [CUSTOMER'S FULL NAME]
[CUSTOMER'S TITLE]
[COMPANY]
[ADDRESS]
[CITY], [STATE] [ZIP CODE]

Dear [Mr./Mrs./Ms./Dr.] [CUSTOMER'S LAST NAME]:

Most of us learn early that life offers few guarantees. No matter how much good faith and judgment we use in our decision making, we learn that change is inescapable. As a business, we recognize this and attempt to make life more manageable by offering a pledge of 100 percent customer satisfaction.

We honor our customer commitment with a money-back guarantee and stand behind this promise concerning your return of [ITEM 1]. Many praise this product, but we recognize that individual needs differ. Therefore, a complete refund has been processed for [COMPANY] and is [ITEM 2].

We trust this action proves to [COMPANY] that there is at least one thing guaranteed in life and one company that truly understands the meaning of customer satisfaction. Hopefully, your faith has been restored, and our faithful adherence to our commitment will allow you to purchase from us again in the future.

Sincerely yours,

[YOUR NAME]
[YOUR TITLE]

[ITEM 1] = Name of product returned
[ITEM 2] = Describe where the refund is or has been posted

[DATE]

[Mr./Mrs./Ms./Dr.] [CUSTOMER'S FULL NAME]
[CUSTOMER'S TITLE]
[COMPANY]
[ADDRESS]
[CITY], [STATE] [ZIP CODE]

Dear [Mr./Mrs./Ms./Dr.] [CUSTOMER'S LAST NAME]:

Not too long ago, businesses tracked activities quite reliably with pen and paper. Computer automation has made all that paperwork seem antiquated. Interestingly, most packages sent throughout the world now carry electronic bar codes that include the package's destination and the date it was shipped.

[YOUR COMPANY NAME] has spent a great deal of time and effort checking and double-checking our computer system and our receiving department's records for any sign of [COMPANY]'s return of [ITEM 1]. So far, nothing has turned up, leading us to believe that the goods have not been received. We have no alternative but to direct the search back to you in hopes that the missing goods may turn up elsewhere.

Contrary to popular belief, the fastest way to get between two points is not always a straight line. The key is finding where the line bent to the left or right. Thank you in advance for helping us come to a quick resolution of this matter.

Sincerely yours,

[YOUR NAME]
[YOUR TITLE]

[ITEM 1] = Name of product supposedly returned

[DATE]

[Mr./Mrs./Ms./Dr.] [CUSTOMER'S FULL NAME]
[CUSTOMER'S TITLE]
[COMPANY]
[ADDRESS]
[CITY], [STATE] [ZIP CODE]

Dear [Mr./Mrs./Ms./Dr.] [CUSTOMER'S LAST NAME]:

Every spring and summer, workers the world over pick fruits and vegetables. Great care is given to selecting only the best quality from the crop. Then, when the produce arrives in the market, consumers' hands put it to still another test, choosing only those fruits and vegetables that have survived the trip from the orchard or field in good condition.

[YOUR COMPANY NAME] prides itself on maintaining the highest total quality management controls. It's so rare for a bruised apple to pass by the inspector and make its way into a customer's order that frankly, I am appalled. Therefore, I have enclosed a complete refund in the amount of $[ITEM 1].

In our [ITEM 2] years of doing business, we have planted the seeds season after season to ensure bountiful crops. Please accept our apologies for an order that was less than what we both strive for. That is, the best for our respective companies and families.

Sincerely yours,

[YOUR NAME]
[YOUR TITLE]

[ITEM 1] = Dollar amount of refund
[ITEM 2] = Number of years [YOUR COMPANY NAME] has been in business

[DATE]

[Mr./Mrs./Ms./Dr.] [CUSTOMER'S FULL NAME]
[CUSTOMER'S TITLE]
[COMPANY]
[ADDRESS]
[CITY], [STATE] [ZIP CODE]

Dear [Mr./Mrs./Ms./Dr.] [CUSTOMER'S LAST NAME]:

We think you'll agree that life would be chaos without rules. Imagine a football game or an airport without them. Clearly, it would be an unpleasant sight.

Similarly, [YOUR COMPANY NAME] abides by rules that guide operations for optimum customer relations and team efficiency. We encourage customers to read the return policy statement found in our [ITEM 1]. When both sides know the rules, potential misunderstandings can be eliminated.

We recently received a [ITEM 2] from [COMPANY]. Unfortunately, this return is not in compliance with our policy, because [ITEM 3]. Therefore, [YOUR COMPANY NAME] cannot provide any credit for the returned goods. If you have any questions or additional information regarding the matter, do not hesitate to contact me. Instant answers are a telephone call away.

Sincerely yours,

[YOUR NAME]
[YOUR TITLE]

––––––––––––––––––––––⬩––––––––––––––––––––––

[ITEM 1] = Name of [YOUR COMPANY NAME] literature in which return policies are located, i.e., "catalog," "contract," etc.
[ITEM 2] = Name of product returned
[ITEM 3] = Describe in detail why return is not acceptable

[DATE]

[Mr./Mrs./Ms./Dr.] [CUSTOMER'S FULL NAME]
[CUSTOMER'S TITLE]
[COMPANY]
[ADDRESS]
[CITY], [STATE] [ZIP CODE]

Dear [Mr./Mrs./Ms./Dr.] [CUSTOMER'S LAST NAME]:

The exigencies of personal and professional growth sometimes require that we leave the familiar behind. I remember, for example, the anxiety and excitement with which I approached adulthood. The possibilities were limited only by my desire to excel in unfamiliar areas.

As I quickly learned, employers play a significant role in our growth. I have spent much time deciding whether [YOUR COMPANY NAME] is complementary to the attainment of my professional goals. It has not been an easy choice, especially given the knowledge that my path may no longer cross the paths of the customers who have become my friends.

Still, I am accepting the challenge to move forward. [YOUR COMPANY NAME] has a very talented staff, and I am confident that [COMPANY] is in good hands. Because ethics are important to me, I do not feel comfortable detailing the new venture until everything is settled. [ITEM 1], thank you for being my customer and friend. I hope our relationship does not end with my new beginning. I'll be in touch soon.

Sincerely yours,

[YOUR NAME]
[YOUR TITLE]

───────────────◆───────────────

[ITEM 1] = First name of person receiving letter

[DATE]

[Mr./Mrs./Ms./Dr.] [CUSTOMER'S FULL NAME]
[CUSTOMER'S TITLE]
[COMPANY]
[ADDRESS]
[CITY], [STATE] [ZIP CODE]

Dear [Mr./Mrs./Ms./Dr.] [CUSTOMER'S LAST NAME]:

My adrenaline pumps when I do a job well. Thank you for sharing your time at the meeting regarding [ITEM 1]. We accomplished a great deal, and I look forward to moving ahead with the knowledge gleaned.

Although I envision a clear path, a few immediate steps must be taken first. I am planning to [ITEM 2]. Your participation in the project is essential, so I hope you don't mind if I keep you advised of any developments. Again, I express my thanks for the opportunity to work with you in making my professional career more fulfilling. I'm in business to help your business succeed.

Sincerely yours,

[YOUR NAME]
[YOUR TITLE]

[ITEM 1] = Describe the subject of the meeting
[ITEM 2] = Describe your next actions as they relate to [ITEM 1]

[DATE]

[Mr./Mrs./Ms./Dr.] [CUSTOMER'S FULL NAME]
[CUSTOMER'S TITLE]
[COMPANY]
[ADDRESS]
[CITY], [STATE] [ZIP CODE]

Dear [Mr./Mrs./Ms./Dr.] [CUSTOMER'S LAST NAME]:

Fewer than 20 percent of the diamonds mined annually reach gem status. Cut and polished by expert hands, diamonds take on worth based on their color, clarity, cut, and weight. I like to think that [YOUR COMPANY NAME] is one of the most valuable business resources a company can have.

Your order for [ITEM 1] confirmed that we are handling your account with care and competence. If there is anything I can do, please remember that you are my customer. [ITEM 2], thank you for trusting me to keep your best interest in mind. When you are successful, I am too. After all, the best diamonds reflect the most light.

Sincerely yours,

[YOUR NAME]
[YOUR TITLE]

———————————————◆———————————————

[ITEM 1] = Describe what the order was for
[ITEM 2] = First name of person receiving letter

[DATE]

[Mr./Mrs./Ms./Dr.] [CUSTOMER'S FULL NAME]
[CUSTOMER'S TITLE]
[COMPANY]
[ADDRESS]
[CITY], [STATE] [ZIP CODE]

Dear [Mr./Mrs./Ms./Dr.] [CUSTOMER'S LAST NAME]:

Have you ever noticed the camaraderie among NBA players on the basketball court? In the spirit of competition, players applaud their teammates; it doesn't matter whether they are watching a winning basket or a missed free throw. The effort expended is worthy of support and recognition.

I believe this example parallels our teamwork over the past [ITEM 1]. Your endorsement of my efforts, during both good and bad times, is appreciated and extends beyond mere reinforcement. More important, it increases my desire for us to be the winning team.

Medals and plaques are unimportant to me. A higher accolade is simply knowing I am a valued player on the court of your business life. Thank you for supporting my efforts and allowing us to become friends and teammates.

Sincerely yours,

[YOUR NAME]
[YOUR TITLE]

[ITEM 1] = Length of time you have known person receiving letter

[DATE]

[Mr./Mrs./Ms./Dr.] [CUSTOMER'S FULL NAME]
[CUSTOMER'S TITLE]
[COMPANY]
[ADDRESS]
[CITY], [STATE] [ZIP CODE]

Dear [Mr./Mrs./Ms./Dr.] [CUSTOMER'S LAST NAME]:

People are justifiably tired of marketing claims and want real-life examples. Who is better able to tell a vendor's story than a current customer? Thank you for your willingness to share [COMPANY]'s favorable experiences.

Your credible professional endorsement regarding our [ITEM 1] was a definite push in the right direction. While it's too soon to predict the outcome, there was no confusion regarding which company [ITEM 2] should buy from. [ITEM 3], thank you for your assistance. I can't tell you how much I appreciate your support of my goals.

Sincerely yours,

[YOUR NAME]
[YOUR TITLE]

[ITEM 1] = Describe [YOUR COMPANY NAME]'s main business emphasis and what you are trying to market to [ITEM 2]
[ITEM 2] = Name of company [YOUR COMPANY NAME] referred to [COMPANY] for an endorsement
[ITEM 3] = First name of person receiving letter

[DATE]

[Mr./Mrs./Ms./Dr.] [CUSTOMER'S FULL NAME]
[CUSTOMER'S TITLE]
[COMPANY]
[ADDRESS]
[CITY], [STATE] [ZIP CODE]

Dear [Mr./Mrs./Ms./Dr.] [CUSTOMER'S LAST NAME]:

If we hang around long enough, trends make a complete circle. While the 80s offered fast-track promises, the 90s have seen an upsurge in conservative ideals. As ethics and integrity assume renewed importance, promptness has also taken on increased significance.

Whether in internal or external company endeavors, we know that consistent and dependable actions inspire confidence. To have this reciprocated by our customers through prompt payments is the highest honor. It leads us to believe that the conservative ideals on which not only [YOUR COMPANY NAME], but our great nation, were founded are appreciated by [COMPANY].

Thank you for upholding admirable principles at a time when so many have become lax in observing the tenets that past generations esteemed most.

Sincerely yours,

[YOUR NAME]
[YOUR TITLE]

[DATE]

[Mr./Mrs./Ms./Dr.] [CUSTOMER'S FULL NAME]
[CUSTOMER'S TITLE]
[COMPANY]
[ADDRESS]
[CITY], [STATE] [ZIP CODE]

Dear [Mr./Mrs./Ms./Dr.] [CUSTOMER'S LAST NAME]:

In politics, private opinions influence public polls. Individual judgments based on experiences, education, and environment combine to produce the will of the masses on election day. Contrary to popular belief, one person's individual vote can affect the outcome of a political candidate's campaign.

I appreciate your personal endorsement and vote of confidence in my career as demonstrated in your referral of [ITEM 1] as a prospective customer. This fine example of private opinion going public serves to reinforce my stand on professional issues. I will let you know how my first meeting with [ITEM 1] at the "primary" turns out. Thank you for casting your vote in the right direction.

Sincerely yours,

[YOUR NAME]
[YOUR TITLE]

———————————————◆———————————————

[ITEM 1] = Name of company that [COMPANY] told to call you

[DATE]

[Mr./Mrs./Ms./Dr.] [CUSTOMER'S FULL NAME]
[CUSTOMER'S TITLE]
[COMPANY]
[ADDRESS]
[CITY], [STATE] [ZIP CODE]

Dear [Mr./Mrs./Ms./Dr.] [CUSTOMER'S LAST NAME]:

Budget consciousness has prompted many companies to make cosmetic changes. Approaching business in this trendy way rarely affects bottom-line performance in the long term. A penny saved here today could cost a dollar there tomorrow.

We want to help [COMPANY] protect the significant investment made when it purchased [ITEM 1]. Certainly, [COMPANY] is planning to benefit from [ITEM 1] for more than the [ITEM 2] covered by the warranty. Therefore, we recommend an extended warranty agreement that lengthens the standard warranty period by [ITEM 3].

An extended warranty protects [COMPANY]'s investment. I will phone to set a time to discuss this additional customer-oriented opportunity with you. It is a budgetary line item well worth its cost. Let me present real dollar examples that make sense.

Sincerely yours,

[YOUR NAME]
[YOUR TITLE]

[ITEM 1] = Name of product
[ITEM 2] = Length of existing warranty
[ITEM 3] = Length of extended warranty

[DATE]

[Mr./Mrs./Ms./Dr.] [CUSTOMER'S FULL NAME]
[CUSTOMER'S TITLE]
[COMPANY]
[ADDRESS]
[CITY], [STATE] [ZIP CODE]

Dear [Mr./Mrs./Ms./Dr.] [CUSTOMER'S LAST NAME]:

Be it in a community, personal, or professional situation, rules meet and create challenges simultaneously. In providing direction, they are not always universally accepted, but rules are an indispensable part of life.

Upon hearing of your problem with [ITEM 1], I spent the better part of today going over our policies and looking for a way to get around our warranty procedures. I know how conscientious you are, and I anticipated your questions. You probably read our warranty coverage agreement and realized that the required repairs on [ITEM 1] fall outside the provisions of the agreement. Unfortunately, I could not uncover a way to abate the estimated repair cost of $[ITEM 2].

At times like this, I wish I could bend the rules for a valuable customer like [COMPANY]. We will get started immediately after receiving your telephone call authorizing the necessary repairs. Thank you for your understanding in this matter.

Sincerely yours,

[YOUR NAME]
[YOUR TITLE]

[ITEM 1] = Name of product needing repair
[ITEM 2] = Dollar amount of repair for [ITEM 1]

[DATE]

[Mr./Mrs./Ms./Dr.] [CUSTOMER'S FULL NAME]
[CUSTOMER'S TITLE]
[COMPANY]
[ADDRESS]
[CITY], [STATE] [ZIP CODE]

Dear [Mr./Mrs./Ms./Dr.] [CUSTOMER'S LAST NAME]:

All successful businesses speak the same language. The identifying accents are best built on action rather than words alone. Today, we are deluged by satisfaction and quality promises in company propaganda and sales literature.

Therefore, performance is the only way a company can differentiate itself from its competition. Our commitment to customer satisfaction and quality is tangible. We prove it by informing [COMPANY] that the problem with [ITEM 1] is covered by a warranty.

The warranty exemplifies our commitment to you, the customer. We expect to have the problem fixed at the earliest possible date and will phone when working order is restored. [YOUR COMPANY NAME] is flattered that its promises are imitated. We hope you now realize that we are never equaled.

Sincerely yours,

[YOUR NAME]
[YOUR TITLE]

[ITEM 1] = Name of product needing repair

SECTION 3

Interoffice Correspondence

No company is free from interoffice politics. Written communications must recognize this fact very tactfully. People's livelihoods and egos, both precious entities, are inextricably linked with their careers. Saying the wrong thing or forgetting this fact can be detrimental to both employers and employees. Recognition of professional worth enhances efficiency when employees and management cooperate.

Higher Ranking Thinking.   Your interoffice correspondence exemplifies your commitment to the organization. High-level managers use, and enjoy seeing, memos written from this perspective. If you are on this level, congratulations; this book should make your job easier. If you are not, your memos may be giving management the wrong impression.

The hardest memos to write are typically requests that may jeopardize your position or stature in the organization. There is no need to fret any longer; these are written for you. Like all letters, interoffice memorandums require a fair amount of diplomacy and compassion. Memos should never be demanding or condescending. A happy worker is a good worker.

Company Lingo.   Executives are alike. We have families. We want a career. We need to make money. We are encouraged by recognition. Don't lose sight of this fact; use the corporate lingo. Certain words are prevalent in annual reports, employee handbooks, and motivational seminars. We hear about accomplishment, excellence, goal setting, networking, objectives, partnering, strategies, and tactics.

These words have entered our daily vocabulary from corporate hallways. Employees must display these ideals to the company, and the company must do the same for the employees. In this section, proper protocol, based on Fortune 500 company guidelines, is exemplified in every memorandum.

Memos for Every Purpose.   We should write more interoffice memorandums to limit interoffice miscommunication and confusion. Yes, more rather than fewer, contrary to popular belief. Passing someone in the hall and yelling the report due date is not very effective or professional.

The basis of any efficient organization is contained in this section. Written announcements, leave requests, policies, procedures, and reprimands promote structure. Current issues, such as AIDS, benefit reductions, discrimination, and sexual harassment, are addressed as well. Memos covering every imaginable topic are only pages away.

Team Spirit.   "All for one and one for all" is a common philosophy in businesses of all sizes. The players have to know the rules so they can play the game properly. Employee relations is a very important factor in a company's success. Unity brings strength. Ensure maximum efficiency through effective interoffice communication. These memos will make it easier for you.

INTEROFFICE MEMORANDUM

TO: All Staff   FROM: [YOUR NAME]

                                                [YOUR TITLE]

DATE: [DATE]   cc: [COPIES TO]

SUBJECT: Reputation for Excellence Confirmed as [YOUR COMPANY NAME] Receives Award

Think of the last time you watched a sports event, perhaps a baseball or football game. Dig a bit deeper into your memory, and you can't help noticing a few characteristics exhibited by the winning team. I'm talking about the team's coordination, determination, and commitment to excellence.

Even though a single player threw the winning pass or hit a home run, that one play alone didn't make the game a success. Every team member played an integral role and brought a different talent to the field, enabling all to reach the ultimate goal. Because of your individual contributions to our company and our team, [YOUR COMPANY NAME] was recognized by [ITEM 1] for [ITEM 2] and received their prestigious [ITEM 3] award.

Thank you for your winning attitude every game, every day. With your support, we can do it again!

––––––––––––––––––◆––––––––––––––––––

[ITEM 1] = Name of organization that gave award
[ITEM 2] = Describe the reason for award
[ITEM 3] = Name of award

INTEROFFICE MEMORANDUM

TO: All Staff   FROM: [YOUR NAME]

                                     [YOUR TITLE]

DATE: [DATE]   cc: [COPIES TO]

SUBJECT: Combining Companies for Maximum Reach

Throughout history, advancements have been attributed to the vision of individuals looking beyond what the consensus deemed acceptable. Futurists saw a need for change, set goals in their minds, and ignored the bantering and negative opinions of others. Whether exploring uncharted territory or finding a cure for a devastating disease, great men and women have always embraced change and recognized potential.

Foresight has enabled [YOUR COMPANY NAME] to accomplish our goal of being a strong company equipped for long-term growth. As market conditions become more competitive and economically driven, this vision must be realigned. [YOUR COMPANY NAME] has determined that our goals will be best met by combining resources with the well-respected [ITEM 1].

For the merger to be successful, we must work together. I ask each of you to promise one thing. That is, challenge yourself to move out of your comfort zone and welcome this change as an opportunity. A bit of initial uncertainty is unavoidable. Be strong and stand by our company in creating the greatest opportunity of all time. You have my promise that the new territory we are about to explore is full of prosperity.

[ITEM 1] = Name of organization being merged with [YOUR COMPANY NAME]

INTEROFFICE MEMORANDUM

TO: All Staff   FROM: [YOUR NAME]

                                        [YOUR TITLE]

DATE: [DATE]   cc: [COPIES TO]

SUBJECT: Welcome Our Newest Employee, [ITEM 1

It's hard being the new kid on the block. While getting coffee or walking through the office, you may have noticed a fresh face. Go up and introduce yourself to our new employee, [ITEM 1], who is a [ITEM 2] working with us to [ITEM 3].

[ITEM 4] is a valuable addition to [YOUR COMPANY NAME], bringing many skills and talents to better our operation. I am confident each of you will agree as opportunities arise to work together. Today, please take a moment from your busy schedule to welcome [ITEM 4] to our company.

[ITEM 1] = First and last name of person hired
[ITEM 2] = Title of person hired
[ITEM 3] = Job function of person hired
[ITEM 4] = First name of person hired

INTEROFFICE MEMORANDUM

TO: All Staff   FROM: [YOUR NAME]

                                            [YOUR TITLE]

DATE: [DATE]   cc: [COPIES TO]

SUBJECT: [ITEM 1]'s Achievements Recognized with Promotion

It gives me great pleasure to acknowledge [ITEM 1]'s dedication and hard work with a promotion and change in responsibilities to [ITEM 2]. In this new position, [ITEM 3] will be directing our [ITEM 4] efforts and is the primary contact for related projects and questions. As in the past, I am sure you will find [ITEM 3] a truly gifted and innovative individual eager to help and to promote our company's growth.

———————————————————————

[ITEM 1] = First and last name of person promoted
[ITEM 2] = Title of person promoted
[ITEM 3] = First name of person promoted
[ITEM 4] = Departmental functions of person promoted

INTEROFFICE MEMORANDUM

TO: All Staff   FROM: [YOUR NAME]

                                      [YOUR TITLE]

DATE: [DATE]   cc: [COPIES TO]

SUBJECT: Never-To-Be-Forgotten [ITEM 1] Is Retiring

It's going to be difficult not seeing [ITEM 1]'s face each day. For [ITEM 2] years, [ITEM 3] has been pursuing new challenges with fierce determination. [ITEM 4] has been a valuable addition to our company. To say simply we'll miss [ITEM 3] is an understatement.

Still, [ITEM 3] is saying goodbye to us for a world without pressure, fixed routines, or pending deadlines. Let's all extend our warmest congratulations and wishes to [ITEM 4] for much health and happiness in the years ahead.

———————————◆———————————

[ITEM 1] = First and last name of person retiring
[ITEM 2] = Number of years employed
[ITEM 3] = Pronoun referring to retired person's gender, i.e., "he," "she," "him," or "her"
[ITEM 4] = First name of person retiring

INTEROFFICE MEMORANDUM

TO: [ITEM 1]   FROM: [YOUR NAME]

                                     [YOUR TITLE]

DATE: [DATE]   cc: [COPIES TO]

SUBJECT: Expand Your Knowledge of [ITEM 2] at Training Seminar

When we were younger, most of us thought we knew it all. No one had anything to teach us; we had the answers. With maturity, we realize that there are those who are far more knowledgeable in certain areas.

Calling upon the experts saves us energy and time. [YOUR COMPANY NAME] wants to expand our employees' knowledge of [ITEM 2]. This not only sustains operations through increased effectiveness, but more important, improves your long-term professional skills.

On [ITEM 3], we have a training seminar planned from [ITEM 4] to [ITEM 5]. Here, experts will give you information regarding [ITEM 6]. To reserve your place, please contact [ITEM 7].

I hope you will recognize the benefits of this training and seize this opportunity to increase your professional skills. The relationship between accomplishment and knowledge stands the test of time. One is dependent on the other for success.

[ITEM 1] = First and last name of person receiving memo
[ITEM 2] = Focus of training seminar
[ITEM 3] = Date of training seminar
[ITEM 4] = Time the training seminar begins
[ITEM 5] = Time the training seminar ends
[ITEM 6] = List up to five separate points covered in training seminar
[ITEM 7] = First and last name of person responsible for R.S.V.P.'s

INTEROFFICE MEMORANDUM

TO: [ITEM 1]   FROM: [YOUR NAME]

                                               [YOUR TITLE]

DATE: [DATE]   cc: [COPIES TO]

SUBJECT: Apology

     In reaching for the gold, challenging circumstances can bring out the darker side of people. We can become so focused on a single goal that we treat normal everyday tasks as annoying interruptions. Although the [ITEM 2] has been a welcome professional challenge, I recognize that it has caused changes in my normal demeanor.

     Have confidence that my acknowledgment of this atypical behavior will have a positive effect. From this point forward, I promise to pay special attention to meeting the challenge with utmost enthusiasm. Thank you for understanding.

[ITEM 1] = First and last name of person receiving memo
[ITEM 2] = Describe the legitimate new task you have been assigned

INTEROFFICE MEMORANDUM

TO: [ITEM 1]   FROM: [YOUR NAME]

                                                    [YOUR TITLE]

DATE: [DATE]   cc: [COPIES TO]

SUBJECT: Apology

There is good in every bad situation. While I do not claim to be an eternal optimist, my recent poor health has had a few positive effects. Specifically, I have gained a greater appreciation of both my family and my career.

The consideration you have shown in understanding the time constraints placed on me by the healing process is greatly appreciated. Please accept my sincerest apologies for any delay this absence has caused in meeting project goals. It is my hope to resume a regular work schedule by [ITEM 2], or sooner, if I can possibly coerce the doctor into granting permission.

[ITEM 1] = First and last name of person receiving memo
[ITEM 2] = Date by which you estimate to resume regular work schedule

INTEROFFICE MEMORANDUM

TO: [ITEM 1]   FROM: [YOUR NAME]

                                   [YOUR TITLE]

DATE: [DATE]   cc: [COPIES TO]

SUBJECT: Apology

Perfectionism is both a blessing and a curse. My desire for excellence has uncovered areas in the [ITEM 2] report that require additional effort and research. Rather than submitting a report that fails to meet our standards, I intend to continue to devote extra energy to ensuring the information's accuracy and validity.

These steps will require that I spend more time on the task. However, I will do my very best to have the complete [ITEM 2] report in your hands no later than [ITEM 3]. Please accept my apologies for any inconvenience this delay has caused.

[ITEM 1] = First and last name of person receiving memo
[ITEM 2] = Name of project, report, or task
[ITEM 3] = Date by which you will provide report

INTEROFFICE MEMORANDUM

TO: [ITEM 1] FROM: [YOUR NAME]

[YOUR TITLE]

DATE: [DATE] cc: [COPIES TO]

SUBJECT: Apology

There are times in our lives when we make terrible mistakes. Afterwards, we realize that, if somehow given the chance to turn back the clock, our actions would have been different. Mistakes that affect only ourselves are far less important than those that influence others.

I am afraid you are the subject of my error in not attending the [ITEM 2] meeting. No excuse could possibly convey my regret for such a display of unprofessionalism. I extend my sincerest apologies with the hope that this action will not reflect negatively on your opinion of my commitment to [YOUR COMPANY NAME].

If possible, I would like to obtain any information or notes resulting from the meeting. Please know that I have learned from this mistake and promise to maintain the professional standards of our company in the future.

———————————◄ ►———————————

[ITEM 1] = First and last name of person receiving memo
[ITEM 2] = One or two words defining meeting's purpose

INTEROFFICE MEMORANDUM

TO: [ITEM 1]   FROM: [YOUR NAME]

                                          [YOUR TITLE]

DATE: [DATE]   cc: [COPIES TO]

SUBJECT: Apology

Occasionally, leaving our personal life at the door each morning on the way to work is hard. We are taught that professional performance requires a separation of business from home life. It's a good lesson and one I mistakenly believed had been perfected in my career.

Upon realizing that my personal life was affecting my work, I listed various ways to avoid similar situations in the future. The solution is simple. With an action plan in hand, I am confident that a dramatic change is imminent. Please accept my apologies for any concern I might have caused. I have recommited myself to giving nothing less than 110 percent of myself to our company's success. You have my commitment from this day forward.

———————————◆———————————

[ITEM 1] = First and last name of person receiving memo

INTEROFFICE MEMORANDUM

TO: [ITEM 1]   FROM: [YOUR NAME]

                                        [YOUR TITLE]

DATE: [DATE]   cc: [COPIES TO]

SUBJECT: We're Looking for the Employee of the Month

"Passing the buck" was first described by the Mark Twain in 1872. During early American card games, a piece of buckskin was passed from player to player indicating the one who was next in line to deal. The phrase referred only to a shift in duty with no hidden meaning.

Today, passing the buck has a negative connotation that is incompatible with [YOUR COMPANY NAME]'s team spirit. We want our players to help one another strive to meet individual and department goals. Whether through a seemingly small or easily recognizable effort, a day does not go by without someone in our company going the extra mile for everyone's benefit.

We thank those special employees for their inspiring actions every month through our Employee of the Month Award. These people don't believe in passing the buck and regularly perform beyond all expectations in their job descriptions. Their careers encompass more than the duties outlined on a piece of paper.

Soon, you will be receiving a nomination form that will help us select the recipient of [YOUR COMPANY NAME]'s Employee of the Month Award. Winners are given [ITEM 2]. Think about how you could win and put those thoughts into action—not just today but every day. Passing the buck is best left in card games and out of our professional careers.

[ITEM 1] = First and last name of person receiving memo
[ITEM 2] = List what award recipient receives

INTEROFFICE MEMORANDUM

TO: [ITEM 1]   FROM: [YOUR NAME]

                                       [YOUR TITLE]

DATE: [DATE]   cc: [COPIES TO]

SUBJECT: [ITEM 2] Receives Employee of the Month Award

Being average is no longer good enough in this competitive world. Information flows and market conditions change faster than ever before.

To continue meeting [YOUR COMPANY NAME] goals, we are taking a proactive position. Promoting above average performance continues monthly in the recognition of special team members with our Employee of the Month Award. It gives me great pleasure to welcome [ITEM 2] into our [YOUR COMPANY NAME] achiever's hall of fame for the month of [ITEM 3].

Time after time, [ITEM 4] has taken the initiative in promoting the highest standards of team activities. A listing of every contribution [ITEM 2] has made to our company would take many pages. The nominations drew particular attention to [ITEM 4]'s efforts in [ITEM 5].

Join me today in personally congratulating [ITEM 2] for a winning performance. Mediocrity certainly has no place in [ITEM 4] vocabulary!

[ITEM 1] = First and last name of person receiving memo
[ITEM 2] = First and last name of award recipient
[ITEM 3] = Month awarded
[ITEM 4] = Pronoun referring to recipient's gender, i.e., "he" or "she," "his" or "her"
[ITEM 5] = Describe the reason [ITEM 2] won award

INTEROFFICE MEMORANDUM

TO: [ITEM 1]   FROM: [YOUR NAME]

                                             [YOUR TITLE]

DATE: [DATE]   cc: [COPIES TO]

SUBJECT: We're Looking for the Winner of [YOUR COMPANY NAME]'s Motivation Award

Winners accept challenges with determination, perseverance, and stamina. Take the example of the man whose life took the following turns before he reached his goal: he failed at a business, was defeated for the legislature, failed again in business, suffered the loss of a love, had a nervous breakdown, was defeated in an election, was defeated for Congress three times in five years, was defeated for the Senate, was defeated for the office of vice president, and was defeated for the Senate one last time.

Abraham Lincoln's struggle to overcome obstacles continued right up until the time he was elected President of the United States. He serves as an excellent model for success. Today, I announce a search for the best among us—the employees with the winning, often contagious, attitude to make themselves and [YOUR COMPANY NAME] better every day. Winners receive [ITEM 2].

We have so many excellent employees that management alone cannot choose the recipient of [YOUR COMPANY NAME]'s prestigious motivational award. We need your help. Therefore, you will soon receive a nomination form that you can use to vote for a peer who demonstrates presidential drive. Thank you for your daily support, which allows our company to be the success we all want it to be.

[ITEM 1] = First and last name of person receiving memo
[ITEM 2] = List what award recipient receives

INTEROFFICE MEMORANDUM

TO: [ITEM 1]   FROM: [YOUR NAME]
                                                   [YOUR TITLE]

DATE: [DATE]   cc: [COPIES TO]

SUBJECT: [ITEM 2] Receives Motivation Award

People who exhibit both ambition and motivation make things happen. These are people who stand apart from the crowd, who chart their destiny through diligence and a solid commitment to excellence. They are the people who create the standards by which others are judged.

While our organization is full of great people, there can be only one winner of [YOUR COMPANY NAME]'s prestigious motivation award. Your votes have been counted and have reaffirmed to management that we have a winning team. Many of you were nominated.

This [ITEM 3], it gives me great pleasure to recognize [ITEM 2] as a model employee who exhibits the characteristics necessary for success in all facets of the our business. Please join me in this celebration by personally congratulating [ITEM 4] on the honor being bestowed for [ITEM 4] achievements in [ITEM 5].

[ITEM 1] = First and last name of person receiving memo
[ITEM 2] = First and last name of award recipient
[ITEM 3] = Frequency motivation award is given, i.e., "month," "quarter," or "year"
[ITEM 4] = Pronoun referring to recipient's gender, i.e., "him" or "her," "his" or "her"
[ITEM 5] = Describe the reason [ITEM 2] won award

INTEROFFICE MEMORANDUM

TO: [ITEM 1]   FROM: [YOUR NAME]

                                            [YOUR TITLE]

DATE: [DATE]   cc: [COPIES TO]

SUBJECT: We're Looking for the Winning [YOUR COMPANY NAME] Team

There are few professions in which competence alone leads to success. A quarterback needs someone to receive the pass; a director needs an actor to follow his directions. Life is full of interdependent relationships in which cooperative efforts achieve the best results.

Teamwork is an overarching goal of [YOUR COMPANY NAME]. We believe that collective enthusiasm, motivation, and perseverance are the factors that separate success from failure. Among our diverse personnel and responsibilities, there are teams that prove and promote this corporate goal.

Soon, you will receive a nomination form for this year's notable team award. We want to know why your quarterback deserves the Theismann trophy. How your defensive ends support strategic plays. And what your team has done to win the Super Bowl of [YOUR COMPANY NAME] team awards.

Look for this form in your mailbox, and be sure to complete it by the requested date. As their coach, you will be in line for a commendation too. A team is only as good as the coach who counsels, educates, and sponsors the players.

[ITEM 1] = First and last name of person receiving memo

INTEROFFICE MEMORANDUM

TO: [ITEM 1]   FROM: [YOUR NAME]

                                                              [YOUR TITLE]

DATE: [DATE]   cc: [COPIES TO]

SUBJECT: [ITEM 2] Receives Team Award

In unity, there is strength enough to construct a colossus. From the foundation to the ridgepole, the parts reinforce and support one another to create a cathedral that will echo with the sounds of success. [YOUR COMPANY NAME] prospers because of the synergism our employees individually and collectively provide in building solidarity.

Recently, we asked several within our organization to select the team that displays productive fellowship and a unified winning spirit. The results clearly show that teamwork is pervasive throughout the ranks. We had so much difficulty selecting the best partnership that we are contemplating bestowing more than one award in the future.

This year, I am pleased to announce that the winners of [YOUR COMPANY NAME]'s team award are: [ITEM 2]. Their coordination and diligence exemplify the principle that mastery of the whole requires mastery of the parts. Please join me in congratulating every team member for this prestigious recognition of their collective contribution.

[ITEM 1] = First and last name of person receiving memo
[ITEM 2] = First and last names of team members

INTEROFFICE MEMORANDUM

TO: [ITEM 1]   FROM: [YOUR NAME]

                                      [YOUR TITLE]

DATE: [DATE]   cc: [COPIES TO]

SUBJECT: Competition Update

Competition in business sparks progress. Knowing that another organization is pursuing the same goal makes us work harder and smarter. Having [ITEM 2] in our industry, therefore, is not a bad thing.

Their market placement reveals an unstable foundation that is working to our advantage. The key is to expose these facts to our customers in an ethical and professional manner. We never want to appear to be "bad mouthing" the competition.

Making negative comments about competitors inevitably lowers our credibility. When asked about [ITEM 2], keep comments brief and vague while communicating your confidence that our [ITEM 3] is of the finest quality. We have a long-standing reputation and a list of satisfied customers behind us.

Our persistence in maintaining standards for excellence will beat the competition. They are not the last challenge we face, only the most recent. Take [ITEM 2]'s very mention as an invitation to advance professionally by focusing a little more on success.

[ITEM 1] = First and last name of person receiving memo
[ITEM 2] = Name of competitor
[ITEM 3] = Name of your product or service

INTEROFFICE MEMORANDUM

TO: [ITEM 1]   FROM: [YOUR NAME]
                                                    [YOUR TITLE]

DATE: [DATE]   cc: [COPIES TO]

SUBJECT: Reduction in Corporate Earnings

Business enterprise is a work-in-process created by the hands of economic and market conditions. As the form takes shape, differing opinions on the right or wrong placement of angles and shading are inevitable. It takes vision to see the big picture.

Likewise, [YOUR COMPANY NAME] is in a development stage that requires a shift of resources. Our assets are many, yet new and exciting projects require funding. These are adding value to our future while reducing corporate earnings.

It is not uncommon for earnings to decrease as a business assumes the form needed for a prosperous future. We have all the human resources and technological tools needed to be a master in our industry. More time is the only thing required to finish this work of art.

[ITEM 1] = First and last name of person receiving memo

INTEROFFICE MEMORANDUM

TO: [ITEM 1]   FROM: [YOUR NAME]

                                           [YOUR TITLE]

DATE: [DATE]   cc: [COPIES TO]

SUBJECT: Delayed Shipments of [ITEM 2]

Salespeople speak of good times when product demand exceeds supply. Economists worry about unbalanced scales. Manufacturing goes into overdrive, and we must be prepared for the delay.

The volume of customer orders for [ITEM 2] has both positive and negative effects. Communication is the key to handling all aspects of this delay. I would like each of you to take a personal interest in maintaining our corporate customer satisfaction standards.

Check your files and advise those customers with pending orders that we are taking all steps necessary to complete these as quickly as possible. Although it is not feasible to provide a firm date, we anticipate being able to fulfill requests for [ITEM 2] by [ITEM 3]. Please let me know of any disgruntled customer responses to the news, and thank for your assistance in the matter.

———————————————————

[ITEM 1] = First and last name of person receiving memo
[ITEM 2] = Name of product delayed
[ITEM 3] = Date the product orders can be filled

INTEROFFICE MEMORANDUM

TO: [ITEM 1]   FROM: [YOUR NAME]

                                        [YOUR TITLE]

DATE: [DATE]   cc: [COPIES TO]

SUBJECT: [YOUR COMPANY NAME] in the Media

Since the late 1950s, quiz shows have provided high ratings for television producers and networks. Starting with CBS-TV's $64,000 Question, hundreds of contestant-oriented shows promising big dollars for the right answers have worked their way into America's homes. ABC-TV had Twenty-One, and The $64,000 Question had a brother, The $64,000 Challenge.

After Charles Van Doren, a Colombia University professor and member of the acclaimed literary Van Doren family, won $129,000 over six weeks, a scandal broke. Newspapers ran an exposé claiming that the shows were rigged. Contestants were coached on the right answers and how to fake dramatics while puzzling out the correct response.

While television learned a valuable lesson, so did the media. Scandals sell newspapers. Newspaper sales stimulate advertising sales. Advertising sales increase profits. The vicious cycle continues, and today we are the subject of the hype created by the media. Unlike those quiz shows, we have nothing to hide. Our comments and position on [ITEM 2] are forthright and accurate.

Information was taken out of context and interpreted in a way that gave the media what they wanted in the first place—increased sales. There is always a victim in these situations. In the quiz show scandal, many innocent people lost their jobs. Be assured that we are taking all steps necessary to rectify this situation and maintain the fine reputation of our corporation and its employees. We have nothing to hide, and we appreciate your support.

[ITEM 1] = First and last name of person receiving memo
[ITEM 2] = Subject of media coverage

INTEROFFICE MEMORANDUM

TO: [ITEM 1]   FROM: [YOUR NAME]

                                                [YOUR TITLE]

DATE: [DATE]   cc: [COPIES TO]

SUBJECT: Reduction in Work Force

Like our climate, businesses have seasons. We emerge in the spring, celebrate in summer, shed in the fall, and hibernate in winter. And we plant seeds throughout the year to assure growth. However, a single storm can destroy the farmer's harvest. Left are difficult decisions affecting many families.

Directional changes occur during economically challenging times when the crop exceeds the demand. Operations must be streamlined, work forces reduced. Unfortunately, our organization is faced with hardships that require us to make drastic changes if we are to maintain our market presence.

It is with utmost regret that I inform our corporate family that there is no way of returning to springtime favor without a work force reduction. Following extensive analysis and review, we have decided to lay off personnel in the [ITEM 2]. Those directly affected will be advised by their managers on [ITEM 3].

This loss places an additional burden of performance on each of us. We are asking all of you to carry more than your share of the load until the seedlings of corporate development have had a chance to take root. Only then will we be able to reap the rewards of a bountiful crop.

———————————————◆———————————————

[ITEM 1] = First and last name of person receiving memo
[ITEM 2] = Name of the department, division, job title, etc. affected by layoff
[ITEM 3] = Date the people let go will be notified

INTEROFFICE MEMORANDUM

TO: [ITEM 1]   FROM: [YOUR NAME]

                                                      [YOUR TITLE]

DATE: [DATE]   cc: [COPIES TO]

SUBJECT: Benefits Costs Increasing

During these inflationary times, it's hard to believe that ten cents once bought a loaf of bread or made a telephone call. Times have certainly changed, and so has the price of health care. Until health care reform becomes more than a political promise, consumers will have to bear the burden.

Unfortunately, we have been notified that [ITEM 2] has increased its premiums by [ITEM 3] percent effective [ITEM 4]. [YOUR COMPANY NAME] is dedicated to providing a comprehensive benefits program for our employees. Upon hearing the news, management requested an examination of the premium increase.

Health care costs have increased across the board; there was nothing we could do. However, [ITEM 2] is still quite competitive in the health care marketplace, offering a comprehensive, cost-effective plan. There is one thing you can do. Write to your representatives in Congress and let them know how increases in health care costs have affected your life. Like a vote, one voice does make a difference.

[ITEM 1] = First and last name of person receiving memo
[ITEM 2] = Name of health care provider
[ITEM 3] = Amount of the increase in percent
[ITEM 4] = Date the price increase takes effect

INTEROFFICE MEMORANDUM

TO: [ITEM 1]   FROM: [YOUR NAME]

                                        [YOUR TITLE]

DATE: [DATE]   cc: [COPIES TO]

SUBJECT: Benefits Program Canceled

Employers and employees are partners in the truest sense. The good of the organization is dependent on the good of the individual contributors. Believing this, [YOUR COMPANY NAME] willingly carries tremendous responsibilities in assuming the roles of caretaker and provider for our employees and their families.

Notifying our colleagues of unfortunate news is a difficult task. Still, increasing costs during economically troubled times have prohibited the continuation of [YOUR COMPANY NAME]'s benefits program. We have no alternative but to recommend private coverage incurred at each employee's expense.

For more information on alternative benefit plans, please contact [ITEM 2]. Thank you for understanding that we had no choice in this matter. [YOUR COMPANY NAME] hopes to resume companywide benefits programs for our employees when the economic tide turns.

[ITEM 1] = First and last name of person receiving memo
[ITEM 2] = First and last name of person responsible for benefits program

INTEROFFICE MEMORANDUM

TO: [ITEM 1]   FROM: [YOUR NAME]

                                                    [YOUR TITLE]

DATE: [DATE]   cc: [COPIES TO]

SUBJECT: Benefit Forms Completion Request

It has been surmised that if the copy machine had been invented before World War II, no one would have won the conflict. Paper, rather than soldiers, would have filled the bunkers. While paperwork can be irritating, it is often the best mode of communication.

The time is here to complete benefits forms for [ITEM 2], and unfortunately, there is no better way than in writing. You do not have to participate in the program; we provide benefits because [YOUR COMPANY NAME] is committed to improving the lives of its employees.

Take a moment to read the instructions that will help you complete the forms accurately and thoroughly. A little extra effort now simplifies information processing later. And this way, we can cut down just a bit on the paperwork for everyone.

[ITEM 1] = First and last name of person receiving memo
[ITEM 2] = Year the benefits forms cover

INTEROFFICE MEMORANDUM

TO: [ITEM 1]   FROM: [YOUR NAME]

                                                        [YOUR TITLE]

DATE: [DATE]   cc: [COPIES TO]

SUBJECT: Benefits Information Contact

Seeking advice from those without expertise or knowledge is a futile effort. Specialization provides maximum organizational operations. That is why we have dedicated, experienced personnel ready to address any benefits-related questions, comments, or suggestions you may have.

Benefits are more than a plan [YOUR COMPANY NAME] offers to our employees. The entire program demonstrates our total human relations approach, offering employees security in, and out of, the workplace. [ITEM 2] is eager to serve as a resource and assist with the program's implementation. [ITEM 3] can be reached at [ITEM 4]. For benefits answers, this is the place.

[ITEM 1] = First and last name of person receiving memo
[ITEM 2] = First and last name of person responsible for benefits program
[ITEM 3] = First name of [ITEM 2]
[ITEM 4] = Telephone number for [ITEM 3]

INTEROFFICE MEMORANDUM

TO: [ITEM 1]   FROM: [YOUR NAME]

                                                [YOUR TITLE]

DATE: [DATE]   cc: [COPIES TO]

SUBJECT: Regaining a Better Perspective

Thinking of your employer as just a place to pick up a paycheck limits your potential. With the right mental attitude, all things are possible. Belief in one's work and chosen profession are among the factors that separate success from failure.

Lately, your actions and relationships with other [YOUR COMPANY NAME] employees do not reflect a winning attitude. It has made management question whether you are willing to cooperate and build a foundation at our company. We are a close-knit group and need everyone's support.

Think about your future with [YOUR COMPANY NAME], and list a few of your personal and professional goals. I would like to discuss these with you on [ITEM 2] at [ITEM 3] in [ITEM 4]. [ITEM 5], the best rewards in life come when we know we are doing our best. I want to encourage your development toward this goal.

[ITEM 1] = First and last name of person receiving memo
[ITEM 2] = Date of meeting with [ITEM 1] to discuss issue
[ITEM 3] = Time the meeting begins
[ITEM 4] = Place within office where meeting will be held
[ITEM 5] = First name of [ITEM 1]

INTEROFFICE MEMORANDUM

TO: [ITEM 1]   FROM: [YOUR NAME]

                                             [YOUR TITLE]

DATE: [DATE]   cc: [COPIES TO]

SUBJECT: Controlling Expenses

Freedom is a precious gift left to businesses and individuals by our founding fathers. Their efforts laid the foundation for the American Dream that people all over the world strive to achieve. We must, however, have rules if we are to maintain order in our independent lives.

We believe that employee autonomy is crucial to [YOUR COMPANY NAME]'s success. Freedom of thought sparks creative action. Yet even when such latitude is given, we must uphold the establishment's rules.

[YOUR COMPANY NAME] has set limits on expenses to eliminate inappropriate spending. These rules, which apply to all of us, benefit the entire organization. Your recent request for reimbursement for [ITEM 2] falls outside the area of approved expenses because it [ITEM 3].

In the future, you must get management approval prior to incurring expenses of this nature. A simple memo detailing the purpose and estimated cost must be submitted to me beforehand. My intention is not to limit your freedom within our corporation; I simply want to ensure that the rules are followed by everyone.

[ITEM 1] = First and last name of person receiving memo
[ITEM 2] = Describe what the expense was for
[ITEM 3] = Describe the reason expense is excessive

INTEROFFICE MEMORANDUM

TO: [ITEM 1]   FROM: [YOUR NAME]

                                                  [YOUR TITLE]

DATE: [DATE]   cc: [COPIES TO]

SUBJECT: Sick Day Discussion

Our corporate team consists of interlocking links that create the chain of accomplishment. Each link is equally important to the strength of the whole. When just one link is weak, the bond lessens and puts additional pressure on the rest.

We have empathy and understand that your recent health problems are not of your own making. Your job is an important link in our team and one that should not be underestimated. For the entire team to prosper, [YOUR COMPANY NAME] needs your resources and talents each day.

Your [ITEM 2] absences during the past [ITEM 3] fall outside the area of acceptability and place additional loads on the rest of the team. Your peers have willingly handled your duties in addition to their own. Still, this is not fair to them.

Please evaluate your present health situation and advise me in writing by [ITEM 4] of the prognosis and estimated time required for you to resume a regular work schedule. We want to help you regain your position in the team's chain. You are a valuable link.

[ITEM 1] = First and last name of person receiving memo
[ITEM 2] = Total number of sick days taken
[ITEM 3] = Time over which sick days have been taken
[ITEM 4] = Date by which you would like to receive [ITEM 1]'s response

INTEROFFICE MEMORANDUM

TO: [ITEM 1]   FROM: [YOUR NAME]

                                  [YOUR TITLE]

DATE: [DATE]   cc: [COPIES TO]

SUBJECT: Dependability

Principles are the backbone of success. Whether we strive for financial gain or a happy family life, the ethical ground upon which we stand serves as the ultimate foundation. People can give us advice, but we determine our own destinies.

We hear the words confidence, integrity, and respect quite often in life. Professionally, one behavior that impairs our relationships with our co-workers and customers is tardiness.

Frankly, tardiness reflects a lack of concern. Being late tells those who are waiting for you that you don't care enough about them or their time to make the effort needed to be on time. For your professional growth, promptness is a necessary habit.

Setting your watch a few minutes fast works. Some people require only a gentle reminder. Thank you for devoting the necessary energy to acquiring this very important professional attribute. The best way to learn promptness is through practice.

[ITEM 1] = First and last name of person receiving memo

INTEROFFICE MEMORANDUM

TO: [ITEM 1]   FROM: [YOUR NAME]
                                              [YOUR TITLE]

DATE: [DATE]   cc: [COPIES TO]

SUBJECT: Clean Air Benefits Everyone

Despite the warnings printed on every pack of cigarettes sold in the United States, millions of people knowingly risk their health. We know cigarette smoking causes cancer in smokers. We know second-hand smoke is detrimental to nonsmokers too.

To guarantee the best work environment for every [YOUR COMPANY NAME] employee, we have policies that must be followed without exception. One of these is our smoking policy. Among other things, the policy clearly states, "Smoking is prohibited in all public areas excluding designated smoking areas." Here at [YOUR COMPANY NAME], the designated smoking area is [ITEM 2].

Take this note as a friendly reminder that your compliance is obligatory. If you have any questions, please do not hesitate to let me know. Thank you for your support of a healthy work environment for all to enjoy.

———————————◆———————————

[ITEM 1] = First and last name of person receiving memo
[ITEM 2] = Place where designated smoking area is located

INTEROFFICE MEMORANDUM

TO: [ITEM 1]   FROM: [YOUR NAME]

                                                [YOUR TITLE]

DATE: [DATE]   cc: [COPIES TO]

SUBJECT: Excellent Report

A good violin contains about 70 separate pieces of wood. Bit by bit, skilled designers shape the highest-sounding instrument of the modern string family. In the hands of a musician, the violin comes alive from the lowest G chord up nearly four octaves.

A review of the [ITEM 2] report makes it clear that many pieces of supporting documentation were gathered to create a thorough presentation. Handing tools to the designer is one thing; having the work done expertly is another. From beginning to end, the report could not have had a better sound.

Thank you for expending the extra effort required to master form and content. It clearly depicts a proficiency in business skills that will enhance your future with [YOUR COMPANY NAME].

[ITEM 1] = First and last name of person receiving memo
[ITEM 2] = Name of the report

INTEROFFICE MEMORANDUM

TO: [ITEM 1]   FROM: [YOUR NAME]

                                              [YOUR TITLE]

DATE: [DATE]   cc: [COPIES TO]

SUBJECT: Outstanding Performance

    "Citius, Altius, Fortius!" This Latin phrase is the Olympic motto, meaning in modern English, "Swifter, Higher, Stronger!" Every four years, athletes from around the globe meet with this phrase ringing in their ears.

    Winners need internal fortitude. The desire for success must drown out any thought of failure. Your performance on [ITEM 2] truly deserves the gold medal.

    In going beyond the call of duty, you displayed the most admirable of professional attributes. It is [YOUR COMPANY NAME]'s pleasure to have you on our Olympic team. Thank you for being a role model, for proving that success is there for the taking when desire is strong.

[ITEM 1] = First and last name of person receiving memo
[ITEM 2] = Reason for the recognition

INTEROFFICE MEMORANDUM

TO: [ITEM 1]   FROM: [YOUR NAME]

                                         [YOUR TITLE]

DATE: [DATE]   cc: [COPIES TO]

SUBJECT: Improved Performance

      The wise person sees constructive criticism as a way to tap into another's experience to better his or her own. Taking advice and putting it into action is a true test of character. We must trust, however, that the person making the recommendations has our best interest in mind.

      I am pleased that you welcomed my appraisal of [ITEM 2] and did not perceive it as a personal or professional attack. You took the initiative and action that resulted in positive growth. Most important, your improvement reflects the commitment I believe you have to yourself, our team, and [YOUR COMPANY NAME]. [ITEM 3], thank you for making the recommended changes and for your continuing support of our business practices.

———————————◆———————————

[ITEM 1] = First and last name of person receiving memo
[ITEM 2] = Problem brought to [ITEM 1]'s attention
[ITEM 3] = First name of [ITEM 1]

INTEROFFICE MEMORANDUM

TO: [ITEM 1]   FROM: [YOUR NAME]
                                                   [YOUR TITLE]

DATE: [DATE]   cc: [COPIES TO]

SUBJECT: New Sale at [ITEM 2]

On the narrow decks of aircraft carriers, pilots routinely land their jet-powered planes with incredible precision. The only thing stopping the jet's 100 mile per hour approach are steel cables across the deck. These landings are considered to be among the most difficult in aviation.

The pilots use a combination of expertise, knowledge, and skill to defy gravity. One wrong move could end in destruction.

Similarly, your handling of the [ITEM 2] account took great diligence and skill. Maneuvering through the sales cycle with such excellence is quite an accomplishment. You are a "Top Gun" in our company, where the sky is truly the limit. Congratulations on your success!

———————————————◆———————————————

[ITEM 1] = First and last name of person receiving memo
[ITEM 2] = Name of the customer

INTEROFFICE MEMORANDUM

TO: [ITEM 1]   FROM: [YOUR NAME]

                                        [YOUR TITLE]

DATE: [DATE]   cc: [COPIES TO]

SUBJECT: The Death of [ITEM 2]

When the ties of friendship and camaraderie are severed abruptly, faith and strength lighten the load of our pain. Grief can be the greatest of teachers, allowing us to have more compassion for our fellow man. Death rekindles in us the very essence and importance of life sometimes left behind in our youth.

We were lucky to have had [ITEM 2] touch us and be part of our lives. [ITEM 3] laughter and smile remain now as we bow our heads in sorrow. [ITEM 4] will remain with us for many years to come in our thoughts and words. If you would like to send your condolences to [ITEM 4]'s family, let me know.

I am sure the family would appreciate knowing how much we miss their loved one. And take a moment today to reflect on what is important in your life. To say we were wronged by so-and-so or this person has more than I do is trivial in loss's pain. While we cannot quickly overcome the grief we feel, perhaps we can learn to cherish our life a little more every day.

[ITEM 1] = First and last name of person receiving memo
[ITEM 2] = First and last name of person who died
[ITEM 3] = Pronoun referring to deceased person's gender, i.e., "his" or "her"
[ITEM 4] = First name of person who died

INTEROFFICE MEMORANDUM

TO: [ITEM 1]   FROM: [YOUR NAME]

                                                  [YOUR TITLE]

DATE: [DATE]   cc: [COPIES TO]

SUBJECT: Our Deepest Sympathies

As night's darkness is followed by dawn, sorrow is followed by comfort. Please know that your [YOUR COMPANY NAME] family extends its deepest, most heartfelt sympathies on the death of your beloved [ITEM 2].

There is not one among us who has not suffered the trauma of a death sometime in our lives. Most have found comfort in paying the ultimate homage to a person who was dear to them. This is to take the characteristics we cherished the most in the departed loved one and pass them on for the benefit of others. If there is anything we can do to lessen your pain, remember we are here to help.

———————————————◆———————————————

[ITEM 1] = First and last name of person receiving memo
[ITEM 2] = Relationship of person who died, i.e., "brother," "child," "father," "mother," "sister," etc.

INTEROFFICE MEMORANDUM

TO: [ITEM 1]   FROM: [YOUR NAME]

                                          [YOUR TITLE]

DATE: [DATE]   cc: [COPIES TO]

SUBJECT: [ITEM 2]'s Health and Our Support

Who among us has not heard that giving to others in time of need is mankind's responsibility? Neither art nor science can possibly replace the understanding human heart and touch. When a comrade falls ill, fellowship helps keep his or her face turned toward sunshine instead clouds.

As many know, our friend and co-worker, [ITEM 2], has been taken ill and will require a lengthy recuperation period. It is our individual responsibility to let [ITEM 3] know we care about [ITEM 4] welfare. While we cannot prescribe a magical cure, there is one important thing each of us can do as our share of the healing process.

A moment is all it takes to extend compassion, whether through a card, a telephone call, a basket of flowers, or a home-cooked meal. Take time from your busy schedule today to do something for [ITEM 3]. There are inevitable rewards in unselfish actions.

----◆----

[ITEM 1] = First and last name of person receiving memo
[ITEM 2] = First and last name of person ill
[ITEM 3] = First name of [ITEM 2]
[ITEM 4] = Pronoun referring to [ITEM 1]'s gender, i.e., "his" or "her"

INTEROFFICE MEMORANDUM

TO: [ITEM 1]   FROM: [YOUR NAME]

                [YOUR TITLE]

DATE: [DATE]   cc: [COPIES TO]

SUBJECT: Community Work Excellence

After the accountants leave, our greatness is not measured by wealth. What counts are our contributions and our willingness to help others. I am delighted to hear of your work with [ITEM 2].

Many talk, but few are willing to dedicate themselves to charitable tasks that will benefit humanity. I am sure the subjects of your hard work are appreciative, and [YOUR COMPANY NAME] respects employees who participate in worthwhile programs. The competitive world in which we spend so much of our time often causes us to lose sight of our true purpose on earth.

Because the indigent sometimes get lost in the shuffle, they need strong people to act and speak on their behalf. It's reassuring to know that there are people like you who genuinely care about humanity. Congratulations, and thank you for enriching our company and world! Please let me know if there is anything I can do to help.

[ITEM 1] = First and last name of person receiving memo
[ITEM 2] = Name of community organization

INTEROFFICE MEMORANDUM

TO: [ITEM 1] FROM: [YOUR NAME]

[YOUR TITLE]

DATE: [DATE] cc: [COPIES TO]

SUBJECT: Your Employment Anniversary

Jukeboxes and the twist faded into obscurity, and poodle skirts lost their glamour. In the following decades, the nation saw everything from peace movements to combat as we moved from the atomic age into the information age. Change is inherent in life's progression.

Helping [YOUR COMPANY NAME] maneuver through past and present trends, you have been a reassuring guiding force over the past [ITEM 2] years of your employment. Don't think for a moment that we could have become what we are today without your skills and talents! From those very first days, you have been a major contributor to [YOUR COMPANY NAME]'s prosperity.

Then, as now, your ideas and steadfast devotion to excellence pervade our entire organization. Please accept as a small token of our appreciation, recognizing your [ITEM 2] years of service, our gift of [ITEM 3]. This is truly a celebration, and we look forward to many more in the future. Thank you for being a reliable team member who possesses talents that will never go out of style.

[ITEM 1] = First and last name of person receiving memo
[ITEM 2] = Number of years [ITEM 1] has been employed
[ITEM 3] = Details of the anniversary gift

INTEROFFICE MEMORANDUM

TO: [ITEM 1]   FROM: [YOUR NAME]

                                             [YOUR TITLE]

DATE: [DATE]   cc: [COPIES TO]

SUBJECT: Your Achievement Recognition

Management principles are ubiquitous. Many believe that the formula for effective management consists of using the right words— "increased productivity" and "team spirit," for example. While good managers may speak the same language, there are often differences in the way they speak that language.

Accenting the proper syllables is one of the keys to success. As my manager, you always used pitches and tones that were pleasing to my ears and spurred me on in my career with [YOUR COMPANY NAME]. It appears now that others more important than I have recognized your management skills as well.

Congratulations on your well-deserved promotion to [ITEM 2]. I could not do justice to a list of all you have given me personally and professionally. Let me just say thank you for being a good, effective manager and facilitating the development of my skills.

———————————————

[ITEM 1] = First and last name of person receiving memo
[ITEM 2] = Title of promotion

INTEROFFICE MEMORANDUM

TO: [ITEM 1]   FROM: [YOUR NAME]

                                              [YOUR TITLE]

DATE: [DATE]   cc: [COPIES TO]

SUBJECT: Congratulations!

      Shared achievement is almost as good as individual achievement. Although I learned this lesson early in life, it has become more meaningful as my experience has increased. I now realize that sharing in another's success inspires me to demand more of myself.

      Your recent accomplishment in [ITEM 2] sparks a greater need within me to be a leader in the truest sense. Your pride in your work is truly admirable. You must know that this trait is rare in our day-to-day pursuits.

      Upon hearing your good news, I reflected on how I could acquire the skills that seem to come so easily to you. Immediately, diligence, hard work, perseverance, and tenacity came to mind. Congratulations on your achievement, and thank you for sharing it with me.

[ITEM 1] = First and last name of person receiving memo
[ITEM 2] = One or two words defining accomplishment

INTEROFFICE MEMORANDUM

TO: [ITEM 1]   FROM: [YOUR NAME]

                                           [YOUR TITLE]

DATE: [DATE]   cc: [COPIES TO]

SUBJECT: Thank you

Acknowledgment of another's efforts in today's fast-paced business environment is often overlooked. It means a great deal to have the appreciation of those you admire. This is especially true for a person like me to whom a career is more than an occupation.

Your recognition of the efforts I put forth to [ITEM 2] reinforces my opinion that we are truly a team here at [YOUR COMPANY NAME]. I could not have done it alone, and your guidance continues to compel me to be the best player possible. Every pennant winner needs a coach directing his or her moves, and I could not have a better one.

Thank you for all you have done for my career and for taking the time let me know that I am a valuable member of our team. I hold your opinion in the highest regard.

[ITEM 1] = First and last name of person receiving memo
[ITEM 2] = One or two words describing accomplishment

INTEROFFICE MEMORANDUM

TO: [ITEM 1]   FROM: [YOUR NAME]

                                         [YOUR TITLE]

DATE: [DATE]   cc: [COPIES TO]

SUBJECT: Your Retirement

Youth holds the most splendid of gifts—our dreams. As we travel the country roads and city highways of life, we turn these visions into realities. Along the way, we give of ourselves continually in return for rewards.

I am envious of you as you embark upon a new stage in your life—a stage that will allow you to appreciate the scenery along the road. No longer will you be tied to the duties and responsibilities that obscure the view. Strange isn't it, that it takes a lifetime to achieve the ultimate freedom of action, thought, and sight?

Now you have time to pursue all the dormant desires life's pressures did not allow you to investigate. I'd like to hear all about the roadside cafes we passed by on our journey because we didn't have the time to stop. Let's meet for coffee at one someday soon.

[ITEM 1] = First and last name of person receiving memo

INTEROFFICE MEMORANDUM

TO: [ITEM 1]   FROM: [YOUR NAME]

                                                   [YOUR TITLE]

DATE: [DATE]   cc: [COPIES TO]

SUBJECT: Business Changes Require Layoffs

There is no good way to tell someone bad news. Inevitably, shock and despair set in no matter how hard one tries to soften the blow. With this in mind, please know that I have taken all steps necessary on your behalf to attempt to change the situation.

[YOUR COMPANY NAME]'s business direction and profits have undergone significant changes. This requires a refocusing of resources that is imperative for survival. To regain our market placement, we must cut expenses immediately throughout the organization. I regret to inform you that effective [ITEM 2], we will no longer require your skills. [ITEM 3] will be contacting you shortly with the layoff details and termination package.

Please be assured that I would change this unfortunate situation if I had the authority and the opportunity. You have been a valuable addition to our company, and you will be missed. I am concerned about your welfare; let me know if we can help. I have always considered you more than an employee; I consider you a valuable team player. It will be my pleasure to provide references to your prospective employers.

—————————————————◆—————————————————

[ITEM 1] = First and last name of person receiving memo
[ITEM 2] = Date [ITEM 1] will be laid off
[ITEM 3] = First and last name of person responsible for handling layoff details

INTEROFFICE MEMORANDUM

TO: [ITEM 1]   FROM: [YOUR NAME]

                                 [YOUR TITLE]

DATE: [DATE]   cc: [COPIES TO]

SUBJECT: Congratulations on Your Promotion

Success is a journey the destination of which changes frequently. From city to city, we walk many paths in search of fulfillment. Lessons get tucked neatly into our pack, and we see other travelers on the same route charting their own futures.

Ambition and motivation separate leaders from followers. Achievement changes the path's direction. The character you have shown in leading your group, often carrying more than your load, is appreciated by [YOUR COMPANY NAME]. It is my pleasure to acknowledge your accomplishments by promoting you to [ITEM 2] effective [ITEM 3].

Besides a more distinguished title, this position carries additional compensation and responsibilities. These will be explained by your new manager, [ITEM 4], soon. You will not need a map to chart your career path at [YOUR COMPANY NAME]; a successful journey is in store. The entire management team thanks you for your participation in our future. We value you as one of our leaders.

**[ITEM 1] = First and last name of person receiving memo
[ITEM 2] = Title of new position [ITEM 1] promoted to
[ITEM 3] = Date the promotion takes effect
[ITEM 4] = First and last name of [ITEM 1]'s new manager**

INTEROFFICE MEMORANDUM

TO: [ITEM 1]   FROM: [YOUR NAME]

                                                          [YOUR TITLE]

DATE: [DATE]   cc: [COPIES TO]

SUBJECT: I Care About You

Strength has nothing to do with one's physical prowess. It is reflected, rather, in the way in which a person survives difficult times. Hardships can result in only one of two things.

They either elevate us to a higher level or deplete our resources until weakness overshadows hope. It takes a strong person to put aside pride and recognize potential problem areas in life. A weak person gives in to the persuasive power of substances that allow different feelings.

Frankly, I worry about the changes I have noticed in your behavior and work patterns, because they are typical of people who are abusing [ITEM 2]. I fear that unless the situation is corrected immediately, I will lose a valuable employee and team member. You are not alone, and I want to help you get on the right track again. We all need assistance in our lives at one point or another.

The ultimate decision to bring back the person you once were belongs to you and no one else. Only you can take the difficult first step—acknowledging that a problem exists. I would like to set up a completely confidential meeting with a professional familiar with [ITEM 2] problems. A strong person acknowledges situations that may be too much to handle alone; that strength increases with another's help. And, this is not a weakness.

[ITEM 1] = First and last name of person receiving memo
[ITEM 2] = One or two words defining the substance [ITEM 1] is abusing

INTEROFFICE MEMORANDUM

TO: [ITEM 1]   FROM: [YOUR NAME]

                                                [YOUR TITLE]

DATE: [DATE]   cc: [COPIES TO]

SUBJECT: Termination Notice

      Misadventures teach many of life's most valuable lessons. When faced with an unfavorable situation, it is best to reflect upon the actions that created the problem. There is never only one action or party totally in the wrong.

      We have the opportunity to learn from our errors. For every action, there is an equal and opposite reaction. Although [YOUR COMPANY NAME] has repeatedly made you aware that a change was needed in [ITEM 2], no improvement has been apparent over the last [ITEM 3].

      Your lack of action leaves us no choice but to terminate your employment with [YOUR COMPANY NAME] effective [ITEM 4]. Your future outside [YOUR COMPANY NAME] is dependent upon your recognizing that we are not alone in finding behavior of this type unacceptable. Learn from your mistakes, and there is a chance you can have all you ever dreamed of.

**[ITEM 1] = First and last name of person receiving memo
[ITEM 2] = Describe why [ITEM 1]'s employment is being terminated
[ITEM 3] = Time lapse between when [ITEM 1] was informed of the problem and when terminated
[ITEM 4] = Date the employment termination takes effect**

INTEROFFICE MEMORANDUM

TO: [ITEM 1]   FROM: [YOUR NAME]

                                          [YOUR TITLE]

DATE: [DATE]   cc: [COPIES TO]

SUBJECT: Conflict of Interest

Ethical standards are a key component of professionalism. Frequently, we must ask ourselves whether our actions will be beneficial to the entire company. [YOUR COMPANY NAME]'s employees have an obligation to practice business ethically, honestly, and unselfishly.

I recently learned that your affiliation with [ITEM 2] could pose a potential conflict of interest in relation to your employment with [YOUR COMPANY NAME]. Conflict of interest covers many areas. In general, the term refers to situations in which an employee is in the position of disclosing information, influencing a decision, or partaking in a venture that results in personal gain.

Because you are innocent until proven guilty, I would like to hear your side of the story. Your relationship with [ITEM 2] alone is not enough to create a conflict of interest. The rumors are circulating, and I want to stop them for the benefit of all concerned—you, me, [YOUR COMPANY NAME], and [ITEM 2].

Whether or not you care to discuss the matter at length, I expect a response by [ITEM 3]. Conflict of interest is a very sensitive matter that demands immediate attention.

[ITEM 1] = First and last name of person receiving memo
[ITEM 2] = Name of company with which [ITEM 1] has affiliation
[ITEM 3] = Date by which you want [ITEM 1] to respond

INTEROFFICE MEMORANDUM

TO: [ITEM 1]   FROM: [YOUR NAME]

                                         [YOUR TITLE]

DATE: [DATE]   cc: [COPIES TO]

SUBJECT: Job Offer Confirmation for [ITEM 2]

Developing a highly effective team is an enduring goal for successful companies like [YOUR COMPANY NAME]. We must strive to integrate only the most knowledgeable, skilled, and talented players into our operation. Clearly, your endorsement of [ITEM 2] as a [ITEM 3] speaks loudly regarding [ITEM 4] abilities as a team player.

I have reviewed [ITEM 2]'s résumé and application for employment along with notes from our conversations. We agree that [YOUR COMPANY NAME] would benefit from [ITEM 4] background and experience. Based upon competitive market salary data, we are prepared to offer [ITEM 2] $[ITEM 5] per [ITEM 6].

Please provide this information to the candidate in writing as soon as possible and advise me when you expect to bring [ITEM 2] on board. Thank you for your assistance in selecting our newest team member.

[ITEM 1] = **First and last name of person receiving memo**
[ITEM 2] = **First and last name of person to be hired**
[ITEM 3] = **Title of position [ITEM 2] will assume**
[ITEM 4] = **Pronoun referring to [ITEM 2]'s gender, i.e., "his" or "her"**
[ITEM 5] = **Dollar amount based on [ITEM 6] to be paid [ITEM 2]**
[ITEM 6] = **Period salary is based on, i.e., "hour," "month," "year"**

INTEROFFICE MEMORANDUM

TO: [ITEM 1]   FROM: [YOUR NAME]

                                        [YOUR TITLE]

DATE: [DATE]   cc: [COPIES TO]

SUBJECT: Nondisclosure

Information holds great power. Because security is its weapon, we need to respect the manner in which proprietary [YOUR COMPANY NAME] information is discussed and handled. Your efforts on [ITEM 2] increase the entire company's vulnerability to inappropriate disclosure.

While I know you would never let such a thing happen, we cannot afford even the appearance of impropriety. Please be aware that any and all discussions, presentations, and meetings that may include confidential or proprietary [YOUR COMPANY NAME] information must be approved beforehand by [ITEM 3].

We trust that all information concerning [ITEM 2] and related plans will be treated in a confidential manner and used only as authorized. Your compliance is mandatory. We wouldn't want this information to get into the wrong hands.

[ITEM 1] = First and last name of person receiving memo
[ITEM 2] = Describe the activity [ITEM 1] is working on with confidential or proprietary information
[ITEM 3] = Person responsible for approval of information

INTEROFFICE MEMORANDUM

TO: [ITEM 1]   FROM: [YOUR NAME]

                                                          [YOUR TITLE]

DATE: [DATE]   cc: [COPIES TO]

SUBJECT: Résumé Handling Policy

Government statistics confirm that finding suitable employment is a trying task. There are many highly qualified people competing for a relatively small number of openings. Because [YOUR COMPANY NAME] is renowned as a reputable organization, we receive many résumés from prospective candidates without any recruitment efforts.

All résumés, whether for an internal job change or a new opening, must be submitted to [ITEM 2]. [ITEM 2] serves as the central point of contact, administering the interview and selection process. Following [ITEM 3] review and preliminary reference check, management is given a list of prospective candidates with which to begin the interview process.

Regulations require [YOUR COMPANY NAME] to hold all résumés for [ITEM 4]. Therefore, your compliance with this policy is mandatory. Thank you for your assistance in ensuring that all candidates are treated equitably.

[ITEM 1] = First and last name of person receiving memo
[ITEM 2] = Name of person or department responsible for résumés
[ITEM 3] = Pronoun referring to [ITEM 1]'s gender, i.e., "his" or "her"
[ITEM 4] = Length of time résumés are held on file by [YOUR COMPANY NAME]

INTEROFFICE MEMORANDUM

TO: [ITEM 1]   FROM: [YOUR NAME]

                                             [YOUR TITLE]

DATE: [DATE]   cc: [COPIES TO]

SUBJECT: Fund Raising Efforts for [ITEM 2]—Immediate Support Encouraged

·The most valuable currency is goodness. Whether sharing a smile or dispelling prejudice, a kind act is priceless. No person among us achieves true greatness without showing kindness to other human beings.

In this world, only a few dedicate their entire lives to charity. They exchange monetary wealth for the riches gained knowing they have made life better for others. [ITEM 2] has asked us for help, and we have given our full support to [ITEM 3].

Most of us are so comfortable that we seldom consider what life must be like for these unfortunate people. They must overcome so many obstacles, and a small contribution makes a difference. It is essential that [ITEM 2] receive money to continue its work.

People like you and me must exchange a small percentage of our salaries for the satisfaction of knowing that we have made a difference through our kindness. Give what you can, and if necessary, forgo that new shirt or piece of sports equipment. When you remember that you have helped to make life more bearable for those less fortunate, you'll be glad you did.

[ITEM 1] = First and last name of person receiving memo
[ITEM 2] = Name of the organization that needs money
[ITEM 3] = Describe how [ITEM 2] will use the funds

INTEROFFICE MEMORANDUM

TO: [ITEM 1]   FROM: [YOUR NAME]

                                    [YOUR TITLE]

DATE: [DATE]   cc: [COPIES TO]

SUBJECT: Fund Raising Assistance for [ITEM 2]

Time must be well-managed when responsibilities are numerous. Decisions must be made whether to dedicate energies to one specific area or another. Otherwise, endeavors undertaken do not receive proper attention and no one likes to do things halfway.

I have found this be true in both my career and my personal life. I have also found that career decisions are easier to make than personal ones, which can affect the lives of the less fortunate. [ITEM 2]'s charitable activities are not unknown to me.

On the contrary, I have been involved in similar efforts for some time, helping people whose lives have run aground in the sea of adversity. But as much as I would like to, I am unable to provide assistance at this time.

The benefits of good deeds are far-reaching; I am continually reminded of the blessings I enjoy in my own life. I am pleased that [YOUR COMPANY NAME] sees value in charity and humanitarian efforts. Please keep me abreast of your progress. We may be able to work together on your next fundraising campaign.

[ITEM 1] = First and last name of person receiving memo
[ITEM 2] = Name of the organization that needs assistance

INTEROFFICE MEMORANDUM

TO: [ITEM 1]   FROM: [YOUR NAME]

                                            [YOUR TITLE]

DATE: [DATE]   cc: [COPIES TO]

SUBJECT: Fund Raising Ideas for [ITEM 2]

Our thoughts are often so focused on the future that we miss the present. When striving for accomplishment, we typically see only the next project on the agenda. Long-range planning occasionally blinds us to the trials our fellow human beings endure in the here and now.

There are unfortunate people among us who have no direct effect on our lives or career success. Yet they warrant our concern today, not tomorrow. [YOUR COMPANY NAME] is taking a proactive stance in helping [ITEM 2]'s charitable efforts for people with [ITEM 3].

Collectively, we are exploring ways to ease their suffering. While [ITEM 2] is making great strides, they desperately need [ITEM 4] to continue. Pull out a piece of paper right now and give their plight the professional consideration you would give to any other worthwhile goal. I want everyone to jot down a few time-dependent ideas. When we have them all in hand, we'll decide exactly what we can do to further [ITEM 2]'s charitable goals.

[ITEM 1] = First and last name of person receiving memo
[ITEM 2] = Name of the organization that needs assistance
[ITEM 3] = Describe the focus of [ITEM 2] efforts
[ITEM 4] = Describe the immediate need of [ITEM 2]

INTEROFFICE MEMORANDUM

TO: [ITEM 1]   FROM: [YOUR NAME]

                                            [YOUR TITLE]

DATE: [DATE]   cc: [COPIES TO]

SUBJECT: Fund Raising Efforts for [ITEM 2]

Our society's emphasis on possessions hurts many people. We buy and buy, believing that one more possession will make us truly happy. The truth is, our survival does not depend on whether we wear designer fashions or own the latest gadgets.

For some, merely having a shirt on their back or a plate of food provides the motivation they need to live one more day. Think for a moment about your home and the appliances, art, electronics, and furniture it contains. Think about the pantry and closets abundant with expensive possessions. Who among us cannot identify unnecessary items or waste somewhere in our lives?

[YOUR COMPANY NAME] has found a worthwhile place for those possessions your family no longer wants. [ITEM 2] focuses on improving the quality of life for people with [ITEM 3]. While any gift is welcome, the items for which there is the most need are [ITEM 4]. Let me know what you can contribute to this worthy cause.

Proverbs speak of the joys of simplicity. Take this opportunity to streamline your home and your life for the sake of humanity. The feeling you get when you know you have helped a needy person cannot be surpassed.

[ITEM 1] = First and last name of person receiving memo
[ITEM 2] = Name of the organization that needs assistance
[ITEM 3] = Describe the focus of [ITEM 2] efforts
[ITEM 4] = Describe the immediate needs of [ITEM 2]

INTEROFFICE MEMORANDUM

TO: All Staff   FROM: [YOUR NAME]

                                         [YOUR TITLE]

DATE: [DATE]   cc: [COPIES TO]

SUBJECT: AIDS and Other Life-Threatening Illnesses

One cannot read the newspaper or watch television without becoming aware of life-threatening illnesses such as AIDS, cancer, and heart disease. We have become concerned about the debilitating effects such illnesses have on the individual and the community. Unfortunately, people afflicted with life-threatening illnesses are often branded as outcasts and suffer the remainder of their lives in exile.

Education is of utmost importance. [YOUR COMPANY NAME] supports continuing employment of workers with life-threatening illnesses. In accordance with the law and acceptable performance standards, we make reasonable accommodations for employees with life-threatening illnesses. We would like them to keep their jobs as long as possible. Medical information is held in strict confidence, and all regulations prohibiting inappropriate disclosure are enforced.

Life-threatening illnesses do not discriminate in choosing their victims. Any one of us could be next. As always, we encourage and support every [YOUR COMPANY NAME] employee, even those whom society isolates because of their maladies.

INTEROFFICE MEMORANDUM

TO: All Staff   FROM: [YOUR NAME]

                                           [YOUR TITLE]

DATE: [DATE]   cc: [COPIES TO]

SUBJECT: Drug Testing Program

      A good work environment clearly includes much more than the right supplies or the latest and greatest equipment. While these are vital, outfitting the office and having good people are not mutually exclusive goals. One clearly depends on the other for an efficient, productive, and safe environment.

      [YOUR COMPANY NAME] is committed to providing a healthy atmosphere for all employees. We never stop searching for ways to better ourselves, whether through additional resources or continuing education programs. In keeping with this philosophy, we want all team members to be aware that they, too, affect the work environment— personally and professionally. Therefore, any employee or job applicant may be requested to provide body substance samples (e.g., blood, urine) to be tested for the presence of alcohol, amphetamines, cocaine, marijuana, opiates, and phencyclidine (PCP). Positive test results will lead to employment reassessment and/or rehabilitation. Any questions about [YOUR COMPANY NAME]'s drug testing policy and program should be directed to [ITEM 1].

      Illegal drug use has no place in any part of our lives. Drugs have proved repeatedly to be a destructive force in the user's personal and professional relationships. [YOUR COMPANY NAME] is a strong enforcer and proponent of a drug-free environment.

ITEM 1 = Name of person responsible for drug testing program

INTEROFFICE MEMORANDUM

TO: All Staff   FROM: [YOUR NAME]

                                       [YOUR TITLE]

DATE: [DATE]   cc: [COPIES TO]

SUBJECT: Equal Employment Opportunity

    In creating a bona fide democracy, our founding fathers established justice as one of the rights to which citizens of this country are entitled. Today, more than 200 years later, [YOUR COMPANY NAME] reaffirms its commitment to equality and fairness.

    All advancement and employment decisions are based on ability, merit, and qualification. Employee relations are not influenced in any manner by an employee or applicant's age, color, disability, national origin, race, religion, or sex. Our affirmative action program further promotes equality throughout the organization.

    Should you have any questions or concerns about [YOUR COMPANY NAME]'s commitment to equal employment opportunities, please bring them to the immediate attention of [ITEM 1]. All reports are held in the strictest confidence. Thank you for your assistance in promoting fairness and equality throughout [YOUR COMPANY NAME].

[ITEM 1] = First and last name of person responsible in human resources or personnel

INTEROFFICE MEMORANDUM

TO: All Staff   FROM: [YOUR NAME]

                                                      [YOUR TITLE]

DATE: [DATE]   cc: [COPIES TO]

SUBJECT: Hiring of Relatives

Family members are often among our most treasured friends. [YOUR COMPANY NAME] is honored when employees' family members want to join our team of professionals. The confidence shown in these referrals confirms our belief that [YOUR COMPANY NAME] is a good place to work.

However, relatives may cause conflicts due to the natural tendency toward favoritism. In addition, we run the risk of having personal problems brought into the workplace. Either of these scenarios could have a detrimental effect on employee morale.

Still, we encourage the hiring of relatives when a reporting or direct relationship will not occur. Of course, relatives are not given any special consideration in the application and hiring process. All applicants are treated equally and must meet the same set of criteria when they apply for employment with [YOUR COMPANY NAME].

[ITEM 1] can answer any questions you may have pertaining to the hiring of relatives. We appreciate your continuous efforts to bring the most qualified employees to our team.

[ITEM 1] = First and last name of person responsible in human resources or personnel

INTEROFFICE MEMORANDUM

TO: All Staff   FROM: [YOUR NAME]

                                          [YOUR TITLE]

DATE: [DATE]   cc: [COPIES TO]

SUBJECT: Overtime

Enthusiasm for one's work is an admirable characteristic. It is often the factor that separates a job from a job done well. [YOUR COMPANY NAME] is proud that so many employees devote themselves to the pursuit of excellence. The responsibilities associated with each job in the company have been assigned with the standard 40-hour workweek in mind.

Realizing there can be extenuating circumstances that call for additional effort, [YOUR COMPANY NAME] compensates our employees accordingly. Working beyond regularly scheduled hours is done on a strictly volunteer basis. The overtime rate is [ITEM 1] times the normal hourly rate for hours worked after the regular workday ends.

However, all overtime is subject to prior authorization. Failure to work overtime scheduled or not obtaining proper approvals may result in disciplinary action, up to and including dismissal.

In fairness to all employees, these overtime policies must be followed. Please do not let the guidelines impair your enthusiasm. We appreciate your willingness to sacrifice personal time in pursuit of corporate goals.

[ITEM 1] = How overtime is calculated, i.e., "one," or "one and a half," "two," etc.

INTEROFFICE MEMORANDUM

TO: All Staff   FROM: [YOUR NAME]
                                             [YOUR TITLE]

DATE: [DATE]   cc: [COPIES TO]

SUBJECT: Personnel Information Changes

Had the renowned Sir Walter Raleigh received this memo, he would not have had much to reply. For 13 years, his contact and status information remained the same while he served time in prison.

Here at [YOUR COMPANY NAME], our records show that it's time again you to update your personnel file. Please look over the following list and advise [ITEM 1] in writing of any changes that may have occurred by [ITEM 2].

1. Home mailing address

2. Office and home telephone numbers

3. Cellular telephone number, if applicable

4. Names of all dependents

5. Emergency contacts

6. Educational accomplishments

7. Any civic and company awards

In addition to needing this information for the obvious contact reasons, management periodically reviews personnel files when jobs become available. Keeping personnel files up-to-date is the employee's ultimate responsibility. While you won't end up in prison if you don't provide the information, it is clearly in your best interest to do so.

[ITEM 1] = First and last name of person responsible for personnel files
[ITEM 2] = Date by which employees must submit changes

INTEROFFICE MEMORANDUM

TO: All Staff   FROM: [YOUR NAME]

                                     [YOUR TITLE]

DATE: [DATE]   cc: [COPIES TO]

SUBJECT: Company Celebration Not to Be Missed

It's easy to decline opportunities to laugh and relax when daily responsibilities mount. The little voice inside cries, "Work-Work-Work," stifling thoughts of sunshine and light conversation with friends. Oddly enough, in our youth it was quite the opposite.

There is a point at which production becomes counterproductive. [YOUR COMPANY NAME] wants our management and staff to strike a balance between work and play by getting together for a [ITEM 1] on [ITEM 2] from [ITEM 3] to [ITEM 4]. Leave your calculators, computers, management theories, paperwork, and suits at home.

The only strategies allowed are those we used when we were children, such as "How much fun can we possibly squeeze into this activity?" Release the carefree kid struggling to get out of your business suit by joining our celebration. Get away from it all. You deserve it!

[ITEM 1] = Type of function, i.e., "barbecue," "party," "picnic," "sports outing," etc.
[ITEM 2] = Date of company get-together
[ITEM 3] = Time the function begins
[ITEM 4] = Time the function ends

INTEROFFICE MEMORANDUM

TO: All Staff   FROM: [YOUR NAME]

                                       [YOUR TITLE]

DATE: [DATE]   cc: [COPIES TO]

SUBJECT: Holiday Time Celebration for Our [YOUR COMPANY NAME] Team

     Reflecting on past holiday seasons shared with family and friends fills us with joy and warmth. Our traditions remind us of the meaning of life. It really is a special time.

     [YOUR COMPANY NAME] considers every employee a member of one family unified in excellence, not only now but throughout the year. We use this calendar marking simply as a date for us to share our celebration of the season and year.

     Please join your [YOUR COMPANY NAME] family and friends at our annual Holiday Party on [ITEM 1] at [ITEM 2] beginning at [ITEM 3]. Your spouses or significant others are welcome to participate in our gala. They are part of your life, so we want them to be part of ours.

     I understand that this is an especially busy time, but I hope you'll make an effort to attend. Let [ITEM 4] know how many will be in your party. It will be my honor to toast the season and the year with my friends and extended family.

———————————◆———————————

[ITEM 1] = **Date of company holiday party**
[ITEM 2] = **Place where company holiday party will be held**
[ITEM 3] = **Time company holiday party begins**
[ITEM 4] = **First and last name of person responsible for tracking R.S.V.P.'s**

INTEROFFICE MEMORANDUM

TO: [ITEM 1]   FROM: [YOUR NAME]

                                      [YOUR TITLE]

DATE: [DATE]   cc: [COPIES TO]

SUBJECT: Career Advancement Opportunity

In a choir, it is difficult to pinpoint by searching the members' faces. All voices are joined to fill the room in perfect unison. Yet, there is always one voice more commanding than the others.

Whether that voice stands out because its owner has learned something others have yet to discover or because its owner was born with special talent, we want to listen. Your accomplishments warrant attention and have not gone unnoticed. Consequently, I thought of you when a [ITEM 2] position became available.

Such a move would enhance your career, allowing you to use the skills you already have and to develop new ones. I invite you to participate in the selection process and learn more about this opportunity through a formal interview on [ITEM 3] at [ITEM 4]. The choir was good training for what could prove to be conductor status. Please advise me if this career move is of interest.

[ITEM 1] = First and last name of person receiving memo
[ITEM 2] = Title of position available
[ITEM 3] = Date of interview
[ITEM 4] = Time interview begins

INTEROFFICE MEMORANDUM

TO: [ITEM 1]   FROM: [YOUR NAME]

                                              [YOUR TITLE]

DATE: [DATE]   cc: [COPIES TO]

SUBJECT: Networking Group Forming to Profit Members

Integrating resources and skills for the mutual benefit of the parties involved is not a new venture. For centuries, people have been using this formula for success. We generate great power when we share ideas.

Networking, as it's called now, is a phenomenon that spans industry segments and professions. [YOUR COMPANY NAME] encourages its management and staff to participate in networking groups, which can be a great source of knowledge and potential business opportunities.

The names of established groups and their meeting times are listed in the business calendar section of our major daily newspaper. Instead of joining an existing networking group, however, you might prefer a new one called [ITEM 2], which is looking for experts in [ITEM 3]. [ITEM 4] is spearheading this effort and can be reached at [ITEM 5].

To appreciate the benefits of networking, you must attend a meeting and experience the synergy created. As John Donne, the English poet, once wrote, "No man is an island." I might add that, in today's competitive business environment, we can't afford to be.

[ITEM 1] = First and last name of person receiving memo
[ITEM 2] = Name of networking group
[ITEM 3] = Specific professional area, i.e., "accounting," "law," "sales," etc.
[ITEM 4] = First and last name of person responsible for networking group
[ITEM 5] = [ITEM 4]'s telephone number

INTEROFFICE MEMORANDUM

TO: All Staff   FROM: [YOUR NAME]

                                          [YOUR TITLE]

DATE: [DATE]   cc: [COPIES TO]

SUBJECT: Good Times Guaranteed at [ITEM 1]'s Retirement Party

With the passage of time, special occasions involving people close to us take on greater significance. The things we do for mere monetary gain lose value as we learn to cherish friendships. One of our friends, [ITEM 1], is about to begin enjoying life without the daily pressures of business.

[ITEM 2] has touched each of us with [ITEM 3] familiar smile and winning attitude. We are toasting [ITEM 3] retirement from [YOUR COMPANY NAME] on [ITEM 4] at [ITEM 5] beginning at [ITEM 6]. It would mean a lot to [ITEM 2] if all of you were able to attend and share the camaraderie.

I have one request. When time allows, write a paragraph describing your fondest or funniest experience with [ITEM 2]. I need your contribution by [ITEM 7]. We plan to read them aloud at the celebration for everyone's enjoyment. I look forward to seeing you there as we give a good friend a great send-off.

[ITEM 1] = First and last name of person retiring
[ITEM 2] = First name of person retiring
[ITEM 3] = Pronoun referring to retired person's gender, i.e., "his," or "her"
[ITEM 4] = Date of retirement party
[ITEM 5] = Place where retirement party will be held
[ITEM 6] = Time retirement party begins
[ITEM 7] = Date by which you want to receive paragraph

INTEROFFICE MEMORANDUM

TO: [ITEM 1]   FROM: [YOUR NAME]

                                              [YOUR TITLE]

DATE: [DATE]   cc: [COPIES TO]

SUBJECT: Leave of Absence Request for Family Reasons

Families cannot be replaced. Possessions and wealth lose their meaning when measured against the joy of holding a loved one's hand or welcoming a new generation into the world. To believe otherwise is to mock humanity's most basic instincts.

Being an important member of a family is a source of tremendous happiness and many responsibilities. I have been forced to make a decision recently between career and family priorities because my [ITEM 2] needs my undivided attention. After exploring various solutions, I believe I am the best one to carry this burden.

The leave, if approved, would be for [ITEM 3] days beginning on [ITEM 4]. Therefore, the date of my return to work date would be [ITEM 5]. I realize that this may be an inopportune time, and I will understand if you should decide not to grant my family's wish. Please advise me of your decision at your earliest convenience. Thank you for your consideration. Again, I will understand if you believe that the burden imposed by the leave would be too great for my other family, [YOUR COMPANY NAME], to bear right now.

[ITEM 1] = First and last name of person receiving memo
[ITEM 2] = Relationship of person needing help, i.e., "brother," "child," "father," "mother," "sister," etc.
[ITEM 3] = Total number of leave days requested
[ITEM 4] = Date the leave begins
[ITEM 5] = Date the leave ends

INTEROFFICE MEMORANDUM

TO: [ITEM 1]   FROM: [YOUR NAME]

                                                 [YOUR TITLE]

DATE: [DATE]   cc: [COPIES TO]

SUBJECT: Leave of Absence Request for Maternity Reasons

For many of us, the ultimate gift is the feeling we get when looking into a small child's eyes. Somewhere in that sparkle, there is a little part of you and your heritage, and there will be so much for the child to see as life unfolds. Birth is nothing less than a miracle.

Amid the exciting preparations, my professional career aspirations have become stronger than ever. Like my parents and their parents, I want my child to have nothing but the best experiences and opportunities.

I am requesting a maternity leave that, barring any unforeseen circumstances, will last from [ITEM 2] through [ITEM 3]. This bonding period is necessary for our family. In addition, plans must be made to assimilate an infant's needs gracefully into our professional lives.

You have my home telephone number; please feel free to call with even the smallest question. I look forward to sharing this gift of life with my [YOUR COMPANY NAME] family. If not in person, I promise to bring in my share of those "Look at my beautiful baby" pictures.

[ITEM 1] = First and last name of person receiving memo
[ITEM 2] = Date the leave begins
[ITEM 3] = Date the leave ends

INTEROFFICE MEMORANDUM

TO: [ITEM 1]   FROM: [YOUR NAME]

                                         [YOUR TITLE]

DATE: [DATE]   cc: [COPIES TO]

SUBJECT: Leave of Absence Request for Medical Reasons

In our day-to-day existence, we tend to take things for granted unless something out of the ordinary forces us to sit up and take notice. The car that starts in the morning and the copy machine that works are just two examples. Until now, I had never given much thought to what I would do if for some reason my health was temporarily taken from me.

The right food, proper exercise, and an active mind has served me well over the years. Today, however, I find myself in a precarious position. Despite my desire to continue doing my job with all the dedication and energy I normally put forth, health limitations have made it impossible for me to do so.

My friends and physicians tell me I am pushing the healing process, which invariably does the opposite and lengthens the cycle. Therefore, for our mutual benefit, I would like to take a medical leave of absence from [ITEM 2] through [ITEM 3].

I expect my health problem caused by [ITEM 4] to be completely under control before returning to work with renewed vitality. Thank you for understanding that this leave is necessary for [YOUR COMPANY NAME] to have this team player back in full force.

[ITEM 1] = First and last name of person receiving memo
[ITEM 2] = Date the leave begins
[ITEM 3] = Date the leave ends
[ITEM 4] = Health reason for leave

INTEROFFICE MEMORANDUM

TO: [ITEM 1]   FROM: [YOUR NAME]
                                                  [YOUR TITLE]

DATE: [DATE]   cc: [COPIES TO]

SUBJECT: Leave of Absence Request for Personal Reasons

No matter how rich a garden's soil may be, seeds must be sown and nutrients added to produce a harvest. The gardener meticulously and patiently cares for the crop as a mother cares for her child. Yet much to the gardener's chagrin, weeds still appear from time to time.

Whether for aesthetic or agricultural reasons, the undesirable is quickly removed from the rows of budding green. Life is a garden that blooms only when the right care and nutrients are applied. Unfortunately, we cannot rely on others to promote growth in our lives.

My personal garden needs attention right now. I prefer not to divulge the exact circumstances. Suffice it to say I am embarrassed by the weeds that are affecting my growth and guilty that I have neglected my harvest.

If at all possible, I would like to take a personal leave from [ITEM 2] through [ITEM 3]. I realize it is a difficult approval in that I am keeping the reason confidential. [ITEM 4], we have known each other for some time. You must trust me when I say I need to rebuild my garden now, not later. It is essential if there are to be any future crops. Please advise me of your decision as soon as possible, and thank you for understanding.

———————————————◆—————————————————

[ITEM 1] = First and last name of person receiving memo
[ITEM 2] = Date the leave begins
[ITEM 3] = Date the leave ends
[ITEM 4] = First name of person receiving memo

INTEROFFICE MEMORANDUM

TO: [ITEM 1]   FROM: [YOUR NAME]

                                             [YOUR TITLE]

DATE: [DATE]   cc: [COPIES TO]

SUBJECT: [ITEM 2] Meeting Confirmation

Once upon a time, a plain ole wall calendar did the trick just fine. Nowadays, we rely on more sophisticated tools as we plan our days. First we embraced notebook sized, then pocket, and now electronic calendar systems to help us organize our lives.

Please check whatever tool you use to track appointments and be sure that our meeting about [ITEM 2] is scheduled. As a quick confirmation, we are gathering at [ITEM 3] in [ITEM 4]. I don't think the meeting will last much longer than [ITEM 5]. This should provide enough time to cover the issues and new developments since we last discussed [ITEM 2].

[ITEM 1] = First and last name of person receiving memo
[ITEM 2] = One or two words defining meeting
[ITEM 3] = Time the meeting begins
[ITEM 4] = Place within office where meeting will be held
[ITEM 5] = Estimated duration of meeting

INTEROFFICE MEMORANDUM

TO: [ITEM 1]   FROM: [YOUR NAME]

                                              [YOUR TITLE]

DATE: [DATE]   cc: [COPIES TO]

SUBJECT: [ITEM 2] Meeting Outline

     When more than one topic is to be discussed in a relatively brief time, preparation can contribute immeasurably to the overall efficiency of the meeting. This is especially true in intricate matters like [ITEM 2]. Therefore, I am providing a topical outline for our upcoming meeting, so you can gather supporting materials that will allow us to deal with the subject thoroughly and quickly.

     To date, our respective expertise and input have been very beneficial in reaching a consensus on some outstanding issues. Areas that require further deliberation and investigation include the following: [ITEM 3].

     Please bring your documentation and ideas concerning the above to the meeting. As a reminder, we are meeting promptly at [ITEM 4] in [ITEM 5]. If you have any questions or items to add to the outline, do not hesitate to contact me. Your suggestions for increasing [YOUR COMPANY NAME]'s productivity are always welcome.

[ITEM 1] = First and last name of person receiving memo
[ITEM 2] = One or two words defining meeting
[ITEM 3] = Describe up to five separate meeting points to cover
[ITEM 4] = Time the meeting begins
[ITEM 5] = Place within office where meeting will be held

INTEROFFICE MEMORANDUM

TO: [ITEM 1]   FROM: [YOUR NAME]

                                              [YOUR TITLE]

DATE: [DATE]   cc: [COPIES TO]

SUBJECT: [ITEM 2] Meeting Summary

      Diligence leads to accomplishment. A cooperative focus on goals, as recently exhibited in our meeting pertaining to [ITEM 2], definitely promotes attainment. In the course of that discussion, areas were revealed requiring a review of the facts to ensure that our future directions are complementary.

      Therefore, the following is a summary of the meeting on [ITEM 3]. While a memo alone cannot do the discussion justice, my interpretation of the conclusions drawn and actions required is as follows: [ITEM 4].

      When you have had a chance to review this summary, I would welcome your comments. We need to move forward as quickly as possible. Thank you for your continued support in upholding our goals and completing our mission. Your recommendations will be given serious consideration.

———————————————◆◆———————————————

[ITEM 1] = First and last name of person receiving memo
[ITEM 2] = One or two words defining meeting's purpose
[ITEM 3] = Date the meeting was held
[ITEM 4] = Describe up to five points covered in meeting

INTEROFFICE MEMORANDUM

TO: [ITEM 1]   FROM: [YOUR NAME]

                                                          [YOUR TITLE]

DATE: [DATE]   cc: [COPIES TO]

SUBJECT: [ITEM 2] Meeting Request

Knowledge lessens the potential for error in business ventures. Especially when a goal's critical point is approaching, detailing efforts expended thus far with a person of experience yields practical results. This is precisely the reason I would like to consult with you about [ITEM 2].

By most indications, we are on track. However, I believe that your valuable input will increase the likelihood of a positive outcome. Specifically, the areas I seek your opinion on are [ITEM 3].

I understand that your time is limited, so I will adjust my schedule to accommodate yours. Thank you in advance for your assistance in ensuring this project's success. Although this is not an emergency situation, I hope to confer with you at your earliest convenience.

[ITEM 1] = First and last name of person receiving memo
[ITEM 2] = One or two words defining meeting
[ITEM 3] = Describe up to five separate meeting points to cover

INTEROFFICE MEMORANDUM

TO: [ITEM 1]   FROM: [YOUR NAME]

                                           [YOUR TITLE]

DATE: [DATE]   cc: [COPIES TO]

SUBJECT: [ITEM 2] Meeting Scheduled

Internal communications affect external events. Maintaining the highest level of internal communication is essential to any organization's success. As in sports, coaches, trainers, and players alike must thoroughly understand strategies before entering the field.

Likewise, no matter what the purpose of the organization, communication among team members is essential if the team is to have a winning season. There are several new directions regarding [ITEM 2] that will influence our business strategies.

This important area for [YOUR COMPANY NAME] warrants your attention and time. There will be a meeting on [ITEM 3] in [ITEM 4] beginning at [ITEM 5]. Your attendance is essential. Should you be unable to attend, please advise me in writing and include the input you would have provided. Thank you for adding strength to our strategic plays.

[ITEM 1] = First and last name of person receiving memo
[ITEM 2] = One or two words defining meeting
[ITEM 3] = Date of meeting
[ITEM 4] = Place within office where meeting will be held
[ITEM 5] = Time the meeting begins

INTEROFFICE MEMORANDUM

TO: [ITEM 1]   FROM: [YOUR NAME]

                                      [YOUR TITLE]

DATE: [DATE]   cc: [COPIES TO]

SUBJECT: Performance Appraisal Meeting

       Action and planning are essential components of a successful career. Implementing one without the other is a futile, often frustrating, experience for the organization and employee. While we do our best to encourage informal discussions on important topics, this casual approach does not provide the opportunity for in-depth reviews.

       We consider formal performance evaluations an example of [YOUR COMPANY NAME]'s commitment to our employees' career development and satisfaction. These [ITEM 2] assessments give us an opportunity to discuss goals, identify and correct weaknesses, acknowledge and encourage strengths, and formulate action plans. Your performance appraisal is scheduled for [ITEM 3] beginning at [ITEM 4] in [ITEM 5].

       There is no reason for any apprehension over a performance appraisal. This scheduled review is truly an opportunity to focus on mutually beneficial actions and plans. I look forward to this chance to discuss in detail your career at [YOUR COMPANY NAME].

[ITEM 1] = First and last name of person receiving memo
[ITEM 2] = Frequency of performance appraisals, i.e., "quarterly" or "yearly"
[ITEM 3] = Date of performance appraisal
[ITEM 4] = Time the performance appraisal begins
[ITEM 5] = Place within office where performance appraisal will be held

INTEROFFICE MEMORANDUM

TO: [ITEM 1]   FROM: [YOUR NAME]

                                         [YOUR TITLE]

DATE: [DATE]   cc: [COPIES TO]

SUBJECT: Performance Improvement Plan

It takes confidence and intelligence to embrace constructive criticism as a beneficial recommendation rather than a personal attack. When we fail to meet company expectations, recommendations help us change our behavior and get back on the road to success. Having the finest team members is important to [YOUR COMPANY NAME].

Each day should be marked with another advancement toward our personal and professional pinnacles of success. I am happy to be a mentor to people who have the ability to accomplish great things.

As your mentor, I must tell you candidly that the probability of success is not very high for you right now. Your performance is being restricted by the following: [ITEM 2].

I believe that your attention and commitment to changing the above inadequacies will bring about an immediate improvement. We will monitor your progress over the next [ITEM 3] to determine whether any further action is necessary. Please do not disappoint us. The way you respond will have a lasting effect on your career.

[ITEM 1] = First and last name of person receiving memo
[ITEM 2] = Describe areas requiring improvement
[ITEM 3] = Time your company policy allots for improvement plans

INTEROFFICE MEMORANDUM

TO: [ITEM 1]   FROM: [YOUR NAME]
                                                    [YOUR TITLE]

DATE: [DATE]   cc: [COPIES TO]

SUBJECT: Performance Appraisal Request Review

Objective opinion is sometimes swayed by subjective thought. Our individual backgrounds and experiences have a tendency to influence our judgments and perceptions. Remaining impartial and unbiased in our dealings can be difficult at times.

Allow me to illustrate. Let's assume that I wanted you to meet one of my friends. In one instance, I told you how often this person has helped me over the years. In the other instance, I told you how often this person has asked for money. In either case, you would have formed an opinion of my friend before ever shaking hands with him or her. This subjective impression would later be confirmed or denied when the introduction took place and you formed an objective judgment.

I may be wrong, but I believe that my performance appraisal for [ITEM 2], contains misconceptions founded on hearsay rather than fact. I cannot tell you how many nights I have lain awake wondering what I could have done better or more effectively to benefit [YOUR COMPANY NAME]. After much deliberation, I decided to find out by taking the first step and asking for a review of my performance appraisal.

I seek additional insight into the criteria and methodology used by [YOUR COMPANY NAME] in determining performance levels. It has always been my goal to exceed my employer's expectations, and I believe that I performed my duties competently during [ITEM 2]. Please let me know as soon as possible when we can meet. I thank you in advance for your professionalism in this matter.

[ITEM 1] = First and last name of person receiving memo
[ITEM 2] = Time the performance appraisal covered, i.e., "second quarter," "1993," etc.

INTEROFFICE MEMORANDUM

TO: [ITEM 1]   FROM: [YOUR NAME]

                                     [YOUR TITLE]

DATE: [DATE]   cc: [COPIES TO]

SUBJECT: Termination Warning Requires Immediate Action

It takes time to figure out our direction in life. We may try our hands at several things before settling on one career pursuit that makes us eager to start the new day. For some time, I have been questioning whether [YOUR COMPANY NAME] does this for you as it does for me.

On many occasions, we have discussed the problem with your performance in the area of [ITEM 2]. I made it perfectly clear that [YOUR COMPANY NAME] wants you to succeed and to continue being a member of our team. To do this, you must change your performance immediately by [ITEM 3].

Should you continue to neglect this area and not show any reasonable improvement, I will be forced to take stronger measures. Please be advised that your employment with [YOUR COMPANY NAME] is in jeopardy. Unless your performance improves by [ITEM 4], I will recommend proceedings that may lead to your immediate termination. [ITEM 5], heed this warning by showing me that your career at [YOUR COMPANY NAME] is important to you. I really would like you to stay.

[ITEM 1] = First and last name of person receiving memo
[ITEM 2] = Describe reason(s) performance is unacceptable
[ITEM 3] = Describe recommendations for improved performance
[ITEM 4] = Date by which improved performance must occur
[ITEM 5] = First name of person receiving memo

INTEROFFICE MEMORANDUM

TO: [ITEM 1]   FROM: [YOUR NAME]
                                         [YOUR TITLE]

DATE: [DATE]   cc: [COPIES TO]

SUBJECT: Organizational Hierarchy Facilitates Communication

Organizations build upon the literal definition of the word: a unit composed of many elements having specific functions that contribute collectively to the whole. There is no doubt that our individual efforts benefit all at [YOUR COMPANY NAME].

In an organization, various specialties create levels of authority and focus. One department understands its charter much better than another does, and vice versa. Therefore, corporate communications must work within established guidelines of authority.

All concerns, comments, and questions should be first directed to your immediate manager or supervisor. It is his or her responsibility to resolve the issue or seek additional support within the corporation at higher levels.

Should you believe your manager or supervisor is not taking every action to address your concern within a reasonable amount of time, you may contact [ITEM 2] for assistance. There are absolutely no exceptions to this policy.

Please direct any comments or questions regarding this policy to your immediate manager or supervisor. Thank you in advance for your respect of [YOUR COMPANY NAME]'s hierarchy and communication channels.

[ITEM 1] = First and last name of person receiving memo
[ITEM 2] = Person responsible for handling policy enforcement

INTEROFFICE MEMORANDUM

TO: [ITEM 1]   FROM: [YOUR NAME]

                                                      [YOUR TITLE]

DATE: [DATE]   cc: [COPIES TO]

SUBJECT: Outgoing Mail Service

More than 2,000 years ago, the Greek historian Herodotus wrote of the Persian courier service, "These men will not be hindered from accomplishing at their best speeds the distance they have to go either by snow, or rain, or heat, or by darkness of night." Interestingly, many mail services throughout the world have taken Herodotus's centuries-old quote as their own.

While technology has made mail service more sophisticated, our policy has not changed. All outgoing mail is for [YOUR COMPANY NAME]-related business only; personal items should not be processed through the company mail system.

There are absolutely no exceptions to our outgoing mail policy, and failure to comply may result in disciplinary action. Please direct any comments or questions regarding this policy to [ITEM 2].

In keeping with [YOUR COMPANY NAME]'s efforts to control costs, individual and managerial support of this policy is imperative. Thank you for your assistance in maintaining our standards.

[ITEM 1] = First and last name of person receiving memo
[ITEM 2] = Person responsible for handling policy enforcement

INTEROFFICE MEMORANDUM

TO: [ITEM 1]   FROM: [YOUR NAME]

                                                     [YOUR TITLE]

DATE: [DATE]   cc: [COPIES TO]

SUBJECT: Personal Appearance

Your personal appearance is a direct reflection of your inner appearance. Like aspirations and goals, dress, grooming, and personal cleanliness contribute to one's professional image. [YOUR COMPANY NAME] has standards of acceptable business attire that have been developed with the best interests of the company, customers, and visitors in mind.

During business hours, all are expected to present a clean and neat appearance. Acceptable dress is defined by your immediate manager or supervisor within general guidelines.

People in management or sales positions are required to wear standard business suits or similar attire. Warehouse employees may wear casual slacks and shirts. Uniforms are provided for certain positions. Should your attire not comply with [YOUR COMPANY NAME] policy, you may be asked to go home and return in proper clothing without compensation for the time away from the office.

There are absolutely no exceptions to our personal appearance policy, and failure to comply may result in disciplinary action. Please direct any comments or questions regarding this policy to your immediate manager or supervisor or [ITEM 2]. Both are able to define in detail what constitutes acceptable and unacceptable attire. Thank you for helping [YOUR COMPANY NAME] maintain the highest professional image.

———————————————————◆———————————————————

[ITEM 1] = First and last name of person receiving memo
[ITEM 2] = Person responsible for handling policy enforcement

INTEROFFICE MEMORANDUM

TO: [ITEM 1]   FROM: [YOUR NAME]

                                          [YOUR TITLE]

DATE: [DATE]   cc: [COPIES TO]

SUBJECT: Sexual and Other Unlawful Discrimination and Harassment

Whether favoritism or discrimination, prejudice is an enemy of a free people. [YOUR COMPANY NAME] does not tolerate any form of discrimination, harassment, or prejudice in our internal or external business affairs.

[YOUR COMPANY NAME] is committed to providing its employees a work environment free of actions, comments, jokes, or words based on a person's age, ethnicity, race, religion, sex, or any other characteristic legally protected. Either blatant or implied, sexual and other forms of unlawful discrimination and harassment are among the worst kinds of employee misconduct and, as such, are strictly prohibited.

Any incident of possible sexual or other unlawful discrimination or harassment should be reported immediately to your manager or supervisor. If you believe this is inappropriate, contact [ITEM 2]. Be assured that your report will be held in the strictest confidence, and have no fear of reprisal. Managers and supervisors must immediately report any incident of sexual or other unlawful discrimination or harassment.

Please direct any comments or questions regarding this policy to your immediate manager or supervisor or to [ITEM 2]. There are absolutely no exceptions to [YOUR COMPANY NAME]'s policy governing the prohibition of any sexual or other unlawful discrimination or harassment. Any employee misconduct of this type will be subject to disciplinary action that may lead to termination of employment. Thank you in advance for your total support of this policy.

[ITEM 1] = First and last name of person receiving memo
[ITEM 2] = Person responsible for handling policy enforcement

INTEROFFICE MEMORANDUM

TO: [ITEM 1]   FROM: [YOUR NAME]

                                                [YOUR TITLE]

DATE: [DATE]   cc: [COPIES TO]

SUBJECT: Smoking Policy

[YOUR COMPANY NAME] company policy entitles every employee to a clean and healthy work environment. Pollutant-free air helps create surroundings in which we can strive for individual and corporate success. [YOUR COMPANY NAME]'s smoking policy is to be followed without exception.

In accordance with state and local laws, smoking is prohibited in [ITEM 2] excluding designated smoking areas. At [YOUR COMPANY NAME], the designated smoking area is [ITEM 3]. Failure to comply with this policy may result in disciplinary action.

There are absolutely no exceptions to our smoking policy, and failure to comply may result in disciplinary action. Please direct any comments or questions regarding this policy to your immediate manager or supervisor. Thank you in advance for your assistance in maintaining [YOUR COMPANY NAME]'s clean and healthy work environment.

[ITEM 1] = First and last name of person receiving memo
[ITEM 2] = Location where smoking is prohibited in office
[ITEM 3] = Location of designated smoking area in office

INTEROFFICE MEMORANDUM

TO: [ITEM 1]   FROM: [YOUR NAME]

                                             [YOUR TITLE]

DATE: [DATE]   cc: [COPIES TO]

SUBJECT: Telephone Use Policy

Like most organizations, [YOUR COMPANY NAME] has gone to great lengths to ensure that employees have the tools they need as they pursue company goals. Telephones are provided to employees to use in conducting company business and should not be used for personal calls.

A personal telephone call is defined as a communication made on, or with, company equipment that is not directly related to your job. This includes local and long distance calls. While local calls are not limited, some job responsibilities require a long distance access code to place calls outside the immediate dialing area.

Long distance access codes are assigned at the discretion of your manager or supervisor. There are absolutely no exceptions to our telephone policy, and failure to comply may result in disciplinary action.

Please direct any comments or questions regarding this policy to your immediate manager or supervisor. Thank you in advance for your support of [YOUR COMPANY NAME]'s policies.

[ITEM 1] = First and last name of person receiving memo

INTEROFFICE MEMORANDUM

TO: [ITEM 1]   FROM: [YOUR NAME]

                                                    [YOUR TITLE]

DATE: [DATE]   cc: [COPIES TO]

SUBJECT: Procedure for After-Hours Office Use

Time management becomes an art when business increases and pressures mount. We try to control our workloads, but projects can take longer than expected. To reach our goals, we must occasionally work extra hours that are not included in our regular work schedules.

[YOUR COMPANY NAME] understands these situations and appreciates its employees' enthusiasm. Therefore, we make our equipment and office resources available to employees after business hours. All we request is that employees secure permission from their immediate managers and supervisors to remain in the building after the majority have left for the day.

In addition to securing permission, please adhere to the following after-hours office use and safety guidelines: [ITEM 2].

Security of information and equipment is a priority. [YOUR COMPANY NAME] trusts you to use common sense and prudence. Suggestions include locking all doors while in, and after leaving, the office; trying not to be in the office alone; and having an escort walk you to your car. If you have any other suggestions in relation to keeping our people and property secure after hours, do not hesitate to give your recommendation to [ITEM 3]. Thank you for your enthusiasm, and please exercise caution and safety in all your pursuits.

[ITEM 1] = First and last name of person receiving memo
[ITEM 2] = Describe all after-hours use guidelines
[ITEM 3] = First and last name of person to receive and/or implement suggestions

INTEROFFICE MEMORANDUM

TO: [ITEM 1]   FROM: [YOUR NAME]

                                            [YOUR TITLE]

DATE: [DATE]   cc: [COPIES TO]

SUBJECT: Procedure for Answering the Telephone

You never get a second chance to make a first impression. Therefore, we want to make sure that our business associates and customers get the right impression the first time, and every time, they call [YOUR COMPANY NAME]. A standard greeting creates continuity and helps to maintain a professional image.

Your primary goal during those first few seconds of conversation is to let the caller know that he or she has reached the right place and that you are glad he or she phoned. Your words and tone should be pleasant at all times.

Job responsibilities and organizational roles require different styles when answering the telephone. In your position as [ITEM 2], the telephone should be answered during business hours in the following manner: [ITEM 3].

Post this script by your telephone as a reminder of the correct way to answer the telephone. [YOUR COMPANY NAME] wants every business associate and customer to get the right impression of every aspect of our business every time. Thank you for contributing to our professional image.

[ITEM 1] = First and last name of person receiving memo
[ITEM 2] = Job title of [ITEM 1]
[ITEM 3] = Describe the greeting to be used by [ITEM 1]

INTEROFFICE MEMORANDUM

TO: [ITEM 1]   FROM: [YOUR NAME]
                                                          [YOUR TITLE]

DATE: [DATE]   cc: [COPIES TO]

SUBJECT: Dealing with Broadcast and Print Reporters

Literally thousands of men and women in our country are charged with the task of keeping the public up to date on happenings in the world. Because of their efforts, we can pick up a newspaper or watch television and become more aware of life as it is today and will be tomorrow. Reporters have a difficult job getting accurate information and then condensing their research to fit in the time or space allotted.

Frequently, media people, whose titles include reporter, editor, researcher, reviewer, and publisher, call upon people like us for information or interviews. We may have specialized knowledge that will help them improve their stories.

To ensure accuracy of information and for the protection of our employees, [YOUR COMPANY NAME] has established one point of contact for media-related people. All inquiries by media personnel, whether written or oral, should be directed immediately to [ITEM 2] at [ITEM 3].

There are absolutely no exceptions to this procedure. Thank you for recognizing the importance of this matter. Your compliance is a personal and professional obligation to maintain the highest integrity of our employees and company.

[ITEM 1] = First and last name of person receiving memo
[ITEM 2] = First and last name of person responsible for media-related communications
[ITEM 3] = Telephone number for [ITEM 2]

INTEROFFICE MEMORANDUM

TO: [ITEM 1]   FROM: [YOUR NAME]

                                                      [YOUR TITLE]

DATE: [DATE]   cc: [COPIES TO]

SUBJECT: Equipment Use

The right tools make our jobs easier. This holds true for everything from yardwork to professional tasks. [YOUR COMPANY NAME] gives its employees the right equipment for maximum efficiency.

When we order tools and supplies, we don't ask our employees to bear the expense. You are never charged for making a business-related call, copy, or printout, nor should you be. These are [YOUR COMPANY NAME]'s responsibilities.

All we ask in return is that you respect [YOUR COMPANY NAME] equipment as if it were your own. Handle our purchases with care. We budget very carefully to obtain the equipment you need to get the job done.

Please follow all operating instructions and observe safety precautions when using company equipment. If you see someone who is not protecting or showing respect for company property, notify [ITEM 2] at [ITEM 3]. Such reports are held in the strictest confidence, so you need not fear reprisal. Thank you for your ongoing respect of company equipment. We are a team, and the equipment is for everyone to use.

[ITEM 1] = First and last name of person receiving memo
[ITEM 2] = First and last name of person responsible for handling equipment misuse
[ITEM 3] = Telephone number for [ITEM 2]

INTEROFFICE MEMORANDUM

TO: [ITEM 1]   FROM: [YOUR NAME]

                                                [YOUR TITLE]

DATE: [DATE]   cc: [COPIES TO]

SUBJECT: Expense Reimbursement

Tight budgetary controls allow [YOUR COMPANY NAME] to operate efficiently and prudently. Successful financial management requires everyone's compliance with a few basic expense reimbursement procedures.

Submitting expenses for reimbursement is each employee's individual responsibility at [YOUR COMPANY NAME]. Expenses estimated to be more than $[ITEM 2] must be approved in advance by [ITEM 3]. The procedure for expense reimbursement is as follows: [ITEM 4].

Please note that expenses, with applicable invoices or receipts attached, must be received by [ITEM 5] within [ITEM 6] days from the date incurred. Otherwise, additional approvals may be necessary prior to reimbursement. Thank you for your cooperation and assistance in maintaining respectable financial ethics.

———————————————◆———————————————

[ITEM 1] = First and last name of person receiving memo
[ITEM 2] = Dollar amount of expense needing prior approval
[ITEM 3] = First and last name of person responsible for [ITEM 1]'s expense approval
[ITEM 4] = Describe step-by-step procedure for expense reimbursement
[ITEM 5] = First and last name of person responsible for releasing money for [ITEM 1]'s expense
[ITEM 6] = Time in days by which the expense must be remitted

INTEROFFICE MEMORANDUM

TO: [ITEM 1]   FROM: [YOUR NAME]

                                         [YOUR TITLE]

DATE: [DATE]   cc: [COPIES TO]

SUBJECT: New Procedures for [ITEM 2]

The shortest distance between two points is a straight line. Management has received many suggestions intended to help us streamline [ITEM 2].

Incorporating employee recommendations is beneficial to [YOUR COMPANY NAME]. Therefore, we have made adjustments to eliminate unnecessary steps in [ITEM 2]. Effective today, the procedure is as follows: [ITEM 3].

Should you have any questions on the new procedure, please do not hesitate to contact [ITEM 4] at [ITEM 5]. As always, we appreciate those who care enough about [YOUR COMPANY NAME] to make suggestions. It truly is beneficial for our entire team.

[ITEM 1] = First and last name of person receiving memo
[ITEM 2] = One or two words describing procedure that changed
[ITEM 3] = Describe step-by-step procedure for [ITEM 2]
[ITEM 4] = First and last name of person responsible for implementing new procedure
[ITEM 5] = Telephone number for [ITEM 4]

INTEROFFICE MEMORANDUM

TO: [ITEM 1]   FROM: [YOUR NAME]

                                           [YOUR TITLE]

DATE: [DATE]   cc: [COPIES TO]

SUBJECT: Attendance and Punctuality Reminder

Let's be candid. Getting to work on time every day is probably not what most would consider fun. We'd rather be fishing, playing sports, reading, or maybe just loafing around in front of the television. We can't though; we have responsibilities to ourselves, our families, and our employers.

When fulfilling these obligations, we make commitments to be dependable and reliable in our actions. Others trust us to honor those commitments.

As your employer, [YOUR COMPANY NAME] expects you to arrive at work at the scheduled time. Absenteeism and tardiness are in direct conflict with the commitment you have made to us.

We don't take very well to people breaking their promises. It puts additional burdens on the company and your co-workers. In the rare instance when you will be late or unable to work as scheduled, advise [ITEM 2] as soon as possible.

Let's be candid again. Continued disregard of your commitment to be on time every scheduled work day may result in disciplinary action, which may include termination of employment with [YOUR COMPANY NAME]. While you could have fun every day then, we think the drawbacks are obvious.

———————————————————————◆◆———————————————————————

[ITEM 1] = First and last name of person receiving memo
[ITEM 2] = First and last name of person [ITEM 1] should contact regarding absenteeism or tardiness

INTEROFFICE MEMORANDUM

TO: [ITEM 1]   FROM: [YOUR NAME]

                                          [YOUR TITLE]

DATE: [DATE]   cc: [COPIES TO]

SUBJECT: Employee Conduct Reminder

Regulations are an important part of our lives. Everywhere we turn, a custom or a guideline dictates acceptable behavior. Whether we personally believe in the soundness of this or that rule, we must believe that most rules were created with the best interests of the majority in mind.

[YOUR COMPANY NAME] has rules that govern every employee's conduct. These rules were made to benefit every member of our team, but it seems that some team members may have forgotten the importance of playing by the rules. Therefore, I highlight the areas where memory loss seems greatest.

[YOUR COMPANY NAME] employee conduct rules include but are not limited to the following: [ITEM 2]. A complete list with explanations is available from [ITEM 3].

There are absolutely no exceptions to our rules, and failure to comply may result in disciplinary action. If you see team rules being broken, notify [ITEM 4] at [ITEM 5]. Such reports are held in strict confidence, so you need not fear reprisal. The confidentiality rule, like the others, is for everyone's benefit. Thank you for reminding yourself and co-workers of [YOUR COMPANY NAME]'s rules of conduct.

[ITEM 1] = First and last name of person receiving memo
[ITEM 2] = Describe rules needing reinforcement
[ITEM 3] = First and last name of person having the rule list
[ITEM 4] = First and last name of person responsible for enforcing the rules
[ITEM 5] = Telephone number for [ITEM 4]

INTEROFFICE MEMORANDUM

TO: [ITEM 1]   FROM: [YOUR NAME]

                                          [YOUR TITLE]

DATE: [DATE]   cc: [COPIES TO]

SUBJECT: Safety Reminder

In the 10 seconds it took you to read this far, an accident probably happened in our community because someone did not observe safety precautions. [YOUR COMPANY NAME] has an established safety awareness program that is a top priority for the entire work force.

I remind you that its success depends on everyone taking responsibility for safe work practices and procedures. One wrong move could endanger yourself and others. Exercising caution protects all employees, customers, and visitors.

Some of the safety guidelines developed within the awareness program are as follows: [ITEM 2]. Equipment operation and safety manuals are located [ITEM 3]. Still, the best safety recommendations come from the people closest to the program.

I encourage our employees to advise [ITEM 4] of any unsafe conditions or suggestions for improving safety in our company. [ITEM 5] is dedicated to administering and monitoring [YOUR COMPANY NAME]'s safety awareness program and can be reached at [ITEM 6]. Thank you for taking the extra time to practice safety in your work area.

[ITEM 1] = First and last name of person receiving memo
[ITEM 2] = Describe safety guidelines needing reinforcement
[ITEM 3] = Location of the equipment operation and safety manuals in office
[ITEM 4] = First and last name of person responsible for enforcing safety rules
[ITEM 5] = Pronoun referring to [ITEM 4]'s gender, i.e., "He" or "She"
[ITEM 6] = Telephone number for [ITEM 4]

INTEROFFICE MEMORANDUM

TO: [ITEM 1]   FROM: [YOUR NAME]

                              [YOUR TITLE]

DATE: [DATE]   cc: [COPIES TO]

SUBJECT: Security Reminder

Security is of utmost importance, both at home and in the workplace. The precautions we take protect us from harm. [YOUR COMPANY NAME] enforces security measures covering both information and property for the good of our employees, customers, and visitors.

[YOUR COMPANY NAME]'s security program requires the cooperation of our entire team of professionals. I remind you that no one is exempt from the rules we have developed to keep the workplace secure. They must be followed by all to serve all.

Briefly, our security program prohibits [ITEM 2]. In accordance with the law, inspections of office furniture may be conducted from time to time with or without your notice. Confidential information should be disposed of by [ITEM 3]. It should be stored in [ITEM 4].

If you have any comments or questions regarding [YOUR COMPANY NAME]'s security policy, contact [ITEM 5] at [ITEM 6]. [ITEM 7] is available to review our security program upon request. Thank you for your continued protection of our environment, information, and property.

[ITEM 1] = First and last name of person receiving memo
[ITEM 2] = Describe security guidelines needing reinforcement
[ITEM 3] = Describe the manner in which you want employees to dispose of confidential information
[ITEM 4] = Describe the manner in which you want employees to store confidential information
[ITEM 5] = First and last name of person responsible for enforcing security rules
[ITEM 6] = Telephone number for [ITEM 5]
[ITEM 7] = Pronoun referring to [ITEM 5]'s gender, i.e., "He" or "She"

INTEROFFICE MEMORANDUM

TO: [ITEM 1]   FROM: [YOUR NAME]

                                        [YOUR TITLE]

DATE: [DATE]   cc: [COPIES TO]

SUBJECT: Continuing Professional Education Request Authorization

Knowledge and proficiency are key factors determining whether a challenge becomes an opportunity or a pitfall. Maximizing professional accomplishment through continuing education is easily neglected when business pressures climb. On the other hand, I have seen very real benefits result from classroom experiences.

I would like to pursue professional education that I think will further [YOUR COMPANY NAME]'s short- and long-range goals. I have spent time during the weekend and evening hours looking for reading material on [ITEM 3]. While the bookstores and library offer a comprehensive selection, one cannot dispute the advantages of an instructor-directed curriculum.

I have found a [ITEM 2] that appears to be exactly what I need to increase my knowledge of [ITEM 3]. After checking the work schedule, I have concluded that the class held [ITEM 4] at [ITEM 5] would be convenient for all concerned. The cost per student is fairly reasonable at $[ITEM 6].

Upon receiving your positive reply, I will confirm my attendance and complete the required expense authorization forms. Thank you in advance for continuing to support my professional endeavors.

[ITEM 1] = First and last name of person receiving memo
[ITEM 2] = Describe the type of professional education, i.e., "class," "conference," "seminar," etc.
[ITEM 3] = Describe [ITEM 2]'s focus
[ITEM 4] = Date(s) and time [ITEM 2] will be held
[ITEM 5] = Location of [ITEM 2]
[ITEM 6] = Dollar amount charged per student for [ITEM 2]

INTEROFFICE MEMORANDUM

TO: [ITEM 1]   FROM: [YOUR NAME]

                                                   [YOUR TITLE]

DATE: [DATE]   cc: [COPIES TO]

SUBJECT: Request Authorization to Purchase [ITEM 2]

Attempting to do a job without the right equipment is frustrating at best. Patience wears thin as the deadline approaches and pressure rises. We just know, "There has got to be a better way."

Recently, I promised to find a solution to the frustration and wasted time caused by [ITEM 3]. Goal attainment is important to our team, and controlling the maximum number of variables is essential.

It have come up with a simple way to enhance our company's efficiency and morale. A [ITEM 2] would accomplish this quickly. A rough cost estimate is between $[ITEM 4] and $[ITEM 5]. Your experience may suggest a solution other than outright purchase.

We both know cost containment is an on-going [YOUR COMPANY NAME] goal. However, I believe this expense is justified. Upon receiving your authorization to procure [ITEM 2], I will perform a thorough analysis of features, manufacturer claims, pricing, and warranty coverage. The research results will then be presented for your recommendation. Thank you in advance for your prompt decision in this matter.

[ITEM 1] = First and last name of person receiving memo
[ITEM 2] = Describe equipment requested, i.e., "computer," "copier," "fax machine," "printer," etc.
[ITEM 3] = Describe problem caused by not having [ITEM 2]
[ITEM 4] = Dollar amount of lowest estimated price of [ITEM 2]
[ITEM 5] = Dollar amount of highest estimated price of [ITEM 2]

INTEROFFICE MEMORANDUM

TO: [ITEM 1]   FROM: [YOUR NAME]

                                                 [YOUR TITLE]

DATE: [DATE]   cc: [COPIES TO]

SUBJECT: Flexible Work Schedule Request

Self-direction is the linchpin of achievement. Organizations count on employees to be diligent, motivated, and productive without constant reminders. Because [YOUR COMPANY NAME] is secure in allowing proven performers to use their judgment daily, I am confident that my work schedule change request will be given careful consideration.

In my role as [ITEM 2], I am linked to [YOUR COMPANY NAME] by a function. The company has determined that my skills are best utilized to [ITEM 3]. My performance ratings are based on my progress toward that goal.

After much consideration, I firmly believe that [ITEM 3] can be accomplished under either a flexible or a traditional work schedule. I propose that my schedule be changed to reflect the following: [ITEM 4]. These hours are equal to those I currently work.

I would like to try a flexible work schedule and recommend that the change be implemented as a temporary move. In three to six months, a situational review could be the deciding factor. Thank you in advance for your prompt consideration of my request.

[ITEM 1] = First and last name of person receiving memo
[ITEM 2] = Your title or position
[ITEM 3] = Describe your job in one or two words
[ITEM 4] = Describe flexible work schedule in days and time reporting to and from work

INTEROFFICE MEMORANDUM

TO: [ITEM 1]   FROM: [YOUR NAME]

                                                [YOUR TITLE]

DATE: [DATE]   cc: [COPIES TO]

SUBJECT: Management Review Request

Mentor relationships—parent-child, teacher-student, coach-player, manager-employee—exist throughout our lives. In every such relationship, the mentor must be willing to teach, and the student to learn. Both parties must agree on the depth and direction of the relationship and the goals they want to realize. Clearly, I am the student to [ITEM 2] in a student-teacher relationship.

Today, I can look at myself in the mirror and honestly say that I have tried earnestly in actions and words to make my professional relationship with [ITEM 2] work. Frankly, I don't think [ITEM 3] can say the same. Under [ITEM 4]'s continued direction, my professional career will not be what is in my, or [YOUR COMPANY NAME]'s, best interest.

I trust you will keep my thoughts on the matter completely confidential until we personally discuss the details and possible alternatives. My concern has always been, and continues to be, for the company and for our team's success. Please call and let me know when we can meet. Thank you in advance for your professional courtesy and understanding; every winning player needs a good coach.

―――――――――――――◆―――――――――――――

[ITEM 1] = First and last name of person receiving memo
[ITEM 2] = First and last name of your manager
[ITEM 3] = Pronoun referring to [ITEM 2]'s gender, i.e., "he" or "she"
[ITEM 4] = First name of [ITEM 2]

INTEROFFICE MEMORANDUM

TO: [ITEM 1]   FROM: [YOUR NAME]

                                            [YOUR TITLE]

DATE: [DATE]   cc: [COPIES TO]

SUBJECT: Position and Title Review Request

     I relish the sort of professional challenge that makes my heart pump faster, keeps my mind alert, and calls forth my inner strength. These are truly invitations to test ambition, knowledge and skills. Thus far in my career, challenge has propelled me through success after success.

     Today, the challenge has been met in my position as [ITEM 2], creating the need to further my career ambitions. While this is not to imply that there is nothing left for me to learn, or no skill remaining to be perfected, I believe a transition to [ITEM 3] would be beneficial.

     To list all my accomplishments thus far on one page of typed text would not do them justice. There are many that demonstrate my ability, experience, and drive.

     If given the opportunity to be [YOUR COMPANY NAME]'s newest [ITEM 3], I would be the company's best defense against failure. You have my pledge that [YOUR COMPANY NAME] will not be disappointed. Thank you in advance for your consideration. I look forward to hearing your decision and welcoming the opportunity to prove further my worth as an employee and member of the [YOUR COMPANY NAME] team.

[ITEM 1] = Full name of person receiving memo
[ITEM 2] = Title of the position you now hold
[ITEM 3] = Title of the position you want

INTEROFFICE MEMORANDUM

TO: [ITEM 1]   FROM: [YOUR NAME]

                                     [YOUR TITLE]

DATE: [DATE]   cc: [COPIES TO]

SUBJECT: Compensation Increase Request

Asking for a raise is a difficult task. I've been writing this memorandum in my head for some time, trying to find the words that will reaffirm my value to [YOUR COMPANY NAME]. I wanted first to draw attention one-by-one to my accomplishments and the daily responsibilities benefiting our team in both the short- and the long term.

Next, there would be a gentle reminder that my salary has not been increased for [ITEM 2]. Inflation continues to increase, and money does not go as far as it once did. And finally, I would close with a standard request for a reevaluation of my total compensation package, trusting that my value as an employee and team member would be reflected in a well-deserved increase.

After further deliberation, I decided that this approach was not necessary, because as an effective coach, you stay close to your players. You are very familiar with my work habits and my dedication to the company. You would want to be fair and reward my efforts.

If you prefer, I can still write the memorandum originally planned. The first few paragraphs would be different; the ending the same. I believe my compensation increase request of [ITEM 3] is reasonable. If the request is not approved, I would like your help in formulating an action plan designed to help me obtain the increase in the very near future. Thank you in advance for acknowledging my value to [YOUR COMPANY NAME].

[ITEM 1] = First and last name of person receiving memo
[ITEM 2] = Length of time since last salary increase
[ITEM 3] = Dollar amount or percentage increase requested

INTEROFFICE MEMORANDUM

TO:	[ITEM 1]	FROM:	[YOUR NAME]
			[YOUR TITLE]
DATE:	[DATE]	cc:	[COPIES TO]

SUBJECT: Account Reviews Scheduled

From the very first "Hello," sales is a series of steps leading up to the customer's door. We may have to knock several times—some days loudly, some softly. Once inside, we offer confirmation of our professionalism and evidence that supports our contention that doing business with [YOUR COMPANY NAME] leads to shared success.

The intricacies of the sales cycle warrant maintaining close contact with your customers and management. As your coach, I want to help our team be successful in opening every door and keeping it open to future business.

I have scheduled an account review for you on [ITEM 2] at [ITEM 3] in [ITEM 4]. Please be prepared to discuss in detail your present, pending, and potential opportunities. In addition, we will discuss quotas and conduct an analysis of business lost. Specifically, list in chart form by customer name the following: [ITEM 5]. I am most interested in [ITEM 6].

If for some reason the account review conflicts with your schedule, advise me in writing immediately. Otherwise, I look forward to hearing all about your stairway to prosperity!

———————————————————

[ITEM 1] = First and last name of person receiving memo
[ITEM 2] = Date of meeting
[ITEM 3] = Location within office where meeting will be held
[ITEM 4] = Time the meeting begins
[ITEM 5] = Describe what you want to know
[ITEM 6] = Describe the information most important to you

INTEROFFICE MEMORANDUM

TO: [ITEM 1]   FROM: [YOUR NAME]

                                         [YOUR TITLE]

DATE: [DATE]   cc: [COPIES TO]

SUBJECT: Sales Contest

     Could you use [ITEM 2]? [YOUR COMPANY NAME] would like to give you this. First, however, you have to win our sales contest. One warning though: only the best members of the sales force should read on.

     It's going to take real effort to win this contest. You must [ITEM 3] by [ITEM 4]. No problem you say?

     Granted, this isn't much of challenge for the performers in the crowd. So, to make it a little tougher, we've added some rules: [ITEM 5]. Get out there and dare your peers! As the date approaches, look for status reports in your company mail. Until then, may the best salesperson win!

[ITEM 1] = First and last name of person receiving memo
[ITEM 2] = Describe the contest prize
[ITEM 3] = Describe what [ITEM 1] has to do to win
[ITEM 4] = Date contest ends
[ITEM 5] = Describe the contest rules

INTEROFFICE MEMORANDUM

TO: [ITEM 1]   FROM: [YOUR NAME]

                                            [YOUR TITLE]

DATE: [DATE]   cc: [COPIES TO]

SUBJECT: Forecast Due

Marketing is what we do to obtain sales. Predicting the future is often a futile effort because so many uncertainties affect the result. Yet, making management aware of your time-based marketing and sales goals enables us to offer assistance and expertise wherever possible.

Please prepare your sales forecast for the next [ITEM 2] and have it in my office by [ITEM 3]. Specifically, list in chart form by customer name the following: [ITEM 4]. I am most interested in [ITEM 5].

Please make your forecast as complete and accurate as possible. If you have any questions, contact me immediately. Contrary to popular belief, we do control our own destinies—with actions taken today.

————————————◆————————————

[ITEM 1] = First and last name of person receiving memo
[ITEM 2] = Period forecast covers
[ITEM 3] = Date forecast is due
[ITEM 4] = Describe what you want to know
[ITEM 5] = Describe the information most important to you

INTEROFFICE MEMORANDUM

TO: [ITEM 1]   FROM: [YOUR NAME]

                                 [YOUR TITLE]

DATE: [DATE]   cc: [COPIES TO]

SUBJECT: Monthly Sales Request

Maintaining communications with the sales force is sometimes difficult. By all means, we want you to be with customers in the field or on the telephone helping customers gain additional insight about [YOUR COMPANY NAME]'s growing placement in the [ITEM 2] industry.

Unless you take a moment out today for paperwork and tell us how you're doing with our customers, we'll never know how we can help you. Please prepare your monthly sales figures for the month of [ITEM 3] and have them in my office by [ITEM 4].

Specifically, list in chart form by customer name the following: [ITEM 5]. I am most interested in [ITEM 6].

If you anticipate a problem getting the report in on time, let me know immediately. I look forward to spreading your success stories throughout the company.

[ITEM 1] = **First and last name of person receiving memo**
[ITEM 2] = **Describe the industry focus of [YOUR COMPANY NAME]**
[ITEM 3] = **Month of the year sales results cover**
[ITEM 4] = **Date monthly sales results are due**
[ITEM 5] = **Describe what you want to know**
[ITEM 6] = **Describe the information most important to you**

INTEROFFICE MEMORANDUM

TO: [ITEM 1]   FROM: [YOUR NAME]

                                                             [YOUR TITLE]

DATE: [DATE]   cc: [COPIES TO]

SUBJECT: Territory Change and Realignment

No prospering business can remain static in today's changing environment. Our sales force, which represents a large segment of our operation, is directly influenced by these changes. Occasionally, territory assignments must be realigned in response to industry and market conditions.

We have given the highest priority to promoting individual opportunities for achievement. When allocating resources, previous success and sales focus are weighed along with potential for growth. Please note the following changes in your territory assignment effective [ITEM 2].

Your new territory consists of [ITEM 3]. A list of sales in process and not yet closed from your previous assignment must be presented to me in writing by [ITEM 4]. The status of these accounts will be determined on a case-by-case basis using established criteria.

If you have any comments or questions, bring these to my attention immediately. I extend my wishes for continued success in this new assignment.

[ITEM 1] = First and last name of person receiving memo
[ITEM 2] = Date territory change is effective
[ITEM 3] = Describe new territory
[ITEM 4] = Date by which [ITEM 1] should advise you of any sales from old territory assignment

INTEROFFICE MEMORANDUM

TO: [ITEM 1]   FROM: [YOUR NAME]

                                                     [YOUR TITLE]

DATE: [DATE]   cc: [COPIES TO]

SUBJECT: Trade Show Announcement

      Tired of the same old routine? Isn't it time you took action? Seized the opportunity to have customers come to you? Mingled with industry leaders? Or just spent time with your existing accounts away from the telephone?

      Get the competitive edge in your marketing and sales future by attending the [ITEM 2] on [ITEM 3] at [ITEM 4] in [ITEM 5]. The literature on the event looks like the latest "Who's Who" register in our industry. [YOUR COMPANY NAME] has endorsed [ITEM 2] by extending personal invitations to our customers.

      For existing customers, the invitation is an act of continued goodwill. New customers are reminded that we haven't forgotten about them. As for prospects, a phone call to invite them provides another opportunity to reaffirm our professional commitment.

      Anyone who attends the show will surely walk away with increased market awareness and knowledge of [ITEM 6]. Please prepare a list of your customers who should be invited and outline what will be gained by their attendance. I need this no later than [ITEM 7]. Salespeople whose customers are selected to attend the event will be advised.

[ITEM 1] = First and last name of person receiving memo
[ITEM 2] = Name of trade show
[ITEM 3] = Date(s) of trade show
[ITEM 4] = Building or physical location of trade show in [ITEM 5]
[ITEM 5] = City and state of trade show
[ITEM 6] = Describe the focus of trade show
[ITEM 7] = Date by which you want to receive [ITEM 1]'s invitation list

INTEROFFICE MEMORANDUM

TO: [ITEM 1]   FROM: [YOUR NAME]

                                        [YOUR TITLE]

DATE: [DATE]   cc: [COPIES TO]

SUBJECT: Resignation Notice

Professional growth is inspiring and isolating simultaneously. While accomplishments are gratifying, the achievement drives us beyond our previous expectations. Standards are raised for the next challenge, and separation from the familiar increases.

In my life, I have learned to seize challenge whenever it crosses my path. I try always to approach my quest for success with zeal. We are truly the ultimate creators of our destinies.

Unfortunately, my professional goals are no longer compatible with those of my position as [ITEM 2]. This warrants a change in direction and focus. After much deliberation, I believe the time has come for me to move forward without [YOUR COMPANY NAME]. I hereby respectfully submit my resignation and provide [ITEM 3] weeks' notice.

I thank you and [YOUR COMPANY NAME] for an unparalleled opportunity to grow, which has allowed me to prepare for my next challenge. [ITEM 4], you have been an inspiration to me, and I hope we can keep abreast of each other's successes.

[ITEM 1] = First and last name of person receiving memo
[ITEM 2] = Title of position leaving
[ITEM 3] = Time in weeks of resignation notice
[ITEM 4] = First name of [ITEM 1]

INTEROFFICE MEMORANDUM

TO: [ITEM 1]   FROM: [YOUR NAME]

                                        [YOUR TITLE]

DATE: [DATE]   cc: [COPIES TO]

SUBJECT: Retirement Notice

Leaving friends behind when circumstances change is one of the most difficult things in life. Promises to keep in touch fade as time goes by. This makes it especially painful for me to leave my friends at [YOUR COMPANY NAME].

Over the years, I have developed many wonderful relationships within our company. There were good times. There were challenging times. Today, I look back while submitting this retirement notice and wonder, "Where did all the time go?"

Yet in doing so, I am confident that the ambitions and goals of the remaining team will guide [YOUR COMPANY NAME]'s continued prosperity. My retirement will take effect in [ITEM 2] weeks. Thank you for such a rewarding professional experience. [ITEM 3], it is my hope that we will, indeed, keep in touch. This would mean a great deal to me.

[ITEM 1] = First and last name of person receiving memo
[ITEM 2] = Time in weeks of retirement notice
[ITEM 3] = First name of [ITEM 1]

INTEROFFICE MEMORANDUM

TO: [ITEM 1]   FROM: [YOUR NAME]

                                        [YOUR TITLE]

DATE: [DATE]   cc: [COPIES TO]

SUBJECT: Vacation Request

Vacations are a necessary evil. I always hesitate to relax and leave projects in process. However, recharging one's batteries away from the office really does wonders.

I am planning a trip [ITEM 2] to [ITEM 3] using [ITEM 4] days of my available vacation time. While figuring out the details, I have noticed that "nonrefundable" and "cancellation penalty" are leisure industry buzzwords lately. Therefore, I await your approval before making final arrangements.

Please let me know as soon as possible if my vacation request meets with your approval. Thank you in advance. As you know, "advance bookings" usually net the best prices.

[ITEM 1] = First and last name of person receiving memo
[ITEM 2] = First day of vacation time
[ITEM 3] = Last day of vacation time
[ITEM 4] = Total number of vacation days used

INTEROFFICE MEMORANDUM

TO: [ITEM 1]   FROM: [YOUR NAME]

                                          [YOUR TITLE]

DATE: [DATE]   cc: [COPIES TO]

SUBJECT: Thank You

There is a tendency to be overconfident when things are going well. We forget to pay attention to details or, worse, fail to give proper thought to our actions. The earlier the problem is recognized, the better.

Although this may sound strange, I want to thank you for voicing your concerns regarding my [ITEM 2]. You helped me recognize the immediate and long-term detrimental effects of this shortcoming.

Please know that I have made a commitment to follow your suggestions and change for my own and [YOUR COMPANY NAME]'s benefit. [ITEM 3], again I extend my thanks for caring enough to make me aware of the problem before it had a chance to damage my career.

[ITEM 1] = First and last name of person receiving memo
[ITEM 2] = Describe the problem [ITEM 1] identified
[ITEM 3] = First name of [ITEM 1]

INTEROFFICE MEMORANDUM

TO: [ITEM 1]   FROM: [YOUR NAME]

                                         [YOUR TITLE]

DATE: [DATE]   cc: [COPIES TO]

SUBJECT: Thank You

     I have often wondered whether goal attainment is encouraged more by managerial support in and of itself or the confidence engendered by that support. Your actions regarding [ITEM 2] clearly lend credence to both hypotheses.

     The extra effort, patience, and time you willingly dedicate to ensuring the accuracy and completeness of my work do not go unnoticed. My experience with other managers gives me an even greater appreciation of you.

     [ITEM 3], thank you for giving me the confidence I need to excel in my life. It means even more coming from a person of your stature.

[ITEM 1] = First and last name of person receiving memo
[ITEM 2] = Describe the most recent job, project, or task [ITEM 1] helped you with
[ITEM 3] = First name of [ITEM 1]

INTEROFFICE MEMORANDUM

TO: [ITEM 1]   FROM: [YOUR NAME]

                                      [YOUR TITLE]

DATE: [DATE]   cc: [COPIES TO]

SUBJECT: Thank You

     Professional accomplishment is not the result of a single day's work. Carefully considered actions build upon one another until the goal is achieved. Look at any successful person, and it will be evident that he or she did not get there alone.

     Achievers acknowledge areas of inadequacy and are not afraid to obtain qualified assistance in reaching their goals. The key is finding a complementary personality who is also compelled to be the best in his or her chosen field. I take this time to say that I found a match while working with you on [ITEM 2].

     You were such an instrumental member of the team, assisting the project by [ITEM 3]. Please know that your dedication and hard work are appreciated, and I look forward to our next opportunity to work together. Thank you again for sharing the expertise that helped bring [ITEM 2] to a positive conclusion.

————————————◆————————————

[ITEM 1] = First and last name of person receiving memo
[ITEM 2] = Name of project
[ITEM 3] = Describe [ITEM 1]'s contribution to [ITEM 2]

INTEROFFICE MEMORANDUM

TO: [ITEM 1]   FROM: [YOUR NAME]

                                        [YOUR TITLE]

DATE: [DATE]   cc: [COPIES TO]

SUBJECT: Thank You

The greater the accomplishment, the greater the significance of receiving acknowledgment from those held in esteem. Since we first worked together, I have admired and respected your judgment and decision-making ability. Frankly, these are both areas I have been working on myself.

The reinforcement of my efforts by a person I hold in high regard is appreciated. Thank you for the positive feedback regarding my contribution to [ITEM 2]. With the additional confidence gained from this accomplishment and your recognition, I feel ready to take on new responsibilities and meet new challenges.

[ITEM 1] = First and last name of person receiving memo
[ITEM 2] = Describe what you did that [ITEM 1] recognized

SECTION 4

Personal Correspondence

Finally, all those necessary life-preservation letters. Until now, writing these letters was a hassle that took time away from your career and family. If you are like most of us, the only time you draft a personal note is when you have something to complain about or something you would rather not say.

Has a product, service, neighbor, politician, or family member slighted you? Don't worry, a letter to deal with it is in this section. In addition, you will find letters for such real-life issues as credit reports, alimony payments, home repairs, child support, job searches, and much more. For best results, take time to describe the problem clearly.

Work the System.   Picture yourself for a moment in the recipient's shoes, say a customer service representative at a major credit card company. Every day, you are handed 20 letters rudely loaded with "your company did this to me" and "I want this now."

About letter number five is your letter from this book saying more or less, "Wow, am I glad you are there to help me out!" You are. Without this person's assistance, you still have the problem. What kind of attention do you think your letter will receive compared to the other 19?

It's astounding. Letters of complaint like the ones in this book elicit telephone calls from customer service representatives who want to tell you that the problem has been solved. No need to send more information. No more asking for the supervisor in charge. We show compassion and receive compassion in return.

Even for the smallest things, like copies of official records, the personal touch ensures that your request is filled quicker than anybody else's.

Strength in Delivery.   There are, of course, times when stronger words are necessary. Pollyannas get used. However, appealing to the conscience of the addressee raises you above him and the situation.

For example, you lent some money to a friend and were never repaid. You want the loan repaid. The person is either financially pressured or lacking in character. Make your friend feel guilty for betraying your trust. Concentrate on that approach rather than demanding the money, and watch what happens.

Ask your local car mechanic if he or she would treat that one, special person in his or her life the way you've been treated. We all have, or had, someone dear to us. If you want a personal loan, explain to your family or friend that you need help and have no one else to turn to. Do it not in a pathetic way, but in way that awakens a desire to help.

And the long lost love letter, which has been replaced by the manufactured greeting card is here to address the stages most relationships pass through. I can't guarantee that the letters in this book will help you find the love of your life, but I do guarantee that the object of your affections will get the message. Communication is the foundation of every beautiful relationship.

[YOUR ADDRESS]
[YOUR CITY], [YOUR STATE] [YOUR ZIP CODE]
[YOUR TELEPHONE NUMBER]
[DATE]

Customer Service Department
[COMPANY]
[ADDRESS]
[CITY], [STATE] [ZIP CODE]

Reference Account Number: [ITEM 1]

Dear Sir or Madam:

It's so easy to make mistakes. Customers are glad to know that [COMPANY] has employees like you who take the time to help correct the errors on our statements. While reviewing my credit card statement dated [ITEM 2], I noticed an incorrect entry.

The problem is identified by transaction code [ITEM 3], with [ITEM 4], and the date of the transaction is [ITEM 5]. After reviewing my records, I find that the correct [ITEM 6] should be [ITEM 7].

I am enclosing supporting documentation to simplify your speedy investigation of the matter. If there are any questions, please write or telephone me at the address and phone provided above. Thank you for your assistance. I do understand that mistakes happen, and I appreciate your help in correcting this one.

Sincerely yours,

[YOUR NAME]

————————◆————————

[ITEM 1] = Your credit card account number
[ITEM 2] = Date of statement on which error appears
[ITEM 3] = Transaction code of error on statement
[ITEM 4] = Name of company involved with transaction
[ITEM 5] = Date the transaction was posted on statement
[ITEM 6] = Describe where error appears
[ITEM 7] = Describe the correction required

[YOUR ADDRESS]
[YOUR CITY], [YOUR STATE] [YOUR ZIP CODE]
[YOUR TELEPHONE NUMBER]
[DATE]

[Mr./Mrs./Ms./Dr.] [FIRST AND LAST NAME]
[TITLE]
[COMPANY]
[ADDRESS]
[CITY], [STATE] [ZIP CODE]

Dear [Mr./Mrs./Ms./Dr.] [LAST NAME]:

A person in your position realizes the importance of credit. More than ever, a consumer's credit rating is the Bible to which companies turn when granting any financial assistance. One wrong entry can have devastating results.

Recently, I discovered that there is an inaccurate entry on my credit report. I request your assistance in challenging and removing this erroneous statement pertaining to [ITEM 1]. It should not there because [ITEM 2].

The following information may be helpful in your professional investigation of the matter:

      1. My social security number is [ITEM 3].
      2. My last address was [ITEM 4].

Please do not hesitate to contact me at the address or telephone number above. Thank you for taking the steps necessary to make my credit report reflect the truth. As the report stands today, it is detrimental to my entire family's financial future.

Sincerely yours,

[YOUR NAME]

[ITEM 1] = Name of company involved with error
[ITEM 2] = Describe why there is an error
[ITEM 3] = Your social security number
[ITEM 4] = Your previous mailing address

[YOUR ADDRESS]
[YOUR CITY], [YOUR STATE] [YOUR ZIP CODE]
[YOUR TELEPHONE NUMBER]
[DATE]

[Mr./Mrs./Ms./Dr.] [FIRST AND LAST NAME]
[TITLE]
[COMPANY]
[ADDRESS]
[CITY], [STATE] [ZIP CODE]

Dear [Mr./Mrs./Ms./Dr.] [LAST NAME]:

Before making a decision, it's best to have all the pertinent information in hand. Credit reports are used so often, I would like to know exactly what mine contains. It is my understanding that a credit report from [COMPANY] costs $[ITEM 1], and I have enclosed a personal check for this amount.

The contact information above is current and may be used to process this request. In addition, my social security number is [ITEM 2], I was born on [ITEM 3], and my current employer is [ITEM 4]. Thank you for your assistance, which will enable me to have the facts in hand.

Sincerely yours,

[YOUR NAME]

[ITEM 1] = **Dollar amount credit report costs**
[ITEM 2] = **Your social security number**
[ITEM 3] = **Your date of birth**
[ITEM 4] = **Your current employer**

[YOUR ADDRESS]
[YOUR CITY], [YOUR STATE] [YOUR ZIP CODE]
[YOUR TELEPHONE NUMBER]
[DATE]

[Mr./Mrs./Ms./Dr.] [FIRST AND LAST NAME]
[TITLE]
[COMPANY]
[ADDRESS]
[CITY], [STATE] [ZIP CODE]

Dear [Mr./Mrs./Ms./Dr.] [LAST NAME]:

Putting the right facts and figures on a credit application is sometimes an uphill battle. The spaces are small, and the details many. It's easy to skip over an area or put something in the wrong place.

This must have happened when I filled out [COMPANY]'s credit application and subsequently received a denial notice. The reason given was [ITEM 1]. That is difficult to understand considering [ITEM 2]. Therefore, I would like to reapply for credit based on the following information: [ITEM 3].

Please do whatever is necessary to have my application reconsidered in light of this information. I cannot imagine that there would be a problem now. This time, I trust you will fill-in-the-blanks for me correctly. Thank you for your assistance and professional handling of the matter.

Sincerely yours,

[YOUR NAME]

[ITEM 1] = Describe [COMPANY]'s reason for denying credit
[ITEM 2] = Describe your reason for thinking there has been an error
[ITEM 3] = Specific information as relates to [ITEM 2]

[YOUR ADDRESS]
[YOUR CITY], [YOUR STATE] [YOUR ZIP CODE]
[YOUR TELEPHONE NUMBER]
[DATE]

[Mr./Mrs./Ms./Dr.] [FIRST AND LAST NAME]
[TITLE]
[COMPANY]
[ADDRESS]
[CITY], [STATE] [ZIP CODE]

Dear [Mr./Mrs./Ms./Dr.] [LAST NAME]:

Applying for credit is a laborious, time-consuming process. Because I devoted much effort and time to completing [COMPANY]'s application, I was disgruntled upon receiving a form letter of denial. I cannot understand why such a negative conclusion was drawn about a person with an honorable financial track record.

No reason was provided. The letter consisted of boiler plate paragraphs saying, "Thanks, but no thanks." Please notify me in writing of the decision criteria used by [COMPANY]. Specifically, I am curious to know whether the decision was based wholly, or in part, on my credit report or another source of credit information.

There may an error I am unaware of somewhere. Perhaps I should be happy I was denied credit by [COMPANY]; my other credit cards have not been used for a while. Regardless, I do extend my thanks for helping me discover the basis on which your company has denied my credit request.

Sincerely yours,

[YOUR NAME]

[YOUR ADDRESS]
[YOUR CITY], [YOUR STATE] [YOUR ZIP CODE]
[YOUR TELEPHONE NUMBER]
[DATE]

[Mr./Mrs./Ms./Dr.] [FIRST AND LAST NAME]
Attorney General's Office
[ADDRESS]
[CITY], [STATE] [ZIP CODE]

Dear [Mr./Mrs./Ms./Dr.] [LAST NAME]:

Consumers have rights that some businesses elect to ignore. I have tried repeatedly, through conversations and letters, to reach a solution regarding my problems with [ITEM 1], located at [ITEM 2] in [CITY]. Finally, having no other place to turn, I am writing to you.

On [ITEM 3], I [ITEM 4] to [ITEM 5]. I did not anticipate any problems based upon [ITEM 1]'s representations, which included [ITEM 6]. However, [ITEM 1] did not adhere to their commitment in the following ways: [ITEM 7].

After making [ITEM 1] aware of my dissatisfaction, all I heard was [ITEM 8]. No consumer should be subject to such a blatant display of bad business practices. I ask only [ITEM 9] from [ITEM 1]. Thank you for your assistance in solving the problem. I need to know that government officials have the power to enforce the law and preserve my rights and those of other consumers.

Sincerely yours,

[YOUR NAME]

[ITEM 1] = Name of company you are having the problem with
[ITEM 2] = Street address of [ITEM 1]
[ITEM 3] = Date the incident first occurred
[ITEM 4] = Describe the action you took on [ITEM 3]
[ITEM 5] = Describe the result of [ITEM 4]
[ITEM 6] = Describe what [ITEM 1] told you on [ITEM 3]
[ITEM 7] = Describe [ITEM 1]'s misrepresentations
[ITEM 8] = Describe what has resulted from your attempts to fix the problem
[ITEM 9] = Describe what you want from [ITEM 1] now

[YOUR ADDRESS]
[YOUR CITY], [YOUR STATE] [YOUR ZIP CODE]
[YOUR TELEPHONE NUMBER]
[DATE]

[Mr./Mrs./Ms./Dr.] [FIRST AND LAST NAME]
[TITLE]
[COMPANY]
[ADDRESS]
[CITY], [STATE] [ZIP CODE]

Dear [Mr./Mrs./Ms./Dr.] [LAST NAME]:

Who is the special person you treasure most? Think for a moment of the last time you were with him or her. I want you to remember those feelings of security and trust as I relate my most recent experience with [COMPANY].

On [ITEM 1], I bought my [ITEM 2] to your establishment for [ITEM 3]. Being familiar with the inner workings of a car, I had no reason to believe that the repair would be difficult. However, [COMPANY]'s actions as shown by [ITEM 4] are clearly beyond the pale.

From the very first time I walked through your doors, "no problem" and "we'll take care of you" were your staff's words. Obviously, they were lying. Is this how you would treat a member of your family or a close friend? Would you expect someone you loved to accept this behavior? Unless you are a person with absolutely no compassion, it's highly doubtful.

My faith in [COMPANY] as an honorable company that will give me the service I deserve as a customer is gone. It will be restored only if [COMPANY] takes the initiative and [ITEM 5]. Undoubtedly, this would be possible for the special person you treasure most. I look forward to hearing from you immediately before the relationship is severed and hope vanishes entirely. A business is never so big that it can afford to lose one customer.

Sincerely yours,

[YOUR NAME]

[ITEM 1] = Date the incident occurred
[ITEM 2] = Describe product repaired
[ITEM 3] = Describe the reason [ITEM 2] was brought to [COMPANY]
[ITEM 4] = Describe the reason you are complaining
[ITEM 5] = Describe what you want [COMPANY] to do now

[YOUR ADDRESS]
[YOUR CITY], [YOUR STATE] [YOUR ZIP CODE]
[YOUR TELEPHONE NUMBER]
[DATE]

[Mr./Mrs./Ms./Dr.] [FIRST AND LAST NAME]
[TITLE]
[COMPANY]
[ADDRESS]
[CITY], [STATE] [ZIP CODE]

Dear [Mr./Mrs./Ms./Dr.] [LAST NAME]:

    Many movements and organizations have been formed to protect our natural surroundings. The world has realized that there is still one thing scientists cannot do in their laboratories. They cannot recreate the Earth; they can only help us preserve it.

    Acid rain, global warming, oil spills, tropical deforestation, and nuclear catastrophes make the newspaper headlines and overshadow local problems, making them seem insignificant. But they are not, and [COMPANY] must be aware that its actions affect the environment. Your company's [ITEM 1] is detrimental to every member of the community.

    Clearly, a person in your position understands the short- and long-term devastation that can be caused by [ITEM 1]. I don't know how you can go home to your own family each night knowing that you are personally contributing to the destruction of their future. The lobbyists, politicians, and environmental organizations do their jobs. I want you to do yours, which goes beyond increasing [COMPANY] revenues for stockholders. The environment is our individual and collective responsibility. Won't you please do your share?

Sincerely yours,

[YOUR NAME]

[ITEM 1] = Describe the environment problem caused by [COMPANY]

[YOUR ADDRESS]
[YOUR CITY], [YOUR STATE] [YOUR ZIP CODE]
[YOUR TELEPHONE NUMBER]
[DATE]

[Mr./Mrs./Ms./Dr.] [FIRST AND LAST NAME]
[TITLE]
[COMPANY]
[ADDRESS]
[CITY], [STATE] [ZIP CODE]

Dear [Mr./Mrs./Ms./Dr.] [LAST NAME]:

Time slips away if it is not watched carefully. Around [ITEM 1], I purchased a [ITEM 2] from [ITEM 3]. Circumstances changed, and rather than returning the [ITEM 2] for a refund, I kept the product in storage. I knew I would use it someday.

Today, for the first time, I attempted to use the [ITEM 2]. Much to my surprise, it did not work. There is a problem with the unit's [ITEM 4]. It might as well still be sitting in the closet.

Because I did not try the [ITEM 2] immediately, the unit is no longer covered by [COMPANY]'s warranty. However, if the purchase and first use were today, the unit would be under warranty. I hope [COMPANY] understands my predicament and will extend the warranty to fix the problem at no charge.

Ever since I made my first [COMPANY] purchase years ago, I have been a fan of your company. The higher price was a trade-off for quality. Therefore, it is my hope that you will uphold your reputation and fulfill my expectation of continued service. I do not want a refund, just the necessary repairs. Please advise me how to proceed. Thank you in advance for your assistance. I would like to use my [ITEM 2] as soon as possible.

Sincerely yours,

[YOUR NAME]

———————————————◆———————————————

[ITEM 1] = Date you estimate product was purchased
[ITEM 2] = Name of product and model number assigned by manufacturer
[ITEM 3] = Name of the place at which you bought the product
[ITEM 4] = Describe why the product does not work properly

[YOUR ADDRESS]
[YOUR CITY], [YOUR STATE] [YOUR ZIP CODE]
[YOUR TELEPHONE NUMBER]
[DATE]

[Mr./Mrs./Ms./Dr.] [FIRST AND LAST NAME]
[TITLE]
[COMPANY]
[ADDRESS]
[CITY], [STATE] [ZIP CODE]

Dear [Mr./Mrs./Ms./Dr.] [LAST NAME]:

It's a terrible feeling to know someone has taken advantage of your good nature. Frankly, I thought [COMPANY] was unlike other repair companies. I mistakenly believed that your work would be done professionally and quickly.

On [ITEM 1], your representative, [ITEM 2], arrived at my home around [ITEM 3] to [ITEM 4]. The fact that [ITEM 5] was late did not cause too much trouble. I was simply happy to have a specialist on the scene to make the necessary repairs.

That lack of punctuality should have been a clue, however. After [ITEM 2] arrived, [ITEM 5] recommended [ITEM 6]. The result was [ITEM 7].

Today, the problem is [ITEM 8]. I believe it would be in [COMPANY]'s best interest to keep this customer satisfied. The only way is to [ITEM 9]. Thank you doing what is required to change my attitude toward [COMPANY]. Your job has made my home-sweet-home havoc.

Sincerely yours,

[YOUR NAME]

[ITEM 1] = Date services were performed
[ITEM 2] = First and last name of repair person
[ITEM 3] = Time the repair person arrived
[ITEM 4] = Describe why [COMPANY] was called
[ITEM 5] = Pronoun referring to [ITEM 2]'s gender, i.e., "he" or "she"
[ITEM 6] = Describe what [ITEM 2] said the problem was and his/her recommendations
[ITEM 7] = Describe what happened after [ITEM 6]
[ITEM 8] = Describe why you are dissatisfied
[ITEM 9] = Describe want you want from [COMPANY] now

[YOUR ADDRESS]
[YOUR CITY], [YOUR STATE] [YOUR ZIP CODE]
[YOUR TELEPHONE NUMBER]
[DATE]

[Mr./Mrs./Ms./Dr.] [FIRST AND LAST NAME]
[TITLE]
[COMPANY]
[ADDRESS]
[CITY], [STATE] [ZIP CODE]

Dear [Mr./Mrs./Ms./Dr.] [LAST NAME]:

Your job can make my life easier. You know more about insurance claim processing than I ever will. Therefore, I request your professional assistance in reevaluating the reimbursement for a [ITEM 1] claim.

On [ITEM 2], I filed a claim for [ITEM 3] as covered by policy number [ITEM 4]. I was advised today in writing that claim number [ITEM 5] was reimbursed only [ITEM 6] percent of the total $[ITEM 7] due. I have attached a copy of this letter for you.

After reviewing my policy and [COMPANY]'s explanation, I am sure that there has been a mistake in the reimbursement amount. Won't you please take a moment today to review both my policy and [COMPANY]'s reimbursement for any errors? Thank you in advance for the extra effort that may be required to correct the amount to which I am entitled. It gives me one less thing to worry about.

Sincerely yours,

[YOUR NAME]

[ITEM 1] = Describe the nature of the claim, i.e., "automobile," "dental," or "medical"
[ITEM 2] = Date claim was filed
[ITEM 3] = Describe the reason for claim
[ITEM 4] = Number of your insurance policy
[ITEM 5] = Number assigned by [COMPANY] to claim
[ITEM 6] = Percent of the total amount of claim reimbursed
[ITEM 7] = Dollar amount of total claim

[YOUR ADDRESS]
[YOUR CITY], [YOUR STATE] [YOUR ZIP CODE]
[YOUR TELEPHONE NUMBER]
[DATE]

[Mr./Mrs./Ms./Dr.] [FIRST AND LAST NAME]
[TITLE]
[COMPANY]
[ADDRESS]
[CITY], [STATE] [ZIP CODE]

Dear [Mr./Mrs./Ms./Dr.] [LAST NAME]:

Newspapers are not always an impartial and unbiased information source. Too often, stories reflect the interests of advertisers, editors, or writers more than the interests of readers. I was reminded of this dismal fact while reading the [ITEM 1] issue of [COMPANY].

On page [ITEM 2], the headline reads, "[ITEM 3]." Underneath that headline, [ITEM 4] asserts that [ITEM 5]. May I remind you that journalists have a responsibility to ensure the objectivity and accuracy of the news items they print?

A more accurate account would have revealed the issue in its entirety by including [ITEM 6]. Unsuspecting readers were left at a loss. Reading between the lines of the story and the situation makes me question [COMPANY]'s motives for stooping so low. Thank you for returning to fact-based stories. Your newspaper is starting to become strikingly similar to the absurd tabloids found at the checkout counter of the grocery store.

Sincerely yours,

[YOUR NAME]

[ITEM 1] = Date of publication
[ITEM 2] = Page number on which story can be found in [ITEM 1] issue
[ITEM 3] = Exact wording of headline above story
[ITEM 4] = First and last name of journalist
[ITEM 5] = Describe your interpretation of the story
[ITEM 6] = Describe what was left out of the story

[YOUR ADDRESS]
[YOUR CITY], [YOUR STATE] [YOUR ZIP CODE]
[YOUR TELEPHONE NUMBER]
[DATE]

[Mr./Mrs./Ms./Dr.] [FIRST AND LAST NAME]
The Honorable [TITLE]
[ADDRESS]
[CITY], [STATE] [ZIP CODE]

Dear [TITLE] [LAST NAME]:

I have no doubt that you are an intelligent human being. Winning a political race requires intelligence as well as the oft-cited perseverance and stamina. However, the stance you have taken on [ITEM 1] makes me question your decision-making abilities.

Perhaps you are simply giving more weight to your advisers' research than to logic. I remind you that [ITEM 1] is [ITEM 2]. It affects not only our future, but the futures of succeeding generations.

In addition, there is [ITEM 3] to consider. The public uproar has merely begun. Once the media get to the bottom of the story, actions detrimental to your political career, or what's left of it at that point, are inevitable. Use your intelligence; sit down with a piece of paper and list the pros on one side, the cons on the other. I am confident that a black-and-white representation of the [ITEM 1] issue will show clearly where your political aspirations are in jeopardy.

Sincerely yours,

[YOUR NAME]

[ITEM 1] = Describe the issue
[ITEM 2] = Describe the major problem with the issue
[ITEM 3] = Describe another major problem with the issue

[YOUR ADDRESS]
[YOUR CITY], [YOUR STATE] [YOUR ZIP CODE]
[YOUR TELEPHONE NUMBER]
[DATE]

[Mr./Mrs./Ms./Dr.] [FIRST AND LAST NAME]
[ADDRESS]
[CITY], [STATE] [ZIP CODE]

Dear [FIRST NAME],

History has not changed the character traits that separate the good from the bad. In our quest for the good, we look for dignity, honesty, integrity, righteousness, and truth. I am sorry for both of us that my opinion of you is changing quickly.

I reached out to you with encouraging words and financial support. It was my way of demonstrating the faith I have in you, your character, and your talents. I trusted that the $[ITEM 1] loan I made would be repaid as promised.

The money is not the overriding issue now. It is the commitment you made to me and the disappointment I feel in your failure to exhibit the characteristics of a forthright person. If you cannot repay me, be strong enough to confront the issue with the confidence that decency rules. We are not handed character; we make it ourselves. I hope to hear from you soon, and I hope further that my original opinion of you was not founded on poor judgment.

Cordially yours,

[YOUR NAME]

_____

[ITEM 1] = Dollar amount of loan

[YOUR ADDRESS]
[YOUR CITY], [YOUR STATE] [YOUR ZIP CODE]
[YOUR TELEPHONE NUMBER]
[DATE]

[GOVERNMENT AGENCY NAME]
[ADDRESS]
[CITY], [STATE] [ZIP CODE]

Dear Sir or Madam:

Our nation's strength lies in the cooperation of the people with the government. There is not one among us who particularly enjoys paying taxes. Yet, we are quick to criticize unacceptable roads, old schools, defunct public programs, declining medical research, and other government-funded efforts.

As a hard-working taxpayer, I am resentful when my fellow citizens do not contribute to the country's welfare. I do, and so should they. Herein lies the problem and why I take time to inform you that [ITEM 1] living in [ITEM 2] is not contributing [ITEM 3] share.

While I do not have facts to prove my claim, [ITEM 3] boasting of techniques to avoid paying taxes must be stopped. This situation is definitely worthy of investigation. Carrying neither more nor less than the next person means carrying your share too. Together, we can make sure this basic principle survives for the benefit of all.

Cordially yours,

A Tax-Paying Citizen

[ITEM 1] = First and last name of tax evader
[ITEM 2] = City and state in which [ITEM 1] resides
[ITEM 3] = Pronoun referring to [ITEM 1]'s gender, i.e., "his" or "her"

[YOUR ADDRESS]
[YOUR CITY], [YOUR STATE] [YOUR ZIP CODE]
[YOUR TELEPHONE NUMBER]
[DATE]

[Mr./Mrs./Ms./Dr.] [FIRST AND LAST NAME]
[ADDRESS]
[CITY], [STATE] [ZIP CODE]

Dear [FIRST NAME],

There are still times when I can remember the feelings I had when I first met you. We were happy and looking forward to a future together. So much has come between us that I sometimes wonder how we could have had even a glimpse of a life together.

The divorce drained me. The lawyers and courts consumed so much money and time. All the while, I kept thinking of your bright promises, like the time we [ITEM 1].

It seems that brightness has been eclipsed in your pattern of behavior. The alimony payments you agreed to pay are late, and I'm disappointed in myself for assuming you would be honorable. I did not force you to sign the agreement; you gave your full concurrence as evidenced by your signature. I wanted you once. Today, I want only what is rightfully mine, the $[ITEM 2] you owe me. Let's not give the lawyers and courts any more of our money. I think we wasted enough of that, and our lives, on petty issues. We have both suffered enough.

Sincerely yours,

[YOUR NAME]

[ITEM 1] = Describe the best time you ever had with letter's recipient
[ITEM 2] = Dollar amount of alimony payment owed

[YOUR ADDRESS]
[YOUR CITY], [YOUR STATE] [YOUR ZIP CODE]
[YOUR TELEPHONE NUMBER]
[DATE]

[Mr./Mrs./Ms./Dr.] [FIRST AND LAST NAME]
[ADDRESS]
[CITY], [STATE] [ZIP CODE]

Dear [FIRST NAME],

Contrary to what you may believe, you have not yet seen the extent of my wrath. Time after time we go around and around with the alimony payments. I call my lawyer, you call yours, I get whatever I can get, and the cycle continues.

I want you to realize what you are doing to me, yourself, and your reputation as an upstanding person. Imagine the stories and multiply them by ten. And they are not coming from me. We like to think this is a big world, but it really isn't.

Your alimony payment has been late once too often with the total amount past due now at $[ITEM 1]. I am forced to pursue stronger measures that I have been avoiding; I do not want to assume the role of a collection agency. I know you're not ignorant of the law. Face facts, [FIRST NAME], this is one situation you won't be able to get out of or avoid. The only way to stop me now is to send the payment so I receive it within five days. If I were you, I would listen to me this time.

Sincerely yours,

[YOUR NAME]

[ITEM 1] = Dollar amount of alimony owed

[YOUR ADDRESS]
[YOUR CITY], [YOUR STATE] [YOUR ZIP CODE]
[YOUR TELEPHONE NUMBER]
[DATE]

[Mr./Mrs./Ms./Dr.] [FIRST AND LAST NAME]
[ADDRESS]
[CITY], [STATE] [ZIP CODE]

Dear [FIRST NAME],

As I am sure you agree, the life we shared once never seems to end. According to our divorce agreement, expenses incurred for [ITEM 1] require joint payment. I have done my best to take care of the situation without exposing you to the details.

Attached are copies of receipts totaling $[ITEM 2], which means you owe me $[ITEM 3]. Since I have already paid the bill, please forward your share to me as soon as possible. Thank you in advance for your attention and full compliance with our mutual divorce obligations.

Sincerely yours,

[YOUR NAME]

[ITEM 1] = Describe reason for bill(s)
[ITEM 2] = Dollar amount of bill(s)
[ITEM 3] = Dollar amount owed you by letter recipient

[YOUR ADDRESS]
[YOUR CITY], [YOUR STATE] [YOUR ZIP CODE]
[YOUR TELEPHONE NUMBER]
[DATE]

[Mr./Mrs./Ms./Dr.] [FIRST AND LAST NAME]
[ADDRESS]
[CITY], [STATE] [ZIP CODE]

Dear [FIRST NAME],

A parent can never replace a child. Watching ours grow and seeing [ITEM 1] sometimes look like me, other times like you, gives me great joy. For this reason and many more, I cannot understand how you can jeopardize your [ITEM 2]'s future.

[ITEM 1] depends on us for love and survival. I give everything I can because I want [ITEM 3] to have more than we had. It's our responsibility for bringing [ITEM 1] into our world. And, I need your help in raising our, not my and not your, [ITEM 2].

Growing up, we didn't have it all that bad. [ITEM 4] deserves more than your total disregard. In school today, [ITEM 1]'s friends asked whether [ITEM 4] had a [ITEM 5] because no word is ever mentioned of you. Please don't force me to turn to the legal system. Think of [ITEM 1]'s face and those eyes. We gave these to [ITEM 3]. I need your help to take care of and protect our [ITEM 2].

Sincerely yours,

[YOUR NAME]

[ITEM 1] = First name(s) of child or children
[ITEM 2] = Singular or plural form of child, i.e., "child" or "children"
[ITEM 3] = Pronoun referring to [ITEM 1], "him," "her," or "them"
[ITEM 4] = Pronoun referring to [ITEM 1], "he," "she," or "they"
[ITEM 5] = Relationship of letter's recipient to [ITEM 1], i.e., "mother" or "father"

[YOUR ADDRESS]
[YOUR CITY], [YOUR STATE] [YOUR ZIP CODE]
[YOUR TELEPHONE NUMBER]
[DATE]

[Mr./Mrs./Ms./Dr.] [FIRST AND LAST NAME]
[ADDRESS]
[CITY], [STATE] [ZIP CODE]

Dear [FIRST NAME],

The [ITEM 1] we brought into this world deserves a future. Responsibility was shared in the creation and continues in the upbringing. You have a moral and legal obligation to our [ITEM 1].

To date, you have not complied with the provisions of the child support agreement. I am forced, for [ITEM 2]'s well-being, to pursue stronger measures in collecting the $[ITEM 3] owed to our [ITEM 1]. I will not jeopardize the future of my flesh and blood any longer. Be warned that if I do not receive the money by [ITEM 4], I intend to pursue legal action.

Sincerely yours,

[YOUR NAME]

[ITEM 1] = Singular or plural form of child, i.e., "child" or "children"
[ITEM 2] = First name(s) of child or children
[ITEM 3] = Dollar amount of total child support payments owed
[ITEM 4] = Date money is due

[YOUR ADDRESS]
[YOUR CITY], [YOUR STATE] [YOUR ZIP CODE]
[YOUR TELEPHONE NUMBER]
[DATE]

[Mr./Mrs./Ms./Dr.] [FIRST AND LAST NAME]
[ADDRESS]
[CITY], [STATE] [ZIP CODE]

Dear [FIRST NAME],

A child of divorced parents can sometimes feel caught in the middle of the struggle. It's good that we are working together so this does not happen. Before planning any activities with [ITEM 1] and in accordance with our custody agreement, I would like to confirm the time [ITEM 2] will be spending with me.

Unless I hear otherwise, I will look forward to seeing [ITEM 1] from [ITEM 3] through [ITEM 4]. The pick-up and drop-off arrangements are as follows: [ITEM 5].

Please ensure that [ITEM 1]'s luggage includes proper clothing for [ITEM 6]. Also, I might suggest a few special things like [ITEM 7] to make [ITEM 8] feel more at home with me. [FIRST NAME], thank you for realizing that [ITEM 8] development requires the support only parents can provide. If you have any questions, do not hesitate to contact me.

Sincerely yours,

[YOUR NAME]

[ITEM 1] = First name(s) of child or children
[ITEM 2] = Pronoun referring to [ITEM 1], "he," "she," or "they"
[ITEM 3] = Date the visit begins
[ITEM 4] = Date the visit ends
[ITEM 5] = Describe the manner in which [ITEM 1] will be picked up from, and brought back to, recipient's home
[ITEM 6] = Describe any activity planned requiring particular clothing
[ITEM 7] = Describe a thing [ITEM 1] likes or plays with
[ITEM 8] = Pronoun referring to [ITEM 1], i.e., "his," "her," or "their"; "him," "her," or "them"

[YOUR ADDRESS]
[YOUR CITY], [YOUR STATE] [YOUR ZIP CODE]
[YOUR TELEPHONE NUMBER]
[DATE]

[Mr./Mrs./Ms./Dr.] [FIRST AND LAST NAME]
[ADDRESS]
[CITY], [STATE] [ZIP CODE]

Dear [FIRST NAME],

No family is perfect like the ones we see on television. Even though we are close, we are all different, so it is not reasonable to assume that there will never be problems between us. We're adults now, not children fighting for attention or independence. Sometimes, I don't like the person you have become and the way I feel when we are together. But I do accept you. We are family, and nothing can change that, not even different opinions about what life is and how it should be lived.

We have both made mistakes over the years. I'm sorry if I have hurt you with things I have done or said. Please know that it was not my intention and that I do care about you. This letter is my first step toward putting the past behind us so we can be family and, more important, maybe friends. [FIRST NAME], I am willing to try. Life is so short, let's not waste any more of it on insignificant matters. I never want to look back and think, "I should have ..." Do you? Let's talk it out. If we devote our energy to making our relationship work, imagine what we could become to each other.

Love,

[YOUR NAME]

[YOUR ADDRESS]
[YOUR CITY], [YOUR STATE] [YOUR ZIP CODE]
[YOUR TELEPHONE NUMBER]
[DATE]

[Mr./Mrs./Ms./Dr.] [FIRST AND LAST NAME]
[ADDRESS]
[CITY], [STATE] [ZIP CODE]

Dear [FIRST NAME],

Families are the only people you can turn to in time of need. It has always bothered me that so many friends disappear the minute you ask for help. During tough times, you really find out who your friends are.

Because of pride, I have not told you the extent of my troubles. I thought things would be better by now and that my feet would be back on the ground. But collection calls have become routine, and I'm afraid to go to my mail box.

Sleep doesn't come easily as my mind races. I wanted to call and tell you this, but I could not work up the courage. I need your help to get through this. If you could spare $[ITEM 1], it would get some of these people off my back so I could concentrate on my future. You have my promise that you'll have the money back in [ITEM 2] months. I am even willing to sign a promissory note to make you feel more at ease. Should you decide not to lend me the money, I understand. I'm sorry I have put you in this position, but I don't have anywhere else to turn. Think about it, and let me know either way.

Love,

[YOUR NAME]

[ITEM 1] = Dollar amount of loan
[ITEM 2] = Duration of loan in months

[YOUR ADDRESS]
[YOUR CITY], [YOUR STATE] [YOUR ZIP CODE]
[YOUR TELEPHONE NUMBER]
[DATE]

[Mr./Mrs./Ms./Dr.] [FIRST AND LAST NAME]
[ADDRESS]
[CITY], [STATE] [ZIP CODE]

Dear [FIRST NAME],

Doesn't it seem like just yesterday that we were all running around at family gatherings waiting for the day when we could sit with the adults? Our lives have taken us in different directions over the years. It's time we got together to reminisce and make new memories.

Bring your camera and plan to spend some time relaxing with those who love you most. The [YOUR LAST NAME] family is having a not-to-be-missed reunion celebration the [ITEM 1] of [ITEM 2] at [ITEM 3].

We have so much to catch up on. Let me know what you would like to bring in the way of [ITEM 4] and if you need directions. Also, I would like to plan something special for [ITEM 5] and am looking for ideas. [FIRST NAME], nothing is as important as this day. Please make every effort to join us. It just wouldn't be the same without you.

Love,

[YOUR NAME]

[ITEM 1] = Day of the month of reunion
[ITEM 2] = Month of reunion
[ITEM 3] = Location of reunion
[ITEM 4] = Describe what you would like letter's recipient to bring to reunion
[ITEM 5] = Name of person who deserves a kind gesture at reunion

[YOUR ADDRESS]
[YOUR CITY], [YOUR STATE] [YOUR ZIP CODE]
[YOUR TELEPHONE NUMBER]
[DATE]

[Mr./Mrs./Ms./Dr.] [FIRST AND LAST NAME]
[ADDRESS]
[CITY], [STATE] [ZIP CODE]

Dear [FIRST NAME],

In business, talk is often limited to the issue on the table, weekend plans, or daily news. We have many acquaintances and few friends. I want you to think of me as your friend now.

I was disturbed to hear of your [ITEM 1]'s death. When pain is masked by shock, everyone offers consolation with clichés. It is strange that although death faces each of us, no one really knows quite what to say.

Grief may be universal, but it is also extremely personal. Let me just say, I care. There is no rule that tells us how long to grieve, so do not place time constraints on your healing process. Any business that is really important will be there when you are ready to return. Your well-being is the top priority. If I can do anything— place phone calls, check on clients, you name it—know that it would be my pleasure. [FIRST NAME], please remember that I am your friend and life is to be lived.

Cordially yours,

[YOUR NAME]

————————————◆————————————

[ITEM 1] = Relationship of person who died, i.e., "brother," "child," father," mother," "sister," etc.

[YOUR ADDRESS]
[YOUR CITY], [YOUR STATE] [YOUR ZIP CODE]
[YOUR TELEPHONE NUMBER]
[DATE]

[Mr./Mrs./Ms./Dr.] [FIRST AND LAST NAME]
[ADDRESS]
[CITY], [STATE] [ZIP CODE]

Dear [FIRST NAME],

Recently, I learned something very important from you that has dramatically affected my life. Hearing the stories and watching you persevere with incredible strength astounded me. I thought initially that if I had been placed in your shoes, I would have given up.

But you didn't, and you pulled determination from within to become stronger and more focused. I asked myself how a person faced with [ITEM 1] moves on. I thought of many answers, but the most important one was, "by having faith in him or herself."

Such power exists when we are forced to call upon it and trust that things will work out. You taught me this valuable lesson, and I wanted to say thank you. If you ever need to rely on another's strength, I am just a telephone call away. Remember, it's harder to ask for help than to give it.

Cordially yours,

[YOUR NAME]

[ITEM 1] = Problem person receiving letter has or had

[YOUR ADDRESS]
[YOUR CITY], [YOUR STATE] [YOUR ZIP CODE]
[YOUR TELEPHONE NUMBER]
[DATE]

[Mr./Mrs./Ms./Dr.] [FIRST AND LAST NAME]
[ADDRESS]
[CITY], [STATE] [ZIP CODE]

Dear [FIRST NAME],

Watching you start your life, I would like to promise you that bad things never happen. Love and grief, joy and strife, will never cross your vision simultaneously. Unfortunately, I cannot, because life is difficult. You may not know pain or limitations yet. This is your right, for youth carries this most splendid gift; age is the culprit that destroys its very essence as experiences mount.

As we mature, a terrible thing called fear can grab hold of our dreams. Whether it's fear of failure, the unknown, or the risk or ramifications of a decision, it limits potential. You must be stronger than your strongest fear but also understand that you are destructible.

Build your spirituality, loving the person within. In my own life, I have learned that this is the source of true strength. [FIRST NAME], I am so very proud of you, and I wish I could make your dreams instant realities by waving a magic wand over your head. But by doing so, I would rob you of accomplishment's satisfaction and that is not my right. No matter what or when, I am here for you to rely on. Congratulations on your accomplishment. I feel fortunate to be part of your life.

Cordially yours,

[YOUR NAME]

[YOUR ADDRESS]
[YOUR CITY], [YOUR STATE] [YOUR ZIP CODE]
[YOUR TELEPHONE NUMBER]
[DATE]

[Mr./Mrs./Ms./Dr.] [FIRST AND LAST NAME]
[ADDRESS]
[CITY], [STATE] [ZIP CODE]

Dear [FIRST NAME],

　　We take our families for granted, assuming they will always be there no matter what happens. There is absolutely no replacement for our family. All the friends and money in the world cannot separate people joined by love.

　　Now I know things have not always been perfect. I remember thinking how much smarter I was than everyone in my early years. Remember the time [ITEM 1]? It is amazing how much everyone else learned in the years between my adolescence and my adulthood.

　　We've had our power struggles, indifference, and hurts, but these occur only because the bond between us is strong. I suppose the greatest compliment I could give you is to say that, had I been given the choice in selecting my family members from all the people I have ever met, I would have chosen you. I don't often get the chance to tell you how much you mean to me, and it's a shame because none of us knows what tomorrow will bring. I took the time today to make up for all the times I haven't said I care and I love you.

Love,

[YOUR NAME]

[ITEM 1] = Describe a funny, light experience person receiving the letter is familiar with

[YOUR ADDRESS]
[YOUR CITY], [YOUR STATE] [YOUR ZIP CODE]
[YOUR TELEPHONE NUMBER]
[DATE]

[Mr./Mrs./Ms./Dr.] [FIRST AND LAST NAME]
[ADDRESS]
[CITY], [STATE] [ZIP CODE]

Dear [FIRST NAME],

There is nothing greater than the unity of friendship and passion. Both must exist for two to be joined. Seeing you and [ITEM 1] together reminds me that life is designed to be shared and makes professional accomplishments pale by comparison.

I wish for you both days full of the joy you feel now. You have found the perfect complement to your life. It's amazing how many people we meet in our search for the right one. Congratulations on finding a friend who loves you for what you are. After the celebration, let's have dinner so I can start to appreciate [ITEM 1] as much as you do.

Cordially yours,

[YOUR NAME]

-------------------------◆-------------------------

[ITEM 1] = First name of person getting married to the letter's recipient

[YOUR ADDRESS]
[YOUR CITY], [YOUR STATE] [YOUR ZIP CODE]
[YOUR TELEPHONE NUMBER]
[DATE]

[Mr./Mrs./Ms./Dr.] [FIRST AND LAST NAME]
The Honorable [TITLE]
[ADDRESS]
[CITY], [STATE] [ZIP CODE]

Dear [TITLE] [LAST NAME]:

A good politician is really a good salesperson. "Buy now or pay later," threats do not yield the best results. Instead, the politician or salesperson must be committed to providing the facts clearly and logically.

This approach moves the prospect to take action based upon accurate information. The manner in which you took control of the [ITEM 1] situation exemplified the very best sales techniques. From what I know, it was your diligence that made [ITEM 2] possible.

Rarely do we praise politicians for their efforts to confront issues under public scrutiny. I respect you for the job you're doing to benefit the people who would rather buy than be sold. Your sales record is excellent, and apparently, an expanded territory is within your grasp. Best of luck. You have this buyer's vote of confidence!

Respectfully yours,

[YOUR NAME]

[ITEM 1] = Describe the political issue
[ITEM 2] = Describe how person receiving letter resolved [ITEM 1]

[YOUR ADDRESS]
[YOUR CITY], [YOUR STATE] [YOUR ZIP CODE]
[YOUR TELEPHONE NUMBER]
[DATE]

[Mr./Mrs./Ms./Dr.] [FIRST AND LAST NAME]
[ADDRESS]
[CITY], [STATE] [ZIP CODE]

Dear [FIRST NAME],

  Money builds the walls and adorns the halls, but the life inside makes a house a home. The happiest moments in my life, by far, have been in my home, sharing time with family and friends. This is why it is especially important for you to know that the [ITEM 1] household has changed addresses.

  The new address and telephone number are:

    [YOUR ADDRESS]
    [YOUR CITY], [YOUR STATE] [YOUR ZIP CODE]
    [YOUR TELEPHONE NUMBER]

  The boxes are gradually making their way to the trash, and we continue to find things we thought were long gone. Moving has certainly made me wonder why we carry so much memorabilia from place to place in our lives. After all, the most important things are best remembered without any reminders. As soon as everything is settled, let's get together in the [ITEM 1]'s new home.

Cordially yours,

[YOUR NAME]

--------------------◆--------------------

[ITEM 1] = Your last name

[YOUR ADDRESS]
[YOUR CITY], [YOUR STATE] [YOUR ZIP CODE]
[YOUR TELEPHONE NUMBER]
[DATE]

[Mr./Mrs./Ms./Dr.] [FIRST AND LAST NAME]
[ADDRESS]
[CITY], [STATE] [ZIP CODE]

Dear [FIRST NAME],

The best tenant treats a leased home as his own. I assume that, as a landlord, you appreciate tenants who care for and respect your property. I know how expensive real estate is these days.

Therefore, I expected a response long before now regarding the problem with [ITEM 1]. On [ITEM 2], you were notified and asked to make the repairs. No action has been taken in the intervening [ITEM 3] days.

I am sure that you want to take action before the situation gets worse and costs you more money, so please let me know when the problem will be fixed. I know my legal rights as a tenant. This is a last resort that will be pursued only if I do not hear from you by [ITEM 4]. Thank you in advance for your prompt attention in the matter. The repairs are really more for your benefit than mine.

Sincerely yours,

[YOUR NAME]

[ITEM 1] = Describe the problem
[ITEM 2] = Date you first contacted landlord
[ITEM 3] = Number of days between [ITEM 2] and when this letter is sent
[ITEM 4] = Date by which you want to hear from landlord

[YOUR ADDRESS]
[YOUR CITY], [YOUR STATE] [YOUR ZIP CODE]
[YOUR TELEPHONE NUMBER]
[DATE]

[Mr./Mrs./Ms./Dr.] [FIRST AND LAST NAME]
[ADDRESS]
[CITY], [STATE] [ZIP CODE]

Dear [Mr./Mrs./Ms./Dr.] [LAST NAME]:

This letter serves as official notification that I will be vacating your property on [ITEM 1] in full accordance with the rental agreement we signed on [ITEM 2]. The residence is in excellent condition with only normal cleaning required for new tenants.

Therefore, I would anticipate a full refund of my $[ITEM 3] security deposit. My new address will be:

[YOUR ADDRESS]
[YOUR CITY], [YOUR STATE] [YOUR ZIP CODE]

If you find any reason to deduct money from my security deposit for repairs, please provide a complete description and cost breakdown. Thank you for your assistance in the past and for prompt remittance of the security deposit. I am sure the property will be leased again quickly.

Sincerely yours,

[YOUR NAME]

[ITEM 1] = Date you are moving
[ITEM 2] = Date you signed the rental agreement
[ITEM 3] = Dollar amount of the security deposit

[YOUR ADDRESS]
[YOUR CITY], [YOUR STATE] [YOUR ZIP CODE]
[YOUR TELEPHONE NUMBER]
[DATE]

Investor Relations Department
[COMPANY]
[ADDRESS]
[CITY], [STATE] [ZIP CODE]

Dear Sir or Madam:

Strategic investments require complete analysis of corporate and market conditions. As I consider moves that will affect my financial future, I find [COMPANY]'s progressive positioning of interest. Brokers, newspapers, and trade publications tell one story; I want to hear yours.

Therefore, please forward your organization's most recent annual report and last two fiscal quarter earnings statements to my attention at:

    [YOUR NAME]
    [YOUR ADDRESS]
    [YOUR CITY], [YOUR STATE] [YOUR ZIP CODE]

Thank you for your assistance. If you have any questions, you may contact me at [YOUR TELEPHONE NUMBER]. I look forward to reviewing firsthand [COMPANY]'s past results, present directions, and future outlook.

Sincerely yours,

[YOUR NAME]

[YOUR ADDRESS]
[YOUR CITY], [YOUR STATE] [YOUR ZIP CODE]
[YOUR TELEPHONE NUMBER]
[DATE]

Birth Certificate Request Department
Vital Statistics Office
County of [COUNTY]
[ADDRESS]
[CITY], [STATE] [ZIP CODE]

Dear Sir or Madam:

Looking for a misplaced document is a frustrating experience. I have been searching and searching for my birth certificate so that I may [ITEM 1]. I understand your office can provide a certified copy of my birth certificate, thus enabling me to make better use of my time.

The following information will be helpful in locating my records and providing the certificate:

Full name on the certificate:	[ITEM 2]
Sex:	[ITEM 3]
Father's full name:	[ITEM 4]
Mother's full name:	[ITEM 5]
Mother's maiden name:	[ITEM 6]
Month/day/year of birth:	[ITEM 7]
Place of birth:	[ITEM 8]

I have enclosed is a personal check in the amount of $[ITEM 9] for one certified copy of my birth certificate. If you have any questions, you may contact me at the address or telephone number shown above. Thank you for relieving my stress.

Sincerely yours,

[YOUR NAME]

[ITEM 1] = **Describe the reason for requesting the birth certificate**
[ITEM 2] = **Your first and last name at birth**
[ITEM 3] = **Your gender**
[ITEM 4] = **Your father's first and last name**
[ITEM 5] = **Your mother's first and last name**
[ITEM 6] = **Your mother's last name before she married**
[ITEM 7] = **Your month/day/year of birth**
[ITEM 8] = **Your physical place of birth**
[ITEM 9] = **Dollar amount charged for certificate**

[YOUR ADDRESS]
[YOUR CITY], [YOUR STATE] [YOUR ZIP CODE]
[YOUR TELEPHONE NUMBER]
[DATE]

Catalog Request Department
Consumer Information Catalog
Post Office Box 100
Pueblo, Colorado 81009

Dear Sir or Madam:

Becoming an educated consumer is a tough job. I understand the Consumer Information Catalog is full of shopping hints and how-to's. Would you please send me the free catalog?

My address is:

[YOUR ADDRESS]
[YOUR CITY], [YOUR STATE] [YOUR ZIP CODE]

My purpose in asking for the catalog is to make a well-founded decision regarding the purchase of [ITEM 1]. If you would be so kind as to include with the catalog any publications relating to the aforementioned, I would be very appreciative. Use your best judgment, and I guarantee I will study whatever you send. Thank you for your assistance in creating another smart shopper.

Sincerely yours,

[YOUR NAME]

[ITEM 1] = Describe the specific area or product you want information on

[YOUR ADDRESS]
[YOUR CITY], [YOUR STATE] [YOUR ZIP CODE]
[YOUR TELEPHONE NUMBER]
[DATE]

Death Certificate Request Department
Vital Statistics Office
County of [COUNTY]
[ADDRESS]
[CITY], [STATE] [ZIP CODE]

Dear Sir or Madam:

The period following the death of a friend or loved one should be a quiet and reflective time. However, the paperwork controlling our lives never seems to end even as the life of another does. To resolve outstanding estate issues, I require [ITEM 1] certified copies of the death certificate for my beloved [ITEM 2].

The following information will be helpful in locating the records and providing the certificates:

Full name of the deceased:	[ITEM 3]
Sex:	[ITEM 4]
Father's full name:	[ITEM 5]
Mother's full name:	[ITEM 6]
Mother's maiden name:	[ITEM 7]
Month/day/year of death:	[ITEM 8]
Place of Death:	[ITEM 9]

I have enclosed is a personal check in the amount of $[ITEM 10] for the certificates. If you have any questions, you may contact me at the address or telephone number shown above. Thank you for easing my grief in the handling of estate affairs.

Sincerely yours,

[YOUR NAME]

[ITEM 1] = **Number of copies requested**
[ITEM 2] = **Your relationship to the deceased**
[ITEM 3] = **First and last name of the deceased**
[ITEM 4] = **Deceased's gender**
[ITEM 5] = **Deceased's father's first and last name**
[ITEM 6] = **Deceased's mother's first and last name**
[ITEM 7] = **Deceased's mother's last name before she married**
[ITEM 8] = **Deceased's month/day/year of death**
[ITEM 9] = **Deceased's place of death**
[ITEM 10] = **Dollar amount charged for certificates**

[YOUR ADDRESS]
[YOUR CITY], [YOUR STATE] [YOUR ZIP CODE]
[YOUR TELEPHONE NUMBER]
[DATE]

Divorce Decree Request Department
Vital Statistics Office
County of [COUNTY]
[ADDRESS]
[CITY], [STATE] [ZIP CODE]

Dear Sir or Madam:

Compiling information is always time-consuming. To [ITEM 1], I require your professional assistance. It appears I have misfiled my divorce decree, and I understand a certified copy is available quickly from your office.

The following information will be helpful in locating the records and providing the certified copy of the divorce decree:

Full name of husband:	[ITEM 2]
Full name of wife:	[ITEM 3]
Month/day/year of divorce:	[ITEM 4]
Type of decree:	[ITEM 5]

I have enclosed a personal check in the amount of $[ITEM 6] for the copy. If you have any questions, you may contact me at the address or telephone number shown above. Thank you in advance for helping me get on with my life.

Sincerely yours,

[YOUR NAME]

[ITEM 1] = Tell why copy is needed
[ITEM 2] = First and last name of husband
[ITEM 3] = First and last name of wife
[ITEM 4] = Month/day/year of divorce
[ITEM 5] = Type of divorce decree, i.e., "Divorce of Dissolution" or "Final Decree"
[ITEM 6] = Dollar amount charged for copy of divorce decree

[YOUR ADDRESS]
[YOUR CITY], [YOUR STATE] [YOUR ZIP CODE]
[YOUR TELEPHONE NUMBER]
[DATE]

Marriage Certificate Department
Vital Statistics Office
County of [COUNTY]
[ADDRESS]
[CITY], [STATE] [ZIP CODE]

Dear Sir or Madam:

It is truly amazing that one little piece of paper can have so much significance in our lives. Not having my marriage certificate in my possession is a burden now as I try to [ITEM 1]. Therefore, I request your immediate assistance in providing one certified copy of my marriage certificate.

The following information will be helpful in locating the records and providing the certificate:

Full name of bride:	[ITEM 2]
Full name of groom:	[ITEM 3]
Month/day/year of marriage:	[ITEM 4]
Place of marriage:	[ITEM 5]

I have enclosed is a personal check in the amount of $[ITEM 6] for the marriage certificate. If you have any questions, you may contact me at the address or telephone number shown above. Thank you in advance for giving me society's proof that two people made a commitment to share a life.

Sincerely yours,

[YOUR NAME]

[ITEM 1] = **Describe the reason for marriage certificate**
[ITEM 2] = **First and last name of bride**
[ITEM 3] = **First and last name of groom**
[ITEM 4] = **Month/day/year of marriage**
[ITEM 5] = **Physical location with city and state where marriage ceremony was performed**
[ITEM 6] = **Dollar amount charged for certificate**

[YOUR ADDRESS]
[YOUR CITY], [YOUR STATE] [YOUR ZIP CODE]
[YOUR TELEPHONE NUMBER]
[DATE]

Administration Office
[SCHOOL NAME]
[ADDRESS]
[CITY], [STATE] [ZIP CODE]

Dear Sir or Madam:

My carefree school days seem so very long ago today, but I am sure we can both still remember that favorite teacher or worst class. Life does change, and I require your assistance in providing the school records for [ITEM 1].

I believe the records should cover the period [ITEM 2] through [ITEM 3]. You may forward these to me at the address shown above. If there is a charge for copying the records, simply include an invoice, and I will remit payment the day I receive the package. Thank you for your assistance. Writing this letter has made me think about what it would be like to say good-bye to adult pressures and return to [SCHOOL NAME]. I'll tell you, it's pretty appealing!

Sincerely yours,

[YOUR NAME]

————————————————◆◆————————————————

[ITEM 1] = First and last name of student, and the relationship, i.e., "my daughter," "my son," or "myself"
[ITEM 2] = Date school records begin
[ITEM 3] = Date school records end

[YOUR ADDRESS]
[YOUR CITY], [YOUR STATE] [YOUR ZIP CODE]
[YOUR TELEPHONE NUMBER]
[DATE]

[Mr./Mrs./Ms./Dr.] [FIRST AND LAST NAME]
Editor
[COMPANY]
[ADDRESS]
[CITY], [STATE] [ZIP CODE]

Dear [Mr./Mrs./Ms./Dr.] [LAST NAME]:

Many wrongly believe they have the discipline and creativity to be a writer. One must be able to endure setbacks, experience solitude, research endlessly, and have confidence that blank page will be filled soon with wonder. Each time we write, a new lesson is learned, greater fortitude developed, and talent enhanced.

I do not read a magazine like the average person scanning headlines and pictures. I analyze every word critiquing structure and delivery strength. You are to be commended for such an outstanding display of editorial content and features.

For these reasons, I would like to receive your writer's guidelines and editorial calendar with the hope that an article query results in placement. My background and interests in [ITEM 1] are a definite complement to [COMPANY]'s target audience. Enclosed is a self-addressed, stamped envelope. Thank you in advance for the opportunity to join your distinguished list of writers.

Sincerely yours,

[YOUR NAME]

————————————◆————————————

[ITEM 1] = Describe your interests and/or writing experiences

[YOUR ADDRESS]
[YOUR CITY], [YOUR STATE] [YOUR ZIP CODE]
[YOUR TELEPHONE NUMBER]
[DATE]

[Mr./Mrs./Ms./Dr.] [FIRST AND LAST NAME]
[TITLE]
[COMPANY]
[ADDRESS]
[CITY], [STATE] [ZIP CODE]

Dear [FIRST NAME]:

Ability and luck are opportunity's prerequisites. Having good fortune present us with a desirable situation is not enough for accomplishment. The key is possessing the skills to recognize and seize that opportunity.

After spending time with you and [COMPANY], I see an opportunity to join forces for success. Therefore, it is with pleasure and pride that I accept the position as [ITEM 1]. It is my understanding that this new career begins on [ITEM 2].

[FIRST NAME], thank you for your assistance and endorsement of my future. The combination of [COMPANY] and my talents will benefit all concerned.

Sincerely yours,

[YOUR NAME]

[ITEM 1] = Name of new position
[ITEM 2] = Date new job begins

[YOUR ADDRESS]
[YOUR CITY], [YOUR STATE] [YOUR ZIP CODE]
[YOUR TELEPHONE NUMBER]
[DATE]

[Mr./Mrs./Ms./Dr.] [FIRST AND LAST NAME]
[TITLE]
[COMPANY]
[ADDRESS]
[CITY], [STATE] [ZIP CODE]

Dear [Mr./Mrs./Ms./Dr.] [LAST NAME]:

The best investment one can make is in his or her future. Goal setting and planning are not enough. Good intentions must be put into action without hesitation.

Today, my need for accomplishment was sparked by [COMPANY]'s employment advertisement in [ITEM 1]. Based on the information in your ad, I believe my knowledge and skills could be benficial to [COMPANY]. However, please know that my approach to the interview process is somewhat different from the approach most people take.

A company and its employee must be unified as they work toward their objectives. Frankly, one cannot excel without the other's commitment. I am looking for a company that is driven to excellence and promotes professional development based on an employee's dedication, loyalty, and work ethic. You have my commitment to success. I look forward to your telephone call. Thank you in advance for exploring the action-oriented person described on the attached résumé.

Sincerely yours,

[YOUR NAME]

[ITEM 1] = Name of publication in which the advertisement was seen

[YOUR ADDRESS]
[YOUR CITY], [YOUR STATE] [YOUR ZIP CODE]
[YOUR TELEPHONE NUMBER]
[DATE]

[Mr./Mrs./Ms./Dr.] [FIRST AND LAST NAME]
[TITLE]
[COMPANY]
[ADDRESS]
[CITY], [STATE] [ZIP CODE]

Dear [Mr./Mrs./Ms./Dr.] [LAST NAME]:

Our business associates and friends are a direct reflection of ourselves. We tend to interact with others who share common interests or goals. I was given your name recently by [ITEM 1] who, after knowing me for some time, believes our professional aspirations are complementary.

My career, outlined on the enclosed résumé, is marked by abilities and skills developed by a strong work ethic. I understand there may be a position available as a [ITEM 2]. This would utilize my talents and hopefully, lead to additional career growth opportunities within [COMPANY].

I have heard nothing but positive stories about your organization's commitment to business and employees. Thank you for your professional courtesy in reviewing my qualifications. I look forward to receiving your telephone call expressing interest soon. It would be an honor to put [COMPANY] on my business card.

Sincerely yours,

[YOUR NAME]

-----------------------------◆-----------------------------

[ITEM 1] = First and last name of person who referred you to letter's recipient
[ITEM 2] = Name of position or title

[YOUR ADDRESS]
[YOUR CITY], [YOUR STATE] [YOUR ZIP CODE]
[YOUR TELEPHONE NUMBER]
[DATE]

[Mr./Mrs./Ms./Dr.] [FIRST AND LAST NAME]
[TITLE]
[COMPANY]
[ADDRESS]
[CITY], [STATE] [ZIP CODE]

Dear [FIRST NAME]:

Life is a series of choices, and far too often, just when a decision is made, the situation changes. Shortly after receiving your offer to join [COMPANY]'s progressive team, I was presented with another choice in career paths. After much deliberation, I have decided to pursue a future without [COMPANY]'s direct involvement.

This was not an easy conclusion to reach. I had anticipated a mutually beneficial relationship. Please do not interpret my decision as a reflection on yourself or [COMPANY].

[FIRST NAME], thank you for your belief in my abilities and the extension of professional support. You have my appreciation, and perhaps at some future date, our professional aspirations will be more complementary.

Sincerely yours,

[YOUR NAME]

—————————————◆—————————————

[YOUR ADDRESS]
[YOUR CITY], [YOUR STATE] [YOUR ZIP CODE]
[YOUR TELEPHONE NUMBER]
[DATE]

[Mr./Mrs./Ms./Dr.] [FIRST AND LAST NAME]
[TITLE]
[COMPANY]
[ADDRESS]
[CITY], [STATE] [ZIP CODE]

Dear [FIRST NAME]:

An opportunity is little more than two forces combining to create a desired effect. After learning more about [COMPANY], I believe that such a situation exists. Thank you for introducing me to what I believe is a mutually beneficial opportunity.

I found your company's beliefs and success orientation complementary to my own. Clearly, your talents are important to the development of the organization. Again, I extend my thanks for your time. I will await your telephone call advising me of the next step on the road to a future with [COMPANY]. Together, we would be an extraordinary team.

Sincerely yours,

[YOUR NAME]

[YOUR ADDRESS]
[YOUR CITY], [YOUR STATE] [YOUR ZIP CODE]
[YOUR TELEPHONE NUMBER]
[DATE]

[Mr./Mrs./Ms./Dr.] [FIRST AND LAST NAME]
[TITLE]
[COMPANY]
[ADDRESS]
[CITY], [STATE] [ZIP CODE]

Dear [FIRST NAME]:

No company is protected from competition. Building the most ambitious and proficient team possible is the only way to guarantee short- and long-term success. Upon receiving your employment offer, my unwavering belief in our compatibility has left me in a precarious position.

You have presented an opportunity for which, in my opinion, the compensation reflects neither my previous accomplishments nor the nation's turbulent economy. As much as I would like to accept your offer, I cannot afford to financially. I hope that a reassessment of my potential value to [COMPANY] will lead you to a reevaluation of the financial terms of the offer.

[FIRST NAME], we've already determined that I am right for the job. I look forward to hearing how we can get started. After all, to be the best, you need the best.

Respectfully yours,

[YOUR NAME]

RECITALS:

    This is a Bill of Sale confirming the exchange of money between [ITEM 1], hereinafter referred to as the "Buyer," whose full address is [ITEM 2], and [YOUR NAME], hereinafter referred to as the "Seller," whose full address is [YOUR ADDRESS], {YOUR CITY], [YOUR STATE] [YOUR ZIP CODE].

Bill of Sale

    Seller in consideration of the sum of $[ITEM 3], receipt of which is acknowledged by this Bill of Sale, sells and delivers to the Buyer the following personal property and goods: [ITEM 4] and all accessories affixed thereto. Seller warrants and represents to Buyer that Seller is the owner of the property with the right to sell the property, that the title conveyed is good, that the property is free from all claims, and that Seller will defend the title against the claims of any person. Buyer acknowledges that the property has been examined and accepts the purchase "as is."

    EXECUTED this [ITEM 5] day of [ITEM 6], [ITEM 7] at [ITEM 8].

_____

Seller

_____

Buyer

[ITEM 1] = First and last name(s) of buyer(s)
[ITEM 2] = Full address, city, state, and zip code of buyer(s)
[ITEM 3] = Dollar amount buyer is paying the seller
[ITEM 4] = Describe property being sold
[ITEM 5] = Date of the month agreement is signed
[ITEM 6] = Month agreement is signed
[ITEM 7] = Year agreement is signed
[ITEM 8] = City and state where agreement is signed

RECITALS:

This is a Home Improvement Agreement between [ITEM 1], hereinafter referred to as the "Contractor," whose full address is [ITEM 2], and [YOUR NAME], hereinafter referred to as the "Owner," whose full address is [YOUR ADDRESS], [YOUR CITY], [YOUR STATE] [YOUR ZIP CODE] for improvements on property owned by the Owner.

Home Improvement Agreement

Contractor shall provide the following work, [ITEM 3], using the following materials, [ITEM 4]. All building permits and licenses shall be secured by [ITEM 5]. The work to be done under this agreement shall be started on [ITEM 6] and completed no later than [ITEM 7]. If Contractor fails to complete the work by [ITEM 7], Contractor shall pay Owner $[ITEM 8] per day every day beyond [ITEM 7] as liquidated damages. Contractor's bond of $[ITEM 9] is in place and a copy is attached. Any damage done to Owner's property is Contractor's responsibility, and Contractor agrees to pay for any damages or theft of materials left on Owner's property. Contractor is responsible for worker's compensation insurance. Owner reserves the right to approve subcontractors. Progress payments will be made to Contractor based on the completion of [ITEM 3] and are as follows: $[ITEM 10]. Final payment will be made to Contractor when the work is completed to Owner's satisfaction. Owner reserves the right to terminate this agreement.

EXECUTED this [ITEM 11] day of [ITEM 12], [ITEM 13] at [ITEM 14].

_____
Owner

_____
Contractor

———————————————◆—————————————————

[ITEM 1] = Name of contractor
[ITEM 2] = Full address, city, state, and zip code of contractor
[ITEM 3] = Describe work to be performed by contractor
[ITEM 4] = Materials to be used by contractor to complete [ITEM 3]
[ITEM 5] = Party responsible for obtaining building permits and licenses
[ITEM 6] = Date contractor starts the job
[ITEM 7] = Date by which contractor is to complete job
[ITEM 8] = Dollar amount per day contractor pays you
[ITEM 9] = Dollar amount of contractor's bond
[ITEM 10] = Dollar amount of progress payments
[ITEM 11] = Date of the month agreement is signed
[ITEM 12] = Month agreement is signed
[ITEM 13] = Year agreement is signed
[ITEM 14] = City and state where agreement is signed

RECITALS:

This is a Promissory Note for a personal loan of $[ITEM 1] from [YOUR NAME], whose full address is [YOUR ADDRESS], [YOUR CITY], [YOUR STATE] [YOUR ZIP CODE] to [ITEM 2], whose full address is [ITEM 3].

Promissory Note

On or before, [ITEM 4], [ITEM 2] agrees and promises to pay [YOUR NAME], at [YOUR ADDRESS], [YOUR CITY], [YOUR STATE], [YOUR ZIP CODE], the sum of [ITEM 1] in United States currency, with interest accruing from the date this agreement is executed on the unpaid principal at the rate of [ITEM 5] percent per annum. Principal and interest will be paid in installments of [ITEM 6], on the [ITEM 7] day of the month until the loan is paid in full. Privilege is hereby granted to [ITEM 2] to pay the note in full at any time with no prepayment penalty.

EXECUTED this [ITEM 8] day of [ITEM 9], [ITEM 10] at [ITEM 11].

_____

[YOUR NAME]

_____

[ITEM 2]

[ITEM 1] = **Dollar amount of loan**
[ITEM 2] = **First and last name of borrower(s)**
[ITEM 3] = **Full address, city, state, and zip code of [ITEM 2]**
[ITEM 4] = **Date the loan is due**
[ITEM 5] = **Interest in percent charged on loan**
[ITEM 6] = **Dollar amount of installments**
[ITEM 7] = **Date of the month [ITEM 6] is due**
[ITEM 8] = **Date of the month agreement is signed**
[ITEM 9] = **Month agreement is signed**
[ITEM 10] = **Year agreement is signed**
[ITEM 11] = **City and state where agreement is signed**

[YOUR ADDRESS]
[YOUR CITY], [YOUR STATE] [YOUR ZIP CODE]
[YOUR TELEPHONE NUMBER]
[DATE]

Dear [FIRST NAME],

Time changes relationships in the strangest of ways. Moment by moment, the ticking of one's heart strikes something deep inside. Like hands moving across the clock's face, a relationship changes even as we try to hold on to the past.

For me, there seems no in between about love. I must either give totally or feel this is an injustice to the other person and myself. Each morning I look in the mirror, and lately, these eyes have not been filled with happiness. It is not me, it is not you. It is what has become of us.

I ask you to let me go, let yourself go, and let us go on in life separately. It's not easy for me to do this, but I must. We are who we are, and no one can, nor should we, mold ourselves to fulfill another's needs. Please respect my decision and do not destroy the chance that this could end as a friendship by asking why. We both need some time to regain our lives, so let's not talk for a while.

Love is the greatest of emotions and bears the most sorrow. We were friends first and foremost, and part of who I am today is because of you. I hope you remember us as two individuals who shared love for as long as time allowed.

All the best now and for the future,

[YOUR NAME]

[YOUR ADDRESS]
[YOUR CITY], [YOUR STATE] [YOUR ZIP CODE]
[YOUR TELEPHONE NUMBER]
[DATE]

Dearest [FIRST NAME],

Manifesting in force behind my eyes, my love for you comes as a complete surprise. Seeking expression entangled in a maze, as love works in the most mysterious of ways. I wish I could give you just one portion or one tenth, to explain the glorious feeling I meant. When I say, "I love you," it's stronger by days, but love works in the scariest of ways.

Escaping the prisons of fear within thoughts race, dreams become real once hidden behind my face. Trappings of the mind have no place to stay, when love works in the strangest of ways. Feeling about you as I do makes me shudder with joy, can there ever be anything more to strive for? Thoroughly content and satisfied in your arms I lay, for love works in the most marvelous of ways.

For you and our love I try to be my very best, respecting the delicacy of life's treasure chest. Thanking my God for our love, I shed tears and pray that love works in the most supreme of ways. Guiding us, protecting us, and making dreams for you, that happiness springs forth bona fide and true. Feel, know, take my love with the onset of each new day's ray, secure our love works in the most spectacular of ways.

I love you,

[YOUR NAME]

[YOUR ADDRESS]
[YOUR CITY], [YOUR STATE] [YOUR ZIP CODE]
[YOUR TELEPHONE NUMBER]
[DATE]

Dear [FIRST NAME],

My heart was stark whiteness, like this page before my thoughts were applied, having no color before I met you. I remember the first time I saw you. Those eyes drew me in from that moment only to find a heart dormant, but alive. You are becoming a special part of my life, as every time we are together, I learn something else wonderful about you.

Each time we share something, it just feels right. You challenge my emotions and mind to grow upward to a higher level exploring the unknown. You ask me what I feel, what I see, seeking an answer for a question that has not been completed yet. We are learning to trust and now move forward in our respective days; there is someone who truly understands us.

How much closer could I feel? I honestly do not know. Never did I believe I could care for another person as much as I care for you. I sometimes wish for all this to end, for me not to enjoy and look forward to our time together, for you to walk away and for us to go on separately.

Then, the thought of our ending frightens me more than the uneasiness of this heart. It's strange how my feelings for you grow. Please know how very grateful I am to have you become more and more a part of my life.

Yours,

[YOUR NAME]

[YOUR ADDRESS]
[YOUR CITY], [YOUR STATE] [YOUR ZIP CODE]
[YOUR TELEPHONE NUMBER]
[DATE]

Dear [FIRST NAME],

Where do I start to divulge my heart? The depth of my emotion is far too extreme for solitary sentences to serve them well. Today, daydreams passed before my eyes. Magical thoughts of you and I. For years, I have wished for you, my star. Come the brightness, teach the songs and poem's meaning.

I once sang words and hummed rhymes, thinking, dreaming, desiring there be a time. To have just a mere glimpse of the poet's elation in such beautiful thoughts, care, and devotion. Seeing you is warmth. Missing you when you are not near. I am falling, dear star, none but you in the sky.

In deepest emotions come highest thoughts of you, my dear heart. You've given life to dreams, such a wonderful force. Friends into lovers, your needs are no longer your own. Hearts into one, may this love's garden become overgrown.

I love you,

[YOUR NAME]

SECTION 5

Letters for Your Computer

Dear Busy Executive:

By now, you have learned the value of effective letter writing and are ready to reap astounding results. Every letter contained in this book is available on disk for use with most IBM-compatible word processing programs. We typed the letters for you so all that's left is customization.

The following pages outline how easy it is to save more time writing letters with the letters on disk all ready to go. *Section 5 pertains to learning how to use only the* 401 Great Letters *software template.* If you have already ordered the disk, read on. Otherwise, we invite you to put *401 Great Letters* on your computer:

1. For more information about purchasing a template containing all the letters in this book that work with your current word processing program, call Business One Irwin at (800) 634-3966.

2. For more information about purchasing a stand-alone, fully functional DOS or Windows application software program containing all the letters in this book, plus editing, searching and file exporting capabilities, call (800) 275-6453.

SOFTWARE TEMPLATE INSTRUCTIONS

Letters Ready for Computer Use.   Every letter contained in this book is on the disk. Like the book, the disk is divided into four categories, or subdirectories. You may find it helpful to look at the organization of the files before attempting to use the letters with your word processing program.

From this point forward in the directions, the word *file* stands for one letter, or one page, in this book. Every letter is saved under its own unique filename. More about that later. Before using the disk, please make a backup copy.

Make a Backup Copy of the Disk.   Backup copies of original computer software are insurance against data corruption. You should keep them in a safe place for those "just in case" situations. We are going to use the DOS DISKCOPY command to make a backup copy of the *401 Great Letters* original disk. DISKCOPY makes an exact copy of the source disk (in this case, the *401 Great Letters* original disk) on the target disk (in this case a blank, formatted, or unformatted disk of the same size and media type as the *401 Great Letters* disk). DISKCOPY reads from the source disk and writes to the target disk; the process continues until all of the files have been copied.

1. Get one blank, formatted or unformatted disk of the same size and media type as the original *401 Great Letters* disk and label it 401 Great Letters Backup. Go to the DOS prompt.

2. From the DOS prompt, type in the following command:

DISKCOPY A: A:

and press the ENTER key.

3. Put the source (the original *401 Great Letters*) disk into drive A and close the drive door. DISKCOPY will copy some, or all, of the *401 Great Letters* files. You will then be asked to put the target disk into drive A. The target disk is the blank formatted or unformatted disk in Step 1.

4. When DOS is finished copying the original disk, you will receive a message asking "Copy another disk (Y/N)?" Press the N key for No.

TIP: The DOS DISKCOPY command only works when the two disks are the same density. Disks have different density levels. If you are having trouble with the DISKCOPY command, verify that the blank formatted disk's density matches that of the *401 Great Letters* disk. Your DOS user's manual also explains the DISKCOPY command.

Files on the Disk.   There are two ways to display the file organization of the disk. The first method uses the DOS command, DIR, as supplied with the DOS operating system on every IBM-compatible personal computer. Place the disk in the disk drive and type DIR at the system prompt.

Experienced word processing users can do the same thing from within their application program's file manager menus. Please note that this will not get you into the letters themselves; see below for instructions on accessing individual letters.

Organized for Efficiency.   Regardless of how you look at the files, be sure the computer knows which disk drive—A or B—the disk is in. When you do use the DIR command, from either DOS or your word processing program, the following, or a slight variation thereof, appears on the screen.

Volume in drive is 401-Letters

Directory of

BUSINESS	**\<DIR\>**
CUSTOMER	**\<DIR\>**
INOFFICE	**\<DIR\>**
PERSONAL	**\<DIR\>**

The \<DIR\> stands for a subdirectory on the disk similar to one file drawer in a filing cabinet. Our 401 Letters disk has four filing cabinets.

All the business letters are in the BUSINESS subdirectory on the disk, all the customer letters are in the CUSTOMER subdirectory, and so on. This makes finding the right letter easy for you. You won't have to waste time sorting through all 401 letters.

Letter Numbers Are File Names.   In the Table of Contents and on every letter, there is a number. Business letters, or files, start with 1; customer letters, with 2; interoffice letters, with 3; and personal letters, with 4.

Let's say you wanted to find a letter on the disk. Take the example of a business letter to an advertising agency requesting the firm's fees. Turn to the Table of Contents and look in Section 1, Business Correspondence, for the letters dealing with advertising. The first letter in that section is the "Advertising Rate Request" you are looking for.

Next to the letter, you see the number 12.1 in parentheses. This tells you that the letter is the first letter in the first category, Advertising, of the first section of the book, Business. Scan the Table of Contents, and you'll quickly get the picture. A filename is also printed on each letter in the book. Turn to page 7, and at the top, notice the 12.1 next to the letter description.

Once you find the letter, you will use its number/ filename to retrieve it from the disk. The letters in each section are contained in the subdirectories that correspond to the Sections.

File Formats. Now that you understand how the letters are named using numbers for filenames, let's talk about file formats. First, the letters were save on the disk in a format called *ASCII*. This means that virtually any of the 50 or so word processors on the market can read the letters on the disk.

When a word processing program saves a file, it puts at the beginning of the document special codes that tell the computer what the file is supposed to look like and what printer is connected. Saving a file in ASCII format eliminates these codes so the text can be loaded into any word processing program. You don't have to worry about the codes; your word processing program will put them in for you.

ASCII files also eliminate formatting problems. It is easier for you to add your own boldface, italics, and underlining than to remove ours.

The item numbers appear in the letters as reminders, so be sure to change them. You don't want your boss to think that you think her name is [ITEM 2].

Getting the Letters. Remember, the letters are stored in separate subdirectories. The computer has to know which subdirectory—BUSINESS, CUSTOMER, INOFFICE, or PERSONAL—the letter is in. Entering the filename alone will not give you access to the letter. You must enter both the subdirectory name and the filename.

Once you have loaded your word processing program, you can retrieve the files from the disk as you would any other files. Let's go back to our example of the Business, Advertising, Advertising Rate Request letter, filename 12.1. We are using WordPerfect, so pressing the Shift and F10 keys simultaneously causes the program to ask you to type in the name of the file you want to retrieve.

To retrieve letter 12.1, enter first the subdirectory name and then the filename. Our example is a letter contained in the BUSINESS subdirectory. Therefore, assuming the disk is in drive B, we type B:\BUSINESS\12.1. If the disk is in drive A, change the B in the above to an A.

No other special commands are necessary. Retrieve the file from within your word processing program as you would any other file. The same goes for changing the letter, saving it, and printing it out.

When You Need Help. If you have any questions about retrieving ASCII files, refer first to your software manual. Look in the index of the word processing manual under "ASCII files" or "retrieving a file." Both topics are explained thoroughly in word processing manuals.

Technical support from your word processing software publisher is just a telephone call away too. The technical support hotlines for the major word processing software publishers are as follows:

Microsoft Corporation: (206) 882-8080

Lotus Development: (800) 223-1662

WordPerfect: (800) 451-5151

WordStar: (812) 323-0062

The publisher of this book, Business One/Irwin, is committed to customer satisfaction. If the disk is damaged, please notify our office at (800) 634-3966.

If you have other problems or questions, you may contact the author. Write a complete description of the problem, including the name and version number of the word processing software you use, and send it via CompuServe, using ID (71062,1071), or Prodigy, using ID (KIMK99A), or fax it to (602) 991-1056. You will receive an answer promptly.

Also available from Business One Irwin . .

Survive Information Overload
The 7 Best Ways to Manage Your Workload by Seeing the Big Picture
Kathryn Alesandrini
Survive the information onslaught and find the time you need to be more productive! Alesandrini gives you a step-by-step action plan to help you manage your workload without resorting to outdated time-management practices.
ISBN: 1-55623-721-9

The Business One Irwin Guide to Using The Wall Street Journal
Fourth Edition
Michael B. Lehmann
More than 165,000 copies in print! Discover how to use the comprehensive information in the *Journal* to make more informed and potentially profitable business and investment decisions! You'll discover how to evaluate the current investment scene and track investments for greater profit, plus much more! (300 pages)
ISBN: 1-55623-700-6

The Corporate Communicator's Quick Reference
Peter Lichtgarn
This essential guide describes the duties, responsibilities, and functions of today's corporate communicator by anticipating the challenges and answering the questions communicators face daily. (200 pages)
1993—May. ISBN: 1-55623-892-4

Available at fine bookstores and libraries everywhere.

Business One Irwin books are excellent resources for corporate training/educational programs, premiums, and incentives. We also offer Custom Publishing, a flexible option that lets you select the information from our books you need to achieve your goals. Call our Corporate Customer Service Group at 1-800-448-3343 ext. 2715 for more information.

NEW HANOVER PUBLIC LIBRARY

3 4200 00311 4168

For Reference

Not to be taken from this room